Pathways to Recovery:

A Strengths Recovery Self-Help Workbook

Priscilla Ridgway, Diane McDiarmid,
Lori Davidson, Julie Bayes & Sarah Ratzlaff

With Contributing Authors:

Cherie Bledsoe
Janice Driscoll
Les Higgins
Randy Johnson
Suzette Mack
Amy Stiefvater
and other Kansas Consumers

Pathways to Recovery: A Strengths Recovery Self-Help Workbook
is published by the University of Kansas School of Social Welfare,
Office of Mental Health Research & Training, Lawrence, KS, and supported through
a contract with Kansas Department of Social & Rehabilitation Services,
Division of Health Care Policy

Authors:	Priscilla Ridgway	Cover Design:	Lori Davidson
	Diane McDiarmid		Tonya Hinman
	Lori Davidson		Suzette Mack
	Julie Bayes		Jan Kobe
	Sarah Ratzlaff		Janice Driscoll
			Diane McDiarmid
Production Coordinator:	Sarah Ratzlaff		Priscilla Ridgway
			Joy Butterfield
Illustrators:	Jan Kobe		
	Lori Davidson		
	Priscilla Ridgway		

Pathways to Recovery: A Strengths Recovery Self-Help Workbook is published by The University of Kansas, School of Social Welfare, Office of Mental Health Research & Training, Lawrence, Kansas, USA. and is supported through a contract with Kansas Department of Social & Rehabilitation Services, Division of Health Care Policy

Printed by Minuteman Press, Lawrence, KS
    Fifth printing: January, 2008

Printed by Data Reproductions Corporation, Auburn Hills, MI
    Fourth printing: October, 2006
    Third printing: July, 2005
    Second printing: April, 2004
    First printing: July, 2002

Recommended Reference:
Ridgway, P., McDiarmid, D., Davidson, L., Bayes, J., & Ratzlaff, S. (2002). *Pathways to Recovery: A Strengths Recovery Self-Help Workbook*. Lawrence, KS: University of Kansas School of Social Welfare.

Foreword

I love this workbook! *Pathways to Recovery* uses the metaphor of a journey to take the reader through a series of exercises. With these exercises, the reader will identify and use personal strengths for engaging in the recovery process. *Getting into gear, motivation as fuel for the journey, recharging batteries along the way, strategies for tune-ups and rest stops* all contribute to the metaphor of the journey and reinforce the idea that recovery is about changing our lives, not just our biochemistry. Along the way, in the margins of the text, are inspiring quotes from consumers, psychiatric survivors and sages. These quotes remind us that recovery, at its core, is about human growth, resilience and triumph over adversity.

I find it refreshing that *Pathways to Recovery* addresses issues of real concern to mature adults diagnosed with mental illness. There are sections about human sexuality, intimacy and economic well-being. The workbook does not have to be approached in a linear fashion. It is geared to meet people where they are. Because the authors were careful to gather consumer/survivor input through advisory boards, focus groups and workshops, the self-help exercises are very practical and easy to learn.

Pathways to Recovery is an important new resource for consumers and psychiatric survivors. It is also a testament to the power of self-help and, as such, will contribute to move the field of mental health towards becoming recovery oriented. I highly recommend it!

Patricia E. Deegan, Ph.D.

Dedication

We would like to dedicate this workbook to all the individuals who have endured the label of psychiatric disability. We are constantly amazed at your resilience, your strong spirit and most of all your courage. We would like to dedicate this workbook to *you, the reader*. We wish you the best as you set forth upon your journey.

~The Authors

I dedicate this workbook to the dynamic Creative Force at the heart of all we see, do and believe. I also want to dedicate this book to Howie the Harp, whose great heartedness, practical organizing and humor inspired so many people in the ex-patient movement, and to the members of the Recovery Paradigm Project writing team and the completion of the next gift.

~Priscilla

I dedicate this book to George. You have my utmost respect, enduring love & deep gratitude. Your support, imagination & "can-do" attitude helped to clarify the vision of what could be & became. You have been there when I needed you the most. For Debbie, whose sense of adventure inspires; for Mike, whose caring & compassion encourages; to Michelle, for sharing your strengths. With gratitude to consumers, families, helping professionals, colleagues & my students, you have taught me so much.

~Diane

…for Tom & Jerome…you gave me so much in life but left me with so much more… for Cherie, Denise, Jan, Joyce, Karen, Millie, Sherrie, Suzette & Tonya…my friends, my mentors & my life-long sisters…your welcoming spirits energize me and gives meaning to the glory of friendship…for Josie, may you always have peace…and to all those over the years who have shared their stories with me…you have taught me that the lines of connection are often blurry if not non-existent…

~Lori

I dedicate this book to the staff and clients at the Bert Nash Community Mental Health Center for giving me the opportunity to be a part of their lives.

~Julie

To all of the authors…for the opportunity to be a part of this project. You taught me more than you know. Your knowledge, creativity and compassion is inspiring.

~Sarah

In Appreciation

Many people across the country are embracing and mobilizing around a vision of recovery. In Kansas we have worked to create a vision of recovery for several years. *Pathways to Recovery* is a tool that can ground the ideals of recovery in day-to-day life.

This project started when several of us from the University of Kansas attended an intensive train-the-trainers recovery education workshop conducted by Mary Ellen Copeland in Putney, Vermont. We were incredibly impressed by her powerful work. By putting useful and practical recovery knowledge and skills directly into the hands of consumers, she grounds recovery in experimental wisdom.

Several of the workshop participants asked us when we were going to offer a Strengths Model train-the-trainers style workshop in Kansas. We decided to "translate" the basic principles, values and processes of the Strengths Approach (which up to that point had been geared to case managers) into a self-help approach, and to link the Strengths Approach more directly to other work we were doing on recovery.

The creation of *Pathways to Recovery* has truly been a team effort and a shared adventure. We chose to use journey and travel metaphors throughout the text to show the progress we are making toward recovery as individuals and as a system as a whole. We gathered ideas from meetings, seminars and panels where people have shared their ideas and stories of recovery. We read literature and analyzed the latest research findings about recovery. The idea that recovery is a movement, a process and a journey, runs through all of these sources.

Pathways to Recovery Advisory Group

The Pathways to Recovery Advisory Group is a collection of enthusiastic and creative people. Participants met every month for a year and a half helping to conceptualize and create the *Pathways to Recovery* workbook. The Advisory Group is made up predominantly of consumers but also includes Kansas Department of Mental Health leaders and innovative community support workers. Advisory Group members provided suggestions on the tone and content of the workbook, brainstormed ideas for chapters, shared their stories, helped gather quotations and resources and made decisions on the workbook's appearance. They critiqued draft chapters and provided helpful feedback. We are deeply appreciative to this group of amazing individuals: Julie Bayes, Barbara Bohm, Janice Driscoll, Darrin Dressler, Elizabeth A. Gowdy, JoAnn Howley, Les Higgins, Tonya Hinman, Randy Johnson, Jan Kobe, Suzette Mack, Shirley Pilger and Amy Stiefvater.

Lori Davidson

Lori completed her first year Masters in Social Work practicum working on this project. Lori authored sections of chapters, pretested the book with individuals and groups and worked in partnership with Jan Kobe to illustrate the workbook. One of Lori's greatest strengths is "getting the word out." She designed and developed materials to promote *Pathways to Recovery* throughout Kansas.

Julie Bayes

Julie is a Consumer as Provider graduate and works at Bert Nash Community Mental Health Center in the psychosocial program. We would like to thank Julie for her important contributions to the text in the areas of motivation, intimacy, detours and supercharging and for sharing her personal experiences and stories.

Sarah Ratzlaff

Sarah served as our research assistant throughout the creation of *Pathways to Recovery*. Sarah staffed the advisory meetings, prepared materials and followed up with participants. She gathered supporting research, articles and other resource materials. Sarah also spent many hours formatting the book so we could print the document. Thanks Sarah, for your fortitude and sharing of your numerous strengths.

Contributing Authors

We want to express gratitude to each and every contributor to this book. We feel a sense of excitement as we learn from courageous and resilient people. Their insights, reflections, first person accounts of recovery, ideas and talents added greatly to this workbook. The following individuals contributed to the main text:
> ~ Suzette Mack on supercharging and the vocational domains.
> ~ Les Higgins on spirituality.
> ~ Randy Johnson on motivation.

Contributing Artists

A special thanks to Jan Kobe for her help in illustrating *Pathways to Recovery*. We are thrilled to have an award-winning artist share her talents with us in this way. Thanks to Lori Davidson for her illustrations and "creative eye" in formatting the workbook. Priscilla Ridgway also contributed drawings to the text. As a group project, Lori, Jan, Tonya Hinman, Suzette Mack, Janice Driscoll and Joy Butterfield capitalized on their creative strengths to design the cover art.

Sharing Stories of Recovery

We want to thank others who shared their stories of recovery:

Consumer as Provider (CAP) Project Graduates

Students attending Consumer as Provider classes through the University of Kansas School of Social Welfare have made many significant contributions to the understanding of recovery. CAP is a 15-week program that trains consumers in basic helping skills, ethics and the Strengths Approach so they may become providers of community support services. We learned a great deal from CAP students, especially by listening to their personal stories of recovery. We solicited their recovery stories and drew out several quotations used in this text. We were given permission to use many of the stories of CAP graduates; unfortunately, we could not use them all. Thanks especially to the following people for permission to use their stories and ideas: Sue Bennett, Beth Clement, Crystal Dirks, Linda Endicott, Jan Hanson, Carrie Hunter, Sandy Hyde, Marc Kelso, Sandy Lewis, Suzette Mack, Cindy Northcraft, David Reed, Shelly Scott, Donna Story, Stormie Woodward, Catherine Scruggs, Kathy Shinn, Chris Shore and other CAP graduates who wish to remain anonymous.

Cherie Bledsoe

We have been fortunate to have Cherie Bledsoe, Executive Director of S.I.D.E. Inc., a consumer-run organization in the Kansas City area, contribute to *Pathways to Recovery* by sharing the text of her speeches.

Vicki Darring

We met Vicki, a consumer leader from Philadelphia, PA, at a conference. We would like to thank her for sharing her struggles with making choices.

Participants in the "Telling Your Story of Recovery" Workshop

The 2001 Kansas Conference on Recovery was held in Wichita. Almost 100 of the 700 participants came to our "Sharing Your Story of Recovery" workshop. People shared parts of their recovery stories in small story circles. Listening to these stories had a powerful effect on everyone in the room. The group brainstormed why telling recovery stories is so important and came up with great ideas that we incorporated in the final chapter. We don't have your names, but you influenced and shaped this book, and for that we are grateful.

Recovery Paradigm Project

We also drew from a group of papers prepared for a meeting held in Lawrence, Kansas in 1999, entitled "Deepening the Mental Health Recovery Paradigm, Defining Implications for Practice." These papers will appear as a separate text. Thanks go to Andrea Blanch and Sally Clay who live in Florida, Kansan Cherie Bledsoe, Kathryn Cohen of Rhode Island, Mary Ellen Copeland of Vermont, Zahirah Duvall of Maine, Patricia E. Deegan, Courtenay Harding and Dori Hutchinson of Massachusetts, Edward Knight from Colorado, Jay Mahler and Stacy Tupper from California and Patrick Sullivan from Indiana.

Kansas Consumer-Run Organizations (CRO) & Community Support Services (CSS)

Creating and championing a Strengths Recovery perspective has been a major thrust of both CROs and CSSs across Kansas over the past few years. In order to evaluate and redesign the content of this workbook, we field-tested each chapter. We gained feedback from consumers in two organizations and from individuals across the state. Thanks go to Wyandot Center in Kansas City, under the leadership of Leslie Young and Tonya Hinman, and Breakthrough Clubhouse in Topeka, under the leadership of Michael Horan, for supporting the field-testing of *Pathways to Recovery*. We learned that people enthusiastically want and need positive strengths based information and processes that help them assume personal responsibility for their recovery and move toward achieving personal goals. People literally pounded on doors to gain access to this material. We thank each person who participated in focus groups or worked individually to pilot this material.

Kansas Social and Rehabilitation Services (SRS)/Division of Health Care Policy

We are also very grateful to Elizabeth A. Gowdy and Randy Johnson from the State of Kansas Adult Mental Health Services. Their strong leadership and vision for recovery is making a difference. SRS funded this project and Liz and Randy have been active participants.

The Strengths Perspective

This volume is based on the Strengths Perspective. The Strength Model of case management was originally developed by The University of Kansas' Ronna Chamberlain when she was a doctoral student, and it was expanded upon and systematized by Charles A. Rapp, Ronna and KU colleagues in the early 1980's. Rapp and Dennis Saleebey, also from KU, have published texts on the Strengths Model that give mental health practitioners both theory and practice skills.

The strengths approach is a natural partner with recovery. Some of the guiding principles of the Strengths Model include: the consumer must direct the helping process; the focus is upon strengths rather than pathology; people having the capacity to learn, grow and change; and community integration and utilization of natural occurring community resources are preferable to segregated program environments. The Strengths Model was originally used with people experiencing severe mental illness, but it has also been adapted to other populations, including aging and child-welfare.

A formal training curriculum for the Strengths Model was developed for mental health practitioners over the course of several years by Charles Rapp, Pat Sullivan, Walter Kisthardt, Diane McDiarmid and others, and workshops have been presented throughout Kansas, across the USA and internationally. A recent update undertaken by the Office of Mental Health Research and Training staff Linda Carlson, Rick Goscha, Diane McDiarmid and Steve Huff brought more recovery content into this training. Staff from the University of Kansas School of Social Welfare now partner with consumers to present this training in Kansas and across the country.

The University of Kansas School of Social Welfare's Office of Mental Health Research and Training enabled us to mount the *Pathways to Recovery* Project. We are especially grateful to our Director, Charles A. Rapp, for his encouragement and support.

Priscilla Ridgway & Diane McDiarmid
June, 2002

Postscript

Since the first printing of *Pathways to Recovery*, we at The University of Kansas have been both honored & humbled at the response this recovery tool has had worldwide. We have heard from hundreds of individuals & organizations who have found the workbook helpful and life-altering. We sincerely thank you for your ideas, comments & stories and trust you will continue sharing these with us.

We'd also like to take this opportunity to remember the memory of at least four individuals who shared their stories in the workbook—Crystal Dirks, Jan Hanson, Carrie Hunter & Shelly Scott. Each of these individuals shared their lives and their stories of hope and compassion within the pages of *Pathways*. We miss them dearly.

And finally, as we all continue on our personal pathways, may the following words by singer Diego Torres (2002) be our guide always:

> *Creer que se puede, querer que se pueda, quitarse los miedos, sacarlos afuera, pintarse la cara color esperanza, tentar al futuro con el corazon.*

> *Believing it is possible, wanting it to be possible, getting rid of fears, taking them out, painting your face with the color of hope, tempting the future with your heart.*

Lori Davidson
January, 2008

What lies behind us
and what lies
before us
are tiny matters
compared to
what lies within us.

~Ralph Waldo Emerson

CONTENTS

Preface: Is this Workbook for You?

Chapter One: Introduction to a Strengths Recovery Approach

Chapter Two: Gearing Up for the Journey

Chapter Three: Setting Ourselves in Motion

Chapter Four: Recovery is Self-Discovery

Chapter Five: Setting a Course for the Recovery Journey

Chapter Six: Moving Forward on the Journey

Chapter Seven: Travel Companions and Social Support for the Journey

Chapter Eight: Developing Your Personal Recovery Plan

Chapter Nine: Making it Past Detours and Roadblocks

Chapter Ten: Rest Stops and Travel Tips

Chapter Eleven: Supercharging the Recovery Journey

Chapter Twelve: Sharing Our Stories of Recovery

Preface and Introduction

This chapter explores what this workbook is about and how it can help you on the road to recovery.

Is this Workbook for You?

☑ **Have you experienced a psychiatric disability?**

☑ **Do you want your life to improve?**

☑ **Are you interested in achieving recovery?**

If you answered yes to any of these questions, this workbook is for you!

Even if you have never thought about recovery, but feel you may need to make some important changes to attain the kind of life you really want, you'll learn a lot by using this workbook! If you simply want to explore the idea of recovery or are just starting out and want to begin a journey of recovery in a positive way, this workbook can open up a new world of possibilities for you!

If you are already well underway on a journey of recovery, this workbook can help you avoid pitfalls and find highly positive and productive pathways to achieve your goals.

This book is <u>not</u> a structured set of "rules of the road" that you must follow. The journey of recovery is different for each person. The workbook will help you develop the inner guidance, self-motivation, self-direction and self-effort that will get you where *you* want to go.

This workbook is full of "travel tips" that you can use to plan your personal pathway to recovery. Exercises are provided that will help you develop a better understanding of yourself and increase your potential for having the kind of meaningful, interesting and full life that *you* want.

Have you ever felt like your life wasn't going in the direction you wanted it to? If so, this book will replace those feeling with a renewed sense of self-control over your life. You'll have a road map that *you have designed* to keep you pointed in the direction of a more positive future.

> "The trail is the thing, not the end of the trail. Travel too fast and you miss all you are traveling for."
> ~Louis L'Amour

What is this Workbook All About?

Unlike most other recovery self-help materials, this workbook does not concentrate on psychiatric disorders, symptoms or treatments. Instead it focuses on how you can use your many strengths and resources to set goals and achieve recovery in broad domains of life such as:

- Having a sense of home
- Increasing your knowledge and education
- Deciding what kind of work you may want to do
- Developing the kind of relationships you want to have with others
- Improving your sexuality and achieving intimacy
- Attaining higher levels of wellness
- Finding enjoyable recreational activities
- Unfolding your spirituality and other important areas

This workbook can be used along with other approaches to recovery that focus on reducing and self-managing disturbing symptoms.

This workbook guides you through processes of self-assessment, self-discovery and planning that help you decide where you want to go in life. You will create personal visions, design long-term goals and action steps to make progress towards your dreams. *Pathways* will help you use your own inner and outer strengths and the resources that are available to you to move you forward on your pathway to recovery. In other words, this workbook is about getting a fuller and more enjoyable life!

How to Use this Workbook

In *Pathways to Recovery* you actively venture onto the path towards recovery and learn from the successful experiences of others who have gone before you. Working this workbook is a little like having a travel agent or tour guide. By doing the readings and completing the self-assessments and exercises provided, you become much more active on your own behalf. As you work through each section you build the

"A journey of a thousand miles must begin with a single step."
~Chinese Proverb

knowledge, skills and plans needed to make your journey a success. Exploration and finding out about yourself and your dreams requires a gradual build-up of activity, particularly if you haven't been actively involved in making important decisions for awhile.

The Strengths Recovery process may look easy as you thumb through this book. You may be tempted to skip ahead to later chapters. The workbook builds upon itself, one chapter after another, so the best way to use this resource is to begin at the beginning and work the workbook on through to the end. Of course, not everyone sticks to the path that is laid out for them! It's possible to find a section that is of interest to you, start there, then work the workbook around that point.

The workbook may seem overwhelming. But take it page-by-page, step-by-step, at your own pace and you'll soon be making important choices about *your* life. You aren't alone in your feelings. People who were very fearful or overwhelmed at first, who began setting goals and persevered to achieve them, have proven the Strengths Approach really works. You are in good company with others who are making the journey of recovery.

This workbook can be a resource for years to come.

- You can work the workbook, then go ahead and do what you planned, then step back and revisit sections that you worked on previously as you keep moving forward.
- It may be helpful and motivating to review the workbook from time to time to see all that you have worked through and record all of your progress to date.
- The workbook can serve as a permanent record of your journey.
- As you learn more about yourself through this workbook, you may want to share information and exercises with mental health providers (i.e. case manager, therapist, nurse, psychiatrist) you work with. This workbook is a very personal record of self-discovery and should only be shared when you feel completely comfortable with revealing such personal information.
- Once you have completed the workbook, you can come back to it again and again, for encouragement, support, advice and validation and to update your personal recovery goals and plans.

There is no magic potion you can swallow to get where you want to go in recovery. There are no short cuts, no uncharted secret passageways to success. The journey is a long one and it requires both dedication and perseverance. Many people are achieving recovery and focusing on your strengths helps move you forward.

Make a commitment to work this workbook, to learn more about yourself, to taking some small steps on your unique pathway to recovery this very day. As you move forward, you will feel better, be healthier and you will become much more satisfied with your life!

Find a Place to Work the Workbook

This workbook is a personal approach to starting or proceeding on the road to recovery. Find a place where you won't be interrupted as you work your workbook. This place may be a corner of your bedroom, a coffee shop, your favorite bench under a tree in the park or a comfortable chair in the corner of the local public library. You'll need a quiet place where you can feel relaxed and comfortable while you think through your feelings, make decisions and do the exercises in the workbook.

Give a Specific Block of Time to Work the Workbook

Plan on setting aside a specific period of time to work your workbook. Don't let a lack of time become a barrier. Many of us feel we don't have enough time for ourselves, we have important responsibilities to others, we have tasks that we must complete and programs and appointments we have to attend. When we have so many competing priorities, we often put ourselves last. We may think we lack the energy to take on something new. It's time to put ourselves and our recovery as a top priority. *We have the power to choose how we will spend our time each day!*

Don't say, "I'll start working the workbook later this month." Set an appointment with yourself and map out a plan to read and do the exercises in this workbook. Here are some ideas people have used to "find time":

- Work the workbook while sipping your morning coffee or tea
- Give up one television show and use that time slot
- Find an hour or two each weekend (i.e. Sunday morning) to devote to the process
- Use part of your lunch hour
- Use a weekly planner or calendar; early in the week write down some dates and times you will work your workbook
- Link working on your workbook to a time of day you enjoy, for example, if you are a night owl and like staying up late, take an hour before going to bed to work on your personal recovery plan

Set aside some time each week to read, think about and complete your workbook. The time you put into working on your recovery plan will be paid back as you act on your own behalf to create a more fulfilling life.

Make a Commitment to Yourself

The *Pathways to Recovery* workbook is personalized to you, it is all about *your* ideas, *your* thoughts and *your* feelings. This workbook should capture your deepest wishes, values, hopes and beliefs.

The path that you travel should reflect your uniqueness. In order for this workbook to be effective, and for you to move forward and stretch and grow, be honest and true to yourself. Being faithful to your inner self, or "authenticity," helps you learn more about yourself, where you have been, where you are now and where you really want to go.

"What we ever hope to do with ease, we must first learn to do with diligence."
~Samuel Johnson

- *You deserve to take care of yourself*
- *You deserve to put your life as the top priority*
- *You deserve to learn, stretch and grow*
- *You deserve to make choices about your life*
- *You deserve to have options to draw from*
- *You deserve to fulfill your personal goals*
- *You deserve to celebrate the steps along the way*
- *You deserve to feel renewed*
- *You deserve to recover!*

You may want to establish clear boundaries about sharing this workbook with other people. It may be best to share the writing you have done only with allies and supporters whom you trust. You don't need to show your writing to anyone who may try to undermine your progress. Find people who support your recovery!

Celebrate Each Step as You Work Through the Workbook

There are ideas for celebrating your progress at the end of most chapters. Try some of the suggested activities and develop your own ways of celebrating your progress in recovery. Be very proud of every step of your recovery journey!

Chapter Format

Most pages of the workbook have large margins. You may want to add notes, things you want to follow-up on or your reactions and ideas in that space. Space has been provided to answer questions, however, if you have large handwriting or need more space you may want to start a notebook to accompany this workbook.

Listings of references and resources can be found at the end of the chapters. These resources can help you explore the content of each chapter more deeply. You may want to add your own resources to the list.

Group Support

Do you think you might want to work through the ideas in this workbook with a group of supportive peers?

If so, information on whom to contact to learn more about support groups that use the content of this workbook is available at the back of this book.

"It takes courage to push yourself to places that you have never been before...to test your limits...to break through barriers."
~Anais Nin

A Special Note to Mental Health Providers and Other Supporters

If you are a case manager, therapist or other mental health provider or serve as a friend or support person for someone who may have an interest in recovery from psychiatric disability, this workbook may help you too.

How to Use the Pathways to Recovery Workbook

- Use this text as a resource in your work with consumers.
- Give copies of this text to individuals you support or serve to encourage their recovery.
- Use part of your time with the person to go through material contained in this workbook.
- Support people in recognizing, recording and developing their strengths.
- Use the *Pathways to Recovery* Plan to help individuals set goals.
- Help people secure resources to achieve their goals.
- Use the supplemental readings and resources at the end of each chapter to increase your knowledge.
- Share the information you learn from this book with colleagues and other supporters.
- Don't try to take over the person's recovery process. Remember recovery is based in self-responsibility and empowerment!

"Formal supports (therapists, case managers, psychiatrists and hospitals) have been the backbone of my recovery. Continued contact with these supports helped me to develop the skills needed to recover."
~Karen Cook,
  Kansas Consumer

Chapter One

Introduction to a
Strengths Recovery Approach

This chapter goes over the basics of the Strengths Recovery Approach. It includes a definition of what recovery is as well as a short history of the consumer movement.

What is the Strengths Approach to Recovery?

This workbook is based on a "Strengths Approach to Recovery."
The "Strengths Approach to Recovery" is a new way to think about
mental health and recovery. It is based on over 15 years of experience
with Strengths Model work in the mental health field. Research has
shown the Strengths Model is highly effective in helping consumers of
mental health services plan and achieve personal goals, attain a higher
quality of life and succeed in roles they want to be successful in. Some
research shows the Strengths Approach can also reduce psychiatric
hospitalization (Rapp, 1995).

Up to this point, the Strengths Approach has been taught to mental
health practitioners, especially case managers, so they can work
effectively with consumers.

- The Strengths Approach does not focus primarily on symptoms,
  problems or diagnoses as many mental health services and
  programs do. Instead, the Strengths Approach looks at each
  person more holistically and focuses on and amplifies the "well"
  part of each person.

- The Strengths Approach helps people identify and use their inner
  strengths and the strengths in their environment to rebound from
  difficulties and create the life they want.

- People with psychiatric histories are empowered to reclaim
  fuller and more satisfying lives by building upon their strengths,
  defining their personal aspirations and goals and identifying and
  using the resources available within their families, friendship
  circles and communities.

- The Strengths Approach honors the inherent potential for
  human growth in each person's life and supports each person's
  search for healing, meaning and wholeness, even in the midst of
  struggle and adversity.

"We have no choice
of what color we're
born or who our
parents are or
whether we're rich
or poor. What we
do have is some
choice over what we
make of our lives
once we're here."
~Mildred Taylor

Now a team of consumers, consumer-providers, Strengths Approach educators, recovery researchers and practitioners have come together to put the valuable information contained in the Strengths Approach and important new information on recovery directly into your hands as a consumer of mental health services.

We believe our work to adapt the Strengths Approach into a personalized *self-help* approach will give you an important tool to plan and work toward recovery. This workbook combines the key steps of the Strengths Approach with important knowledge on recovery from psychiatric disability to create a new "Strengths Approach to Recovery."

By putting this information on a Strengths Approach to Recovery directly into your hands, the authors hope you will gain more control over your life and be more successful on your unique journey of recovery.

What Will You Get Out of the Strengths Recovery Process?

As you move through this self-help workbook you are guided through important self-discovery and decision-making processes.

- You will become more aware of your own values, cultural resources, talents, hopes, commitments and aspirations.

- You will determine what is important to you in many areas of your life.

- You will set long-term and short-term goals for your life—goals that truly reflect what is important to you.

- You will plot out a course to move toward the kind of life you want.

- You will create a step-by-step plan to guide you on the path toward your recovery.

- You will discover resources that you never knew were available to you that will help you reach your goals.

- You will find ways to celebrate every step that moves you closer to the life you want.

What is Recovery?

Recovery is an important idea that is sweeping the mental health field. Recovery is a word that is used to describe the many positive changes that can happen in people's lives after the experience of prolonged psychiatric disability.

There are many definitions of recovery from consumers, researchers and leaders in the rehabilitation and mental health field. Here are two that are often used:

"There are as many ways to live and grow as there are people."
~Evelyn Mandel

Recovery is a process, a way of life, an attitude, and a way of approaching the day's challenges…The need is to meet the challenge of the disability and to re-establish a new and valued sense of integrity and purpose within and beyond the limits of the disability; the aspiration is to live, work and love in a community in which one makes a significant contribution.

~Patricia E. Deegan,
National Consumer Leader

Recovery is a deeply personal, unique process of changing one's attitudes, values, feelings, goals, skills, and/or roles. It's a way of living a satisfying, hopeful, and contributing life even within the limitations caused by the illness. Recovery involves the development of new meaning and purpose in one's life as one grows beyond the catastrophic effects of mental illness.

~William Anthony,
Director, Center for Psychiatric Rehabilitation,
Boston University

Here are some definitions of recovery that were collected at the National Summit of Mental Health Consumers and Survivors held in Oregon in 1999:

What does recovery mean to me? To have hope. To feel like a useful, needed person. To be able to use the abilities I have. To be able to help others and be a contributing member of society. To have a positive attitude. To be out of the victim role and be able to transcend the experience I had. To feel connected to the Creator and other people. To take responsibility and take charge of my life. To lead a productive life. Inner healing. Enjoy living. Spiritual wholeness. Living effectively. It's giving back. Forgiveness. Helping other people. Believing in yourself. Overcoming obstacles in achieving my goals.

~Sheila Hill

Recovery means to be free to sing no matter how weak or quivery your voice. When I was a child, I was abused; one form this took was my mother telling me my voice was so ugly that no one could stand it. I refused to sing even in church or in private, because if I did, I would drive everyone away with my voice. It was through recent friends and self-help that during the last year I have felt free enough to sing again in my home. I know I am on the road to recovery because I start each day with a song. And I feel this freedom to 'sing' is applicable to the very core of recovery.

~Anonymous

An inner healing. Accepting the 'whole of me.' Having a life — your own — with its dreams, goals, and consequences — with or without symptoms. Being in charge of your own self. Living the kind of life that is of value to me — in my community — contributing to my community — with mutual acceptance and support. Enjoyment of living.

~Cherie Bledsoe,
Kansas Consumer Provider

How would you define recovery for yourself?

"Our own life is
the instrument with
which we experiment
with the truth."
~Thich Nhat Hanh

Priscilla Ridgway, one of the authors of this workbook, researched the life stories many mental health consumers have told about their own experience of recovery. From this research she created the following definition (Ridgway, 1999):

"The world is divided
into two classes,
those who believe
the incredible, and
those who do
the improbable."
~Oscar Wilde

A Definition of Recovery Based on Consumer Life Stories

- Recovery is an ongoing journey of self-healing and transformation.

- Recovery is re-claiming a positive sense of self despite the challenge of psychiatric disability.

- Recovery is actively self-managing one's life and mental health, in order to control psychiatric symptoms, create a positive lifestyle and achieve higher levels of wellness.

- Recovery is reclaiming roles and a life beyond being a consumer in the mental health system.

Is Recovery Something New?

Those of us with psychiatric disabilities have *always* recovered, but the mental health system has paid little attention to this fact until the last few years.

When we received services from the mental health system, we were often told we had a lifelong disorder and that there was *no chance that we would recover*. When we did recover, despite these negative predictions, we were often told we had been wrongly diagnosed!

What were you were told about your chances for recovery?

Until recently, we lacked positive role models of recovery. Those of us who achieved recovery often stopped attending formal programs. Most of us who recovered actively covered up our experience in the mental health system because of the social stigma attached to mental illness. We did not discuss our experience of recovery openly. Even though some mental health professionals had the experience of extreme emotional distress, psychiatric symptoms or a history of mental health treatment, we hid these facts. But this is changing…

Until recently, the mental health system was almost exclusively geared toward *stabilizing symptoms* and *maintaining or controlling* those of us who were diagnosed with a severe and persistent mental disorder and we were considered permanently disabled. But this is changing…

Until recently, those of us who experienced psychiatric disabilities were not expected to continue to grow, learn and function well in important social roles. Instead, we were expected to assume the "sick role." The sick role teaches us to turn important decisions in our lives over to experts, become passive, accept our disability and remain out of the mainstream of life. But this is changing…

What are some of the positives and negatives you have experienced by being in the "sick role"?

It turns out we were hiding or ignoring the successful recovery of many former patients/clients/consumers!

Now there is a growing emphasis on recovery that is spreading across the country. Consumers, family members, advocates, professionals and program directors are all refocusing our efforts around recovery as a primary goal.

More and more frequently, advocates, professionals and program directors are consumers. Many of us who are recovering from psychiatric disorders now serve as role models and service providers in a way that helps others recover.

We are finding there is much we can do to improve our lives and mental health. We are also finding peer support is invaluable and are helping one another along the pathway to recovery.

We are participating in recovery-oriented programs that help us live, work and learn in the community. We are regaining our rightful social roles as tenants, students, friends, intimate partners, parents and employees.

We are taking a much more active role in designing our own treatment. We are using alternative and complementary health approaches and are taking much more responsibility for our own health and mental health.

Programs are encouraging us to become much more active consumers of services and are listening to our feedback as consumers and stakeholders.

"With the new day comes new strength and new thoughts."
~Eleanor Roosevelt

"New opportunities await and abound. Never stagnate and settle."
~Katherine Negermajian

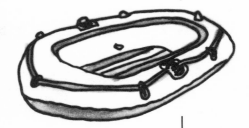

Recovery and Resilience

When people face hard times and challenges, but go on with their lives and do well anyway, they are said to be "resilient." Resilience also comes into play when people rebound or recover from serious trauma or stressful events in their lives.

It turns out that most of us find ways to rebound from the experience of psychiatric disorder and go on to live productive and full lives over the course of time.

- Psychiatric problems lessen as we develop coping techniques or learn ways to contend with stress or control our symptoms. Over time our symptoms diminish and sometimes completely fade away.

- We no longer need to be full-time recipients of services. Our disability no longer serves as the core of our sense of identity. We create a positive structure for our daily lives that is not centered on our psychiatric disability.

- We stop being so vulnerable to stress. We find better ways to deal with the stressful events that we experience in our life. We become "hardy" in the face of stress.

- We overcome a tendency to isolate ourselves and no longer withdraw from social relationships. We develop positive, supportive, mutual give-and-take social relationships. We find satisfaction through peer support, intimate relationships and helping others. We become less dependent on formal helpers for human contact.

"When we are motivated by goals that have deep meaning, by dreams that need completion, by pure love that needs expressing, then we truly live life."
~Greg Anderson

- We return to work, and/or become involved in other meaningful activities that contribute to our communities.

- Our lives become much more hopeful and more meaningful.

Every one of us has self-righting tendencies, or the ability to achieve a more balanced life after having our life disrupted by overwhelming stress, problems, trauma or illness. We know some people are naturally more resilient than others, they heal faster, seem to bounce back more easily from difficult life experiences, adapt better to life and seem more able to deal with, and overcome, difficult situations.

All of us can become more resilient by learning and practicing some of the attitudes and skills that those who are most resilient use. Every one of us has some degree of resilience, something inside us that urges us to heal, or we wouldn't have made it this far in life. We need to learn about ourselves and our environment and find both inner and outer resources that will support our capacity to rebuild our lives.

What are some of the inner and outer resources that have helped you make it through everything you have been through so far in your life?

What made it possible for you to keep on going and not give up?

What Does Research Say About Our Chances for Recovery?

Research from around the world has shown the common belief that people *don't* recover from prolonged psychiatric disorder is a myth or falsehood. Both short-term and long-term studies are more hopeful about the chance for recovery than many mental health practitioners have traditionally been (Sullivan, 1994).

Studies from around the world indicate the chances that we will achieve recovery are better than 50-50. This is true, even when we have been told there is *no chance at all that we will recover.* Recovery can take place even when mental health programs and systems are not designed to support our recovery (Harding, Zubin & Strauss, 1987).

One long-term outcome study followed a large group of people who had been in a state hospital in Vermont for many years and who had not responded to any available medication. The group of people received a model rehabilitation program and were discharged. Most stayed out of the hospital for good. Most went on to having good relationships with others, most had meaningful work and very few had on-going psychiatric symptoms (Harding, Brooks et al., 1987).

Other studies from America and countries such as Switzerland and Japan also found most people recover from psychiatric disability over the course of time. In fact, all the studies conducted around the world that follow up on people who have severe psychiatric disorders have found that most people do recover (Jimenez, 1988; Harding, 1988; Hubert, 1980).

One-half to two-thirds of all people with psychiatric disabilities recover even when told they can't expect to recover, are given little or no help to recover and face barriers to recovery (Harding, 1988).

We don't know how many people can recover now that we are beginning to have more positive information, role models, supportive systems and recovery-facilitating services!

"Both tears and sweat are salty, but they render different results. Tears will get you sympathy, sweat will get you change."
~Jesse Jackson

In 1999, the Surgeon General of the United States (U. S. Department of Health and Human Services, 1999) recommended that all mental health systems assume a recovery orientation. As mental health systems change to support recovery, barriers are removed and information on resilience and recovery become more available, the proportion of people with psychiatric disabilities who recover will certainly increase as well.

WHERE AM I ON MY JOURNEY OF RECOVERY?

- Take the following self-assessment to see where you currently are on the journey of recovery.

- I have never really thought about recovery from psychiatric disability.

- I don't feel I need to recover.

- I have so much going on that I can't think about recovery right now.

- I'm thinking about recovery, but haven't decided to move toward recovery.

- I am committed to my recovery, but have not begun to act on recovery.

- I was on a journey of recovery but am having a setback right now.

- I am actively involved in recovering from psychiatric disability.

- I feel that I am fully recovered and now I have to maintain my gains.

"No matter how far you have gone on the wrong road, turn back."
~Turkish Proverb

"Where you are is where you start from."
~Anonymous

Thirteen years ago, I was diagnosed with a mental illness and it changed the course of my life's journey. I experienced a loss of my self. The mental illness became my identity. I played only one life role — a client of the mental health system. My own internal stigmas, struggling with symptoms, medications, hospitalizations, shame, fear, and a lack of confidence kept me hopelessly trapped within myself. Added to that, the pressures of surviving within my family and community — where I increasingly felt the sting of misunderstanding, miseducation, stigma, and fear — painted for me a bleak picture of the life ahead.

At the time, I didn't know the 'language' of recovery. I measured my own success in terms of the length of the time out of the hospital or other treatment facilities. Measures of success also included things like keeping custody of my children, being my own payee, living in my own place, and participating in the mental health center's day program.

A big turning point in my life was the connection that I made to key people who saw something in me beyond my illness. They pushed me to disclose my dreams and wishes. Through this process of support, motivation, self-advocacy and my own determination, I began my recovery journey.

Unlike thirteen years ago, we now use that word 'recovery.' The impact of the recovery vision has helped me refocus my life. It has put my illness in perspective for me. I can now acknowledge my other life roles — being a daughter, wife, mother, church member, advocate, employee, and friend.

Recovery enables me to have options and choices within these roles. It goes way beyond my mental illness. It has opened pathways for opportunities and new discoveries.

Most importantly, recovery has given me hope — believable hope — for a future that I can design myself. This hope comes through different channels — spirituality, education, and a support system that includes my peers, coworkers, family members and mental health professionals.

Recovery is contagious! The concepts I have learned have also empowered my children, my family, and my friends. I feel better about myself. I am comfortable with who I am. Others around me seem more accepting as I continue to accept myself.

Continued...

> *I feel recovery changes people by giving them a language — an understanding — in which everyone can relate. I think most people are recovering or have recovered from something in their life — perhaps a disaster, a death, divorce, or a financial or job loss. Most importantly, the message of recovery challenges consumers not to define themselves exclusively within a framework of an illness.*
>
> *I believe recovery gives my peers and me the simple message...enough is enough of the same old stigmas and beliefs. It is time to take charge of our lives...it is time for us to 'GET A LIFE!'*
>
> *~Cherie Bledsoe,*
> *Kansas Consumer Provider*

What are the Foundations of the Movement Toward Recovery?

There are many reasons for the major changes that are taking place in our basic understanding of the potential for positive change after psychiatric disability. Factors that range from increased consumerism to hard science all support a shift toward a recovery perspective.

Consumerism in Health Care

A consumer orientation has grown in the entire health care field. We are no longer passive recipients of health care services. Those of us with serious health or mental health conditions have more rights — we have the right to know what our treatment is, what the risks and benefits and reasonable alternatives are and we have the right to consent to treatment or refuse treatment under almost all circumstances.

There is a growing emphasis on self-management or self-care in many long-term health conditions. More and more, we are expected to help ourselves in order to control and lessen the impact of all kinds of health challenges, from being overweight to heart disease and diabetes. In most long-term health conditions, the few hours of expert professional treatment we receive often have less impact on our quality of life than

"Each time a man stands up for an ideal, or acts to improve the lots of others, or strikes out against injustice, he sends forth a tiny ripple of hope, and crossing each other from a million different centers of energy and daring, those ripples build a current which can sweep down the mightiest walls of oppression and resistance."
~Robert F. Kennedy

do our personal decisions, the relationships we have, our attitudes and how we live our lives day-by-day. Self-care and self-management of our health and mental health are crucial. We are finding that psychiatric problems follow this general trend; improved self-care and self-management of our condition greatly improves our mental health!

There is a growing emphasis on the interaction of day-to-day lifestyle and health and mental health. The decisions we make about how we live our lives have a strong influence on our health. Choices we make each day either help us stay healthy and promote healing or cause our health or mental health to worsen. We have a hand in how healthy we are!

More and more people are using forms of complementary and alternative health care. Many of us are finding that alternative and complementary approaches to traditional medical-model services can help us improve our health and mental health. Support groups, nutrition and exercise, friendships and meaningful activities are now seen as having a positive impact on many health/mental health conditions. Those of us with psychiatric disabilities are also using alternative and complementary health strategies as tools to move toward recovery. For example, we are using support groups, herbal medicine, nutrition, meditation, stress reduction techniques and exercise. Some of these approaches seem to have a direct impact on our psychiatric symptoms, while others operate more indirectly to promote our wellness. In many cases, we are finding that when we act to improve our general wellness our mental health also improves.

Disability Rights

The Disability Rights Movement has changed the way we view people with disabilities. The Disability Rights Movement has made it clear that the opportunities and supports that people with physical and mental disabilities have are usually more important to our active participation in life than is our personal condition. The Disability Rights Movement has shown us that those of us with disabilities can live positive, contributing lives if we have the right resources and supports.

"Just as everybody else, we need to be in charge of our lives, think and speak for ourselves."
~Adolf Ratzka
Disability Rights
Activist

"They cannot take away our self respect if we do not give it to them."
~Mahatma Gandhi

Prior to the Disability Rights Movement, which began having a major impact in the 1970s, many people with serious disabilities were socially segregated. We were forced to live out our lives in closed institutions. Now society has acknowledged the legal and moral responsibility to make all communities more accessible to those of us with disabilities. People with disabilities, including those of us with psychiatric disabilities, have won the right to live fully in the community and we have the right to have reasonable accommodations that assist us to succeed in the workplace and many other areas of life.

In the past, those of us with disabilities were often treated as though we were children, rather than as adults. Our human rights were often violated rather than upheld. We were treated in ways that were very disrespectful and injured our dignity. Important decisions were made without our involvement.

The Disability Rights Movement increased consumer involvement in policy-setting and decision-making and increased attention to basic human, civil and legal rights. One of the major slogans of the Disability Rights Movement is "Nothing about us without us!" In fact, consumer-controlled and consumer-provided services have increasingly been promoted in the disability field.

The Ex-Patient or Consumer/Survivor Movement in the mental health field has increased attention to our rights as consumers and increased the availability of consumer-run programming. Leaders in our movement have become role models of recovery. A whole new generation of consumer providers has recently emerged to run or work in mental health programs who serve as recovery role models.

Evidence-Based Psychiatric Rehabilitation Practice

New models of mental health programming, such as supported housing, supported employment and supported education, have proven to be very effective in helping us succeed in roles such as tenant, student and employee. As research evidence has mounted to show that a high percentage of those of us with serious psychiatric

"Equal rights are not special rights."
~Disability Rights Slogan

17

problems can perform well in typical social roles, the idea that people with psychiatric disabilities cannot recover has completely lost credibility.

Recovery and a Strengths Orientation

We know that we increase our chances of recovery when we focus on our strengths, hopes and aspirations and the positive resources around us, rather than focusing primarily on our problems, psychiatric symptoms or deficits. Consumers have written about the importance of strengths to the whole process of recovery. Here's what Jay Mahler, a California consumer leader, has to say:

> *When we begin to feel more confidence in ourselves, we begin to acknowledge positive aspects of ourselves that are also a part of our reality. People are not a collection of psychiatric symptoms. We also have many talents, strengths and inner wisdom. We have important relationships with family, friends and helpers…As we gradually begin to identify with positive aspects within ourselves and our surroundings we come to realize we can call upon our inner and outer resources and strengths to move us forward in our recovery. The mental illness gradually becomes a less dominating and all-encompassing part of our lives.*
>
> *~Jay Mahler,*
> *California Consumer Leader*

As we enter the pathway to recovery, we find we can interact with our environment and other people in ways that help us move forward. There are many powerful sources of help and healing all around us.

Perhaps most importantly, we have many sources of hope and healing *within ourselves*. We can have more control over our lives and have a more positive future by building upon our own resources.

"When people tell you that you can't do something, you kind of want to try it."
~Senator Margaret Chase Smith

"You gain strength, courage and confidence by every experience in which you really stop to look fear in the face. You must do the thing which you think you cannot do."
~Eleanor Roosevelt

18

Watch Out for "Recovery Whiplash"!

Some people previewing this chapter found the ideas of strengths and recovery were very new to them, and these ideas challenged their view of both the world and themselves. They felt really excited about the whole idea of recovery and their potential for positive change. But, excitement wasn't the only thing people were feeling! Some people felt like their world had tilted and they had suddenly hit warp speed and been sucked into a new dimension. They came up with the term "recovery whiplash" to describe this sensation!

Some felt like they were riding an emotional roller coaster—very excited about the prospects of recovery, awakened to new ideas and more than a little scared. Some felt very, very angry that they hadn't been given this information earlier! This mixture of emotions can be hard to take!

What are you feeling about the idea of recovery?

"You must be the change you wish to see in the world."
~Mahatma Gandhi

"Courage doesn't always roar. Sometimes courage is the quiet voice at the end of the day saying, 'I will try again tomorrow.'"
~Mary Anne Radmacher-Hershey

If you have mixed feelings, you are not alone. A nationally known consumer-researcher from Maine, Ruth Ralph, also found that people setting out on the journey of recovery feel many things such as determination, fear, the desire to fight back, the sense that their world would never be the same again and anger. All of these emotions can be used constructively to speed us forward on our pathway to recovery!

Let's go!

A RECOVERY PLEDGE

I acknowledge that I am in recovery.

I believe that all people are made up of more than just their mental illness.

I believe in the principles of recovery...that the journey is unique for each person, it requires the will to recover, it is a self-directed process of discovery, it is nonlinear with unexpected setbacks and it requires self-effort, endurance and courage.

I believe in the essence of recovery that all individuals can live a full life and participate as citizens of our community.

I understand that education and self-advocacy are keys to my recovery.

I believe that it is important for family, friends, professionals, and my peers to join together as partners to build a community of hope.

I will strive to support others on their journey of recovery.

I believe that I have a tomorrow and that I can shape my future, by enjoying life to the fullest and sharing my own story of hope with others.

A recovery pledge Cherie Bledsoe, director of S.I.D.E., Inc., a consumer-run organization, and her peers developed for a recovery group they designed
(Drawn from writings by Patricia E. Deegan, Mary Ellen Copeland & Priscilla Ridgway).

 References & Resources

Chapter 1

References

Anthony, W.A. (1993). Recovery from mental illness: The guiding vision of the mental health service system in the 1990s. *Psychosocial Rehabilitation Journal, 16*(4), 11-22.

Chamberlain, J. (1990). The ex-patients movement: Where we've been and where we're going. *The Journal of Mind and Behavior, 11*(4), 323-336.

Chamberlain, R., & Rapp, C. A. (1991). A decade of case management: A methodological review of outcome research. *Community Mental Health Journal, 27,* 171-188.

Cohler, B. M. (1987). Adversity, resilience, and the study of lives. In E. J. Anthony & B. M. Cohler (Eds.), *The Invulnerable Child* (pp. 363-424). New York, NY: Guilford.

Deegan, P. E. (1988). Recovery: The lived experience of rehabilitation. *Psychosocial Rehabilitation Journal, 11*(4), 11-19. Reprinted with revisions in W. A. Anthony & L. Spaniol (Eds.), *Readings in Psychiatric Rehabilitation* (pp. 149-162). Boston, MA: Boston University, Center for Psychiatric Rehabilitation.

Deegan, P. E. (1992). The Independent Living Movement and people with psychiatric disabilities: Taking back control over our own lives. *Psychosocial Rehabilitation Journal, 15*(3), 3-19.

DeJong, G. (1979). Independent Living: Social Movement to analytic paradigm. *Archives of Physical and Medical Rehabilitation, 60,* 435-446.

DeSisto, J.J., Harding, C. M., McCormick, R.V., Ashikaga, T., & Brook, G. W. (1995). The Maine and Vermont three decade studies of serious mental illness. *British Journal of Psychiatry, 167,* 331-342.

Fisher, D. (1994). Health care reform based on an empowerment model of recovery by people with psychiatric disabilities. *Hospital and Community Psychiatry, 45*(9),913-915.

Harding, C. M. (1988). The outcome of schizophrenia. *The Harvard Medical School Mental Health Letter, 4,* 3-5.

21

Harding, C. M., Brooks, G. W., Ashikaga, T., Strauss, J. S., & Breier, A. (1987). The Vermont longitudinal study of persons with severe mental illness. I. Methodology, study sample, and overall current status. *American Journal of Psychiatry, 144*(6).

Harding, C. M., Brooks, G. W., Ashikaga, T., Strauss, J. S., & Breier, A. (1987). The Vermont longitudinal study of persons with severe mental illness: II. Long-term outcome of subjects who retrospectively met DSM-III criteria for schizophrenia. *American Journal of Psychiatry, 144*, 727-735.

Harding, C. M., Zubin, J., & Strauss, J. S. (1987). Chronicity in schizophrenia: Fact, partial fact, or artifact? *Hospital and Community Psychiatry, 38*(5), 477-484.

Hubert G. et al. (1980). Longitudinal studies of schizophrenic patients. *Schizophrenia Bulletin, 6*, 592-605.

Jimenez, M. A. (1988). Chronicity in mental disorders: Evolution of a concept. *Social Casework, 69*(10), 627-633.

National Summit of Mental Health Consumers and Survivors. (1999, August). Retrieved November 16, 2001, from www.selfhelp.org/plank.html.

Ralph, R. (2000). *Review of Recovery Literature: A Synthesis of a Sample of Recovery Literature.* Alexandria, VA: National Association of State Mental Health Program Directors, National Technical Assistance Center.

Rapp, C. A. (1995). The active ingredients of effective case management: A research synthesis. In C. A. Rapp, R. W. Manderscheid, M. J. Henderson, M. Hodge, M.B. Knisley, D.J. Penny, B.B. Stoneking, P. Hyde, & L.J. Giesler (Eds.), *Case Management for Behavioral Managed Care* (pp. 7-45). Rockville, MD: Center for Mental Health Services (SAMHSA) and the National Association of Case Management.

Rapp, C. A. (1998). *The Strengths Model: Case Management with People Suffering from Severe and Persistent Mental Illness.* New York, NY: Oxford University Press.

Rapp, C. A., & Wintersteen, R. (1989). The strengths model of case management: Results from twelve demonstrations. *Psychosocial Rehabilitation Journal, 13*, 23-32.

Ridgway, P. (1999). *Deepening the Mental Health Recovery Paradigm: Defining Implications for Practice.* Lawrence, KS. Office of Mental Health Research and Training, The University of Kansas, School of Social Welfare.

Saleebey, D. (1997). *The Strengths Perspective in Social Work Practice. Second Edition.* New York, NY: Longman.

Spaniol, L., Koehler, M., & Hutchinson, D. (1994). *The Recovery Workbook.* Boston, MA: Boston University, Center for Psychiatric Rehabilitation.

Sullivan, P. (1994). Recovery from schizophrenia: What can we learn from the developing nations. *Innovations & Research, 3*(2), 7-12.

Sullivan, W. P. (1994). A long and winding road: The process of recovery from mental illness. *Innovations and Research, 3*(3), 19-27.

U.S. Department of Health and Human Services (1999). *Mental Health: A Report of the Surgeon General.* Rockville, MD: U.S. Department of Health and Human Services, Substance Abuse and Mental Health Services Administration, Center for Mental Health Services, National Institutes of Health, National Institute of Mental Health.

Resources

Back from the Brink: A Family Guide to Overcoming Traumatic Stress by D. R. Catherall (Bantam, 1992).

Building Resiliency: How to Thrive in Times of Change by Mary Lynn Pulley & Michael Wakefield (Center for Creative Leadership, 2001).

Full Catastrophe Living: Using the Wisdom of Your Body and Mind to Face Stress, Pain and Illness by J. Kabat-Zin (Dell, 1991).

Resilience: Discovering a New Strength in Times of Stress by F. Flach (Random House, 1988).

Resiliency in Action: Practical Ideas for Overcoming Risks and Building Strengths edited by Nan Henderson, Bonnie Benard, & Nancy Sharp-Light (Resiliency in Action, 1999).

Resilient Adults: Overcoming a Cruel Past by G. O. Higgins (Jossey-Bass, 1994).

The Gifts of Suffering: Finding Insight, Compassion and Renewal by Polly Young-Eisendrath (Addison-Wesley, 1996).

The Resilient Spirit by Polly Young-Eisendrath (Perseus Books, 1996).

www.resiliency.com
Take a resiliency quiz and find books on resiliency. The website provides links to other resources on resiliency and the opportunity to sign up for a free newsletter.

Chapter Two
Gearing Up for the Journey

This chapter explores the "ABC"s of recovery — some of the attitudes, behaviors and ways of thinking (cognitions) that can help us prepare for the journey of recovery.

Introduction: The ABC's that Get Us Into Gear

In this chapter we explore some of the attitudes, behaviors and ways of thinking (cognitions) that can prepare us for the journey of recovery. We focus on the attitudes of hope and courage, the behavior of dignity of risk and ways of changing our thinking from a focus on the negative to a more positive outlook. Before setting out, we must gather the basic resources that support our journey. Let's take a look at some of the ABC's that can support us and get us into gear for the recovery journey.

A=ATTITUDES

The Importance of Our Attitudes

The attitudes we bring to our recovery journey set the stage for everything that follows. Here's how one person, Charles Swindoll (1987), a clergyman, describes the importance of attitude:

> *The longer I live, the more I realize the impact of attitude on life. It is more important than the past, than education, than money, than circumstances, than failures, than successes, than what other people think or say or do. It is more important than appearance, giftedness or skill.*
>
> *The remarkable thing is that we have a choice every day of our lives regarding the attitude we embrace for that day. We cannot change the past. We cannot change the fact that people will act in a certain way. We cannot change the inevitable. The only thing we can do is play on the one string we have, and that is our attitude. I'm convinced that life is 10% what happens to me and 90% how I react to it. And so it is with you. We are in charge of our attitudes.*

Two attitudes are very important as we begin our journey of recovery—hope and courage.

"Every intention is a trigger for transformation."
~Deepak Chopra

"My ruts were so deep they had their own tunnels."
~Julie Bayes, Kansas Consumer Provider

27

The Attitude of Hope

What is hope?

Definitions suggest that hope is the feeling that what we wish for or want can be had, that events will turn out well in our lives. It's an inner feeling or positive emotion that allows us to believe good things can happen for us in the future. To have hope means that we look forward to something with desire and have a reasonable expectation that our desire will be fulfilled.

How do you define hope?

In the past, many of us with psychiatric diagnoses were told straight out that there really wasn't anything to hope for, that we would never be able to reclaim a full or productive life. It's no wonder so many of us fall into a state of hopelessness. If we hold no prospects that our life will change for the better, it's hard to get up the energy to act on our own behalf.

Hope is a vital ingredient in enhancing our quality of life and life satisfaction. Our degree of hope or hopelessness influences how we contend with the challenges we face. Hope has been found to have a positive influence on health and general well-being, and can even have an effect on life itself. For example, research has shown a hopeful attitude plays a positive role in life expectancy for older adults and increases survival rates in women with breast cancer. On the other hand, hopelessness has many negative health and mental health effects. Many people agree that hope is one of the major supports for a successful recovery journey. The very idea that recovery is possible gives us renewed reason to hope.

"Don't be afraid of the space between your dreams and reality. If you can dream it, you can make it so."
~Belva Davis

"...a lack of hope has the danger of almost paralyzing a person, preventing them from going after their dreams."
~Donna Orrin, Consumer who was hospitalized 30 times over the course of 26 years, who went on to get her MSW and become a recovery consultant

How hopeful are you?

People feel hopeful to varying degrees. Some of us are generally more "up" and hopeful throughout life. Others of us have to struggle to feel hopeful and must reach deep inside ourselves to try to find even a tiny flicker of hope. Some of us have to gut it out and get started on our recovery journey without any sense of hope. We start out, and over time, we begin to gain hope through direct experience, as we see progress and positive changes happening in our lives.

> *I feel like I am starting to take control of my life. I see the light at the end of the tunnel, and hope to reach it. I think it is now possible with a lot of hard work still ahead of me. At least I see hope.*
>
> ~Jan Hanson,
> *Kansas Consumer Provider*

Chances are, if we are having more good days than bad, we can begin to feel more hopeful. At other times, when nothing seems to be going right for us, hope is much harder to keep alive. Sometimes despair wins and pulls us down and we struggle to renew an attitude of hope. Sometimes the only thing that gets us through the day is the knowledge that others are holding out hope for us.

Was there a time when you felt really hopeless? What made the difference that allowed you to feel hope again?

"There are times in life when a person has to rush off in pursuit of hopefulness."
~ *Work for Justice Newsletter*, Lesotho, South Africa

Use the following self-assessment to see how hopeful you are feeling.

HOPE SELF-ASSESSMENT

How hopeful you are at this time in your life?

☑ Check out your current level of hope
from the following statements:

❑ I am feeling completely without hope.

❑ I don't feel much hope, but others around me are holding hope for me.

❑ Some days I feel hopeful and other days I feel hopeless about the future.

❑ I feel somewhat hopeful and believe I will have a better future.

❑ I have some positive things going on in my life that make me quite hopeful.

❑ On a day-to-day basis I'm seeing my hopes fulfilled.

❑ I have so much hope that I share it with others and spark their hopefulness.

"If we were logical, the future would be bleak indeed. But we are more than logical. We are human beings, and we have faith, and we have hope."
~Jacques Cousteau

Hope helps us look forward and orients us toward action. Hope always involves some degree of uncertainty—if everything were completely certain, we wouldn't need to have hope. When we feel hopeful we become interested in planning our future. We may have only a vague or general notion about what we want our life to look like in the future. For example, we may hope to "have a good life."

> *Hearing people saying positive things about me was very hard and foreign to me. I had to learn to say thank you. Someone told me those were positive affirmations and gave me an assignment to come up with 10 each day. I struggled and struggled with trying to do this. I amended the assignment by listing 10 positive things about myself that other people had said about me and said those. For the longest time, it was a complicated matter, but finally the day came when a glimmer of hope peeked through and I started to begin to have hope and believe in myself.*
> ~Chris Shore,
> *Kansas Consumer*

What are some of the general hopes that you have for your life?

"Hope is not a dream, but a way of making dreams become reality."
~L.J. Cardina Suenens

Our hopes may be more focused and specific. We may have objectives in mind, achievements we want to attain, things we want to do or have or experiences that are on our "to do" list for our life. For example, we may hope to pay off an old bill by October or we may hope to make a new friend. Most of us have several specific, or particular hopes, in mind for our lives.

What are some of the specific hopes that you have for how things will go for you in the near future?

"Hope is like a road in the country; there was never a road, but when many people walk on it, the road comes into existence."
~Lin Yutang

Hope can be very difficult to hold onto when we experience prolonged psychiatric disability. One national consumer leader, Patricia E. Deegan (1998), tells us that the experience of psychiatric disorder and the negative messages she received from professionals and others around her caused a catastrophic shattering of her world, hopes and dreams. However, she also tells us about the "birth of hope" as an important stage in the process of her recovery. Focusing on the birth or rebirth of hope in our lives is important.

How Can We Renew or Build Hope?

There are several ways we can develop a more hopeful outlook:

Build positive relationships

Many first person accounts of recovery tell of a few very special people who help spark positive change. When people tell such stories they are often about people who really listened, who tried to understand them, and viewed them as a worthwhile person, who stuck by them and gave them hope.

Who are the people in your life that have helped you to feel hopeful or who held hope for you, even when you were feeling hopeless?

Actively seek small successes

Setting and reaching personal goals builds hope. Seeing ourselves as successful—feeling that "I can do this"—gives us an increased sense of control over our life.

List a few successes and achievements that have taken place in your life that you can look back on to help you feel hopeful.

"Hope works in these ways: it looks for the good in people instead of harping on the worst; it discovers what can be done instead of grumbling about what cannot; it regards problems, large or small, as opportunities; it pushes ahead when it would be easy to quit; it 'lights the candle' instead of 'cursing the darkness.'"
~Anonymous

32

HOPE EXERCISE:
Proving Positive Change is Possible

Ed Knight, a national consumer leader, defines hope as "knowing that positive change is possible." He suggests the following exercise:

Pick an activity you have wanted to do, or a small goal you really want to accomplish. Break the activity or goal down into very small steps. Take some steps. You'll experience that positive change is possible!! If you find you cannot take those small initial steps, spend time thinking about the barriers that stand in your way. Take positive steps to address the barriers. For example, if you found you didn't have the time to take the steps you had planned, you may want to work on scheduling. Step-by-step you'll build a history of positive change and bring hope into your life.

Jot down a few small things you will accomplish in the next few days. What will add to your gathering of small successes?

> "Hope is crucial to recovery, for our despair disables us more than our disease ever could."
> ~Esso Leete, consumer leader

Connect with successful role models

We can actively seek out people whom we consider to be positive role models of hope. This includes people who share the same experiences or life challenges we have had, who have been successful in some area of their life. Connecting with others who share common experiences eases our sense of isolation or loneliness.

We can find positive role models in self-help groups or through newsletters, magazines, internet web sites, conferences or newspaper articles. We can also read biographies of inspirational people who give us hope.

Who are some of the people you consider to be role models for you? Why?

How might you go about making a connection with them?

> "Hold your chest high,
> stick your chest out.
> You can make it!
> It gets dark sometimes
> but morning comes...
> keep hope alive!
> Keep hope alive!"
> ~Jesse Jackson

Increase spirituality

Many of us find that spirituality is a deep source of hope. Spiritual traditions provide comfort and ways to understand our suffering. They give us instructions about activities, such as prayers and rituals that can heal deep feelings of hopelessness. Many of us find spiritual writings to be uplifting. Being a part of a spiritual or faith community can also give us a sense of spiritual community and hope.

How can you build your spirituality?

Use many other strategies to build hope

Here are some more ways you can build hope in your life:

- Make good things happen in your life, even if it seems like a very small thing—put fresh sheets on your bed, make yourself a cup of cocoa, smile at someone on the bus. As the popular bumper sticker says, "Practice random acts of kindness and senseless acts of beauty."

- Use humor. It has been said, "If you can laugh, you still have hope."

- Develop hope-filled rituals. Light a candle. Put up a picture of yourself taken when you were a small child, tell that little person everyday that you have hope for him or her.

- Make a pact to join a friend on the phone once a week to share at least one positive experience each of you have had. This will help you keep your eye out for good things around you.

- Surround yourself with symbols of hope. This can be anything—a picture of a special person, an image or an object, whatever reminds you of hopefulness.

- Find ways to share hope with others. This could include something as simple as talking with a friend when they are feeling down, to getting involved in a support group or a consumer-run organization.

"And the day came when the risk to remain tight in a bud was more painful than the risk it took to bloom."
~Anais Nin

> *Recovery has given me hope — believable hope — for a future that I can design myself. Recovery has normalized life for me. It has been a catalyst for me to expand my life beyond the mental health world.*
>
> *~Cherie Bledsoe,*
> *Kansas Consumer Provider*

HOPE EXERCISE

Choose one of the strategies for renewing hope described earlier, or make up one of your own, and write about how you will incorporate it into your life. Be specific.

Are there other strategies that you want to use to enhance your hope?

Remember—hope is contagious! Convey the hope you feel to others. Hope increases your sense of what is possible. A belief in a better future can be a strong motivator for your personal recovery!

What can you do today to make another person feel more hopeful?

An Attitude of Courage

An attitude of courage is important to the recovery journey. When we first think of courage we may remember the cowardly lion in *The Wizard of Oz* or the phrase, "the courage of your convictions," or the line in the Alcoholics Anonymous creed that says, "the courage to change the things I can."

The word *courage* is derived from the French word *"cuer,"* meaning "heart." It is the quality of mind or spirit that enables us to face challenges or difficult experiences without completely shutting down or running away. It is the willingness to forge ahead even though we don't know what the future may hold for us.

Courage gives us the ability to face the "fear of fear" itself. It allows us to open ourselves to the process of change. Courage is part of the human spirit that enables us to face down seemingly insurmountable challenges, stay focused and go forward.

Courage may not feel like courage. It may feel like fear. On the journey of recovery, we experience growth, but even good changes can be scary when we have shut ourselves down for a long time. Amazing strength can be gained by sharing the truth about our life with others, even the truth about our deepest fears. We find many other people who are facing down their fears and finding courage in their own hearts to create positive change in their lives. They are finding freedom from fear by meeting challenges head on, and so can we!

Courage allows us to live a life that we choose for ourselves, rather than a life that others would choose for us. Courage allows us to break through the bounds of the limited existence that has traditionally been predicted for those of us with psychiatric disabilities. We can't control what goes on around us, but we can respond to what we face with courage.

The author of the following poem is a special education teacher. Her writing speaks volumes about hope and courage:

"To dream anything that you want to dream. That is the beauty of the human mind. To do anything that you want to do. That is the strength of the human will. To trust yourself to test your limits. That is the courage to succeed."
~Bernard Edmonds

Don't think of me as "mentally ill" for I am on a "journey."

My "journey" is one of recovery, and for the first time I have hope for my future.

I may appear different than you, but please give me the opportunity to follow a path that will lead to a successful future.

Don't think of me as "mentally ill" for it is not a "label" that I want to be known as, but as a person.

I don't want to be known as a person who is "crazy" or "looney," please give me the chance to have a life free of stigma.

Don't think of me as "mentally ill."

I have capabilities, which make me a strong, courageous person.

Let me follow a path that will allow me to demonstrate I am a SURVIVOR of life's most difficult journey.

My "journey of recovery" is a chance to recover from the pain of my illness and create a new life for myself.

~Kathy S. Shinn,
Kansas Consumer

How Can We Build Courage?

Make the intent to act with courage

The first step we can take to build courage is to formulate the intent or desire to be more courageous in our lives, to face our situation and not deny it or run from it.

Warm up to courage

The next step to building courage is to warm up to the idea of moving forward, before taking any particular action. One way to warm up our courage is to identify with other people who have committed acts of courage.

Do you know of others who have had the courage to face serious challenges and adversity in their life?

What are some of the courageous things that you have seen them do when facing adversity?

What have you learned from watching these people or hearing about their lives?

When someone looks into the mirror they more than likely just see their reflection. Is their hair combed, did they get a close shave, or is their makeup on right? Rarely do they look any deeper. When I look into a mirror, my reflection shows a 54-year-old woman, usually neat, combed and put together. When I look deeper it surprises me that I am here and functioning. As I look even deeper, I see a person who somehow has survived. Not only survived, but lived, raised three children and took control of my life. I find courage. It took courage for me to live and start over when I divorced my husband of 32 years. I know that I am willing and able now to go out on my own. To make a new life for myself, and at the same time acknowledge my past. As I turn from my reflection I realize how far I've come and also how far I have to go.

~Stormie Woodward,
Kansas Consumer

"Courage is being scared to death...and saddling up anyway."
~John Wayne

"It takes courage to grow up and become who you really are."
~e.e. cummings

Take small steps and small risks to build courage

We can try new things without letting fear overtake us. We can start by taking small risks, those that seem realistic for our current level of courage. We can identify something that scares us a little. This may be the fear of having to say something about a conflict we are having with a friend, the fear of rejection in reaching out and asking for help, ambivalence about looking for a job when we haven't worked in a long time or the fear of talking in a peer support group. Everyone's courage is at a different level, so we should choose something that is a reasonable stretch for us. Then do it! If we fall on our first attempt, we can pick ourselves up, dust ourselves off and pat ourselves on the back for trying!

What is one small risk that you can take today?

What kind of support or assistance will you need to carry this out?

As we develop courage, we experience fear and painful moments. We nurture ourselves and let any pain and embarrassment heal, and we continue challenging ourselves in small ways, until we have the courage to take on more. As we face our fears, we find some things become easier—things that we found impossible before, things that have kept us down for years!

Join with another person to build courage

Developing courage and taking risks can seem overwhelming at times. If we are feeling overwhelmed we may want to join with another person who can support us through the process. By working together, each of us becomes stronger and more courageous.

> "Courage is the price that life exacts for granting peace."
> ~Amelia Earhart

> "Any life truly lived is a risky business, and if one puts up too many fences against the risks one ends by shutting out life itself."
> ~Kenneth S. Davis

If you choose to work on deepening your courage with the support of another person, find someone who will not be affected by the outcome of your actions. Ask a friend or a peer who understands what it is you want to do, who is willing to support you and provide you with feedback, not advice. You don't want someone to tell you what to do or try to steer you away from what you really want to accomplish.

Pick a person who cares about you, and who has shown you this by his or her actions, not just in words. The person should agree to be your supporter and cheerleader, but should not try to direct your course of action. Make sure the person is someone who has demonstrated his or her own courage in facing challenges. Be honest with your ally about what you want to accomplish. The person will probably feel honored to be asked to support you!

Is there someone in your life who you think would be willing to help support you as you grow more courageous? Who are they?

Why would you choose this person? What qualities do they possess that you think make them a good supporter for you?

Adopting an attitude of courage moves us out of the role of victim and toward a life that gives us freedom to seek new things. A life without risk and courage is a life that can be stale and boring.

What are you <u>truly</u> afraid of?

"Courage is doing what you are afraid to do. There can be no courage unless you are scared."
~Eddie Rickenbacker

"In great attempts it is glorious even to fail."
~Anonymous

What are you willing to change today?

> "If your life is ever going to get better, you'll have to take risks. There is simply no way you can grow without taking chances."
> ~David Viscott

Being open to our fears and willing to face them is a very important part of beginning our recovery journey. It is possible for us to embrace our own fear, build courage and travel the path toward recovery. We are not alone!

B = BEHAVIOR

Behaviors that Support Recovery

Moving Out of Our Comfort Zone: Accepting the Dignity of Risk

Traditional mental health systems often tried to protect us from taking risks in order to maintain our stability. Most of us have been counseled by professionals against taking on new challenges, such as going to work, going back to school, forming an intimate relationship, even getting a driver's license.

What have you been told about taking risks?

> "Living is a form of not being sure, not knowing what next or how. The moment you know how, you begin to die a little. We never entirely know. We guess. We may be wrong, but we take leap after leap into the dark."
> ~Agnes de Mille

At times the mental health system can insulate us from life and become a kind of separate world. Charlene Syx (1995), a consumer provider who once was a state hospital patient, wrote an article, *The Mental Health System: How We Have Created a Make Believe World,* about the tendency for the mental health system to become an invisible protective bubble.

42

She says:

> ...*mental health providers ensconce people in a protective bubble, shielding them from their community and ultimately from their future... It's a safe and comfortable place for people to spend the rest of their lives. Service bubbles create dependencies. Frequently service systems attempt to solve all problems for all people at all times. But having problems and dealing with them is a natural part of life.*

Have you ever felt you were caught in a protective bubble? What were your experiences like?

To recover, we have to stretch ourselves and break out of our protective bubble. We have to move beyond our personal "comfort zone" in order to grow. Our comfort zone can be very small and contracted. We can feel like our life is in a kind of suspended animation. We may sit for much of the day just smoking cigarettes, wondering how we ended up being retired from life in our 20s, 30s and 40s. We may feel we have to trade in our dreams and goals for an SSI check that we are terrified of losing. We don't want to risk anything because we have so very little.

The field of developmental disabilities has a concept of the "dignity of risk" that national consumer leader Patricia E. Deegan brought into the mental health recovery movement. Dignity of risk promotes the idea that taking risks is a normal part of life. A life without risks unnaturally insulates us or closes us off from making choices and learning from our own experience. We have to take risks because the biggest risk in life is not to risk at all. We may avoid suffering, but we won't learn, change or grow.

What seems risky for one person may seem easy for another. Each person's experience of what feels risky is unique. Deegan's article *Recovery: The Lived Experience of Rehabilitation* (1988), tells about the early days of her recovery, when she had to challenge herself to undertake many "simple acts of courage" that included riding in a car and calling a friend. Taking a college course or going back to work may feel risky for some of us, while for others getting out of bed feels very, very scary.

"Don't let life discourage you; Everyone who got where he is had to begin where he was."
~Richard Evans

"Only those who will risk going too far can possibly find out how far one can go."
~T.S. Eliot

Learn From "Wrong Turns" on the Road to Recovery

There is an old saying that "life is trial and error, not trial and success."

> *Our freedom to make mistakes is one of our greatest assets, for this*
> *the way we learn humility, persistence, courage to take risks, and*
> *better ways of doing things (Hazelden Foundation, 1991).*

As we start out on the journey of recovery we find not everything we try works out. But even "wrong turns" on the road to recovery can move us forward. It's just as important to learn what we don't want, as it is to learn what we do want in our life. We may try living with others and find we really don't enjoy it; what we really want to do is to live alone or with a pet. We may take a job to get work experience, and leave when we find that it is not the right kind of situation for us. It's important to see such experiences as a source of learning rather than viewing them as failures.

Even though we may feel we have lost our way on the path to recovery, such experiences are important sources of learning and are certainly not a sign that it's the end of the road.

Can you think of an experience where you took on a challenge and weren't successful, but through that experience you learned something about yourself or your goals? Write about it here.

"We all know what we need to do, but it takes will, determination and even courage to face yourself and others and begin to make changes. Remember that you are not alone."
~Judy Molnar

Recovery is a mysterious journey. We don't know exactly where it will take us or what we will learn along the way. We do know that if we refuse to take on challenges our progress will be limited. We have to give ourselves the opportunity to step out into the mystery and take some chances.

What other behaviors do you think will get you ready for recovery?

C=COGNITION

The Ways of Thinking that Get Us in Gear: The Importance of Positive Self-Talk

The Problem of Negative Self-Talk

One of the best ways to be slowed down or sidetracked on the journey of recovery is to stay tuned to "negative self-talk." Negative self-talk is like having our radio dial set to a station that gives out only bad weather forecasts for our journey. The negative self-talk station announcer constantly tells us: "For the next 1,000 miles expect freezing drizzle, snowy conditions, slippery roads, rock slides, incredible wind chills and impassable surfaces. Stay off the highway if possible. Low visibility and injury accidents ahead."

We may have become such an expert at negative self-talk that our ongoing negative inner monologue is our most severe critic. Negative self-talk can come about from many experiences:

- It can develop from outer criticism, the negative things we have been told about ourselves by others.

- It can come from experiences of failure we have had in the past, from betrayals in important relationships or from the experience of trauma.

- Negative self-talk can happen when we constantly compare ourselves with ideals that are impossible to reach, such as the physical beauty and slimness of a fashion model or the behavior of a saint.

- We may develop negative self-talk by taking in or internalizing the social stigma associated with psychiatric problems.

"When nothing is sure, everything is possible."
~Margaret Drabble

"The thing always happens that you really believe in; and the belief in a thing makes it happen."
~Frank Lloyd Wright

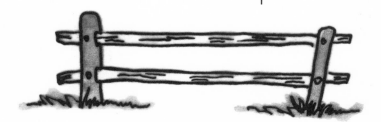

A SELF-TALK SELF-ASSESSMENT

☑How strongly does negative self-talk affect you?
(Check all that apply)

❑ When I listen to my inner negative self-talk I don't even feel like getting out of bed in the morning.

❑ Negative self-talk makes me feel unmotivated to make needed changes in my life. Why should I try anything when I know it won't work out?

❑ Negative self-talk makes it difficult for me to feel joy in life.

❑ I am constantly putting myself down inside my own head.

❑ I often find things to criticize about other people to make me feel a little better about myself, but it only seems to make me feel worse.

❑ Negative self-talk sometimes keeps me from doing things I want to do and keeps me away from people I want to be with.

❑ I don't use negative self-talk.

"I was going to buy a copy of 'The Power of Positive Thinking,' but then I thought: What the hell good would that do?"
~Ronnie Shakes

However negative self-talk arises, it can become a relentless inner voice that keeps us from even trying to make positive changes in our lives.

How has negative self-talk harmed your recovery?

The results of negative self-talk

What can negative self-talk do?
- It can make us less healthy
- It can make it more difficult for us to succeed in a job
- It can lower our quality of life
- It can contribute to depression
- It can make it harder to build or maintain relationships

Shifting to Positive Self-Talk

How can we "tune out" negative self-talk and "tune in" a more positive mindset? Positive self-talk can motivate us to reach beyond difficult experiences. Feeling more positive and reorienting our thinking away from the negative can enhance feelings of wellness and build realistic optimism.

There are many ways you can shift from negative to positive self-talk. Here are some steps you can take:

Tune into your mental mindset

Become aware of your mental habits. Listen in on your own thoughts. Throughout the day, pay attention to what you are telling yourself about how things are going now and how they will go in the future. Identify the thoughts that make up your "negative self-talk vocabulary".

- Do you call yourself names (e.g. stupid, a jerk)?
- Do you put yourself down ("I'll never do anything right")?
- Do you second-guess others' feeling toward you ("John is just pretending to like me; once he gets to know me he won't want me as a friend")?
- Do you predict negative outcomes ("I'm going to mess this up and get fired")?
- Do you "awfulize" ("My life sucks. It's too hard to even try")?
- Do you "catastrophize" ("If I get another roommate he will just rip me off like Paul did")?
- Do you generalize from one experience to all other such experiences ("My relationship with Jean was so bad I don't even want to have another girlfriend; they're all the same!")?

"You have to have confidence in your ability, and then be tough enough to follow through."
~Rosalynn Carter

EXERCISE:
My Negative Self-Talk Inventory

After monitoring your thoughts for several days, write down
the negative self-talk patterns you identify.

My negative self-talk patterns include:

Stop the Pattern!

Now that you have identified any negative thought patterns that you
have, begin to neutralize or counteract them. There are many ways to do
this; you can try out suggested techniques or be creative and make up a
method or visual symbol of your own.

- One way to stop negative thoughts is to picture negative
  thoughts as a separate person—say a nasty troll who is trying to
  keep you under a spell. Your task becomes to break the spell of
  negative thoughts so you can go forward on your quest for your
  true being.

- A simpler way to counteract negative thoughts is to create
  a mental picture or visualization of a stoplight or stop sign.
  When you become aware that you are using the negative thought
  patterns, think "STOP!!!" while visualizing the stoplight or stop
  sign in your mind.

Substitute positive self-talk for negative self-talk

The next step is to actively substitute positive thoughts in place of the old negative thought patterns. There are many ways to substitute positive self-talk.

- One way to counteract the negative thought is by immediately substituting an opposing thought. For example, when you begin to think, "I can't do this!" say, "I find it easy and rewarding to do this."

- Another way is to think of exceptions to the thought and dwell on the exceptions for a few moments. If you are feeling, "I'll never succeed at 'X' task," think about a time when you did succeed at something. Tell yourself "I succeeded at 'Y' so I can certainly also succeed at doing 'X'."

- Counteract negative self-talk by substituting a general encouraging thought such as, "I love and respect myself," or "I am safe," whenever you find yourself beginning to think negative thoughts.

- You can also substitute an uplifting phrase or a short prayer from your spiritual tradition for the negative thought.

- The section on affirmations in Chapter 11 will also give you helpful techniques to begin to use positive self-talk.

"I am in the present. I cannot know what tomorrow may bring forth. I can only know what the truth is for me today. That is what I am called upon to serve."
~Igor Stravinsky

"Life is an immense mural that requires each of us to pick up the brush and paint a bold stroke."
~Holly Near

What are some positive thoughts you will use to counter negative *self-talk?*

Create a wealth of positive thoughts

You can gather a set of positive and uplifting thoughts that you can draw upon. They can be found in self-help books, magazines, spiritual writings and on many websites.

> *I received a book filled with quotes and sayings. It didn't say anything particularly positive, but the quotes helped me to forget how worthless I was feeling. As time went on I discovered these sayings everywhere (magazines, books, other people) and I began to log the sayings that had an impact on me. Soon I began making gifts of tiny booklets of quotes for people I cared about. The more I made, the more I memorized the quotes. Then I found myself applying them to my life. Through certain quotes and sayings, I was able to feel compassion for other people and their suffering. In turn, I eventually was able to apply them to myself and grew to appreciate who I was and what I had endured. I was able to turn my negative thoughts into a form of strength and hope, and to believe that I mattered and there was a reason for all that had taken place in my life.*
>
> *~Beth Clement,*
> *Kansas Consumer*

We didn't develop our negative self-talk vocabulary overnight; it took us years to develop the negative ruts our mind can spin in. Similarly, it can take a long time to consciously change negative thought patterns— several weeks or months, or even a few years. **Be persistent! Monitor your thought patterns for negative self-talk, stop the thoughts using a creative visualization, substitute positive self-talk for negative self-talk and build your own personalized set of positive thoughts that support your recovery!**

SPECIAL PROJECT:
Create Your Own Book of Positive Quotations

We can follow Beth Clement's lead and create our own booklet of uplifting quotations and phrases to help us on our recovery journey.

Here are a few of the quotes Beth included in her booklet:
- "…it takes a deep commitment to change but a deeper commitment to grow."
- "I don't know what the future holds, but I do know who holds the future."
- "To live happily is an inward power of the soul."

Here is how you can develop a similar book for your self:

Materials:
A bound journal or small notebook. A pen or several colored felt-tip pens.

Resources:
Inspirational, motivational books, books from spiritual traditions.

Process:
1. Select quotations that you find inspiring or uplifting.
2. Ask other people for their favorite quotations.
3. Enter your favorite quotes into your book.
4. Read your quotations often to support your shift to more positive thinking.
5. Memorize the most important quotes and use them to substitute for negative thoughts you may have.

Repeat all the steps described above many times!

Negative self-talk can become **_more intense_** when we are under stress and **_much more intense_** when we are initially paying attention to our inner self-talk and trying to make changes in our thought patterns. This is a very common experience! It is good to accept this condition and keep going.

Getting Out of the Shoulda-Woulda-Coulda Cul-de-Sac and Into the Present Moment

Do you ever find yourself going 'round, and 'round, and 'round in your thinking, constantly going over, and over, and over what you or others *could* have done, *should* have done, *would* have done, if only you had...or if only they had...Stop that thinking!

We cannot successfully second guess ourselves, nor can we change anything that happened to us in the past! We cannot change anyone else's behavior, especially their behavior in the past! The more we try to change the past, the more we will find ourselves stuck and unable to move toward a more positive future.

The only time we have to act on our recovery is in this moment! We can try to be more present in the moment. We can learn to release regrets from the past, and fears of the future, whenever we find ourselves dwelling on them. Don't let negative thoughts steal the time you have to work toward recovery!!

What other ways of thinking about things (cognitions) do you think would help your recovery?

What are a few ways you will work to bring new attitudes, behaviors and cognitions into your life?

 References & Resources

References

Byrne, C., Woodside, H., Landeen, J., Kirkpatrick, H., Bernardo, A., & Pawlick, J. (1994). The importance of relationships in fostering hope. *Journal of Psychosocial Nursing, 32*(9), 31-34.

Carter, S. C. (1989). *Negaholics: How to Overcome Negativity and Turn Your Life Around.* New York, NY: Fawcett Columbine.

Deegan, P. E. (1988). Recovery: The lived experience of rehabilitation. *Psychosocial Rehabilitation Journal, 11*(4), 11-19. Reprinted with revisions in Anthony, W. A. & Spaniol, L. (Eds.), *Readings in Psychiatric Rehabilitation* (pp. 149-162). Boston, MA: Boston University, Center for Psychiatric Rehabilitation.

Hazelden Meditations (1991). *Today's Gift: Daily Mediations for Families.* Center City, MN: Hazelden Softcover.

Jackson, M., & Jevne, R. (1993). Enhancing hope in the chronically ill. *Humane Medicine, 9*(2), 121-130.

Jeffers, S. J. (1998). *Feel the Fear and Do it Anyway.* New York, NY: Random House.

Kirkpatrick, H., Landeen, J., Byrne, C., Woodside, H., Pawlick, J., & Bernardo, A. (1995). Hope and schizophrenia: Clinicians identify hope-instilling strategies. *Journal of Psychosocial Nursing, 33*(6), 15-19.

Littrell, K. H., Herth, K. A., Hinte, L. E. (1996). The experience of hope in adults with schizophrenia. *Psychiatric Rehabilitation Journal, 19*(4), 61-65.

Roger, J. & McWilliams, P. (1991). *You Can't Afford the Luxury of a Negative Thought.* Los Angeles, CA: Prelude Press.

Seligman, M. E. P. (1998). *Learned Optimism: How to Change Your Mind and Your Life.* New York, NY: Simon and Schuster.

Swindoll, C. (1987). *Living Above the Level of Mediocrity: A Commitment to Excellence.* Waco, TX: Word Publishers.

Syx, C. (1995). The mental health service system: How we've created a make-believe world. *Psychiatric Rehabilitation Journal, 19,* 83-85.

Resources

A Grateful Heart: Daily Blessings for the Evening Meal from Buddha to the Beatles edited by M.J. Ryan (Conari Press, 1994).

A is for Attitude: An Alphabet for Living by Patricia Russell-McCloud (Quill, 2002).

Embracing Fear: How Facing, Exploring, Accepting and Responding to Fear Can Transform Your Life by Thom Rutledge (Harper San Francisco, 2002).

I Hope You Dance by Mark D. Sanders & Tia Sellers (Rutledge Hill Press, 2000).

Life is an Attitude: How to Grow Forever Better by Dottie Billington (Lowell Leigh Books, 2001).

The Little Book of Courage by Sarah Quigley (Conari Press, 2002).

How to be Happier Day by Day by Alan Epstein (Viking, 1993).

Prisoners of Belief by Matthew McKay and Patrick Fanning (New Harbinger Publications, 1991).

The Body Image Workbook: An Eight-Step Program for Learning to Like Your Looks by Thomas F. Cash (New Harbinger Publications, 1997).

The Depression Workbook: A Guide to Living with Depression and Manic Depression by Mary Ellen Copeland (New Harbinger Publications, 1992).

The Essence of Attitude: Quotations for Igniting Positive Attitudes edited by Katherine Karvelas (Career Press, 1998).

The Feeling Good Handbook by David Burns (Plume, 1999).

The Power of Your Spoken Word: Change Your Negative Self-Talk and Create the Life You Want by Louise L. Hay (Hay House, Inc., 1991).

The Relaxation and Stress Reduction Workbook by Martha Davis, Elizabeth Robbins Eshelman & Matthew McKay (Fine Communications, 1997).

Thoughts and Feelings by Matthew McKay, Martha Davis & Patrick Fanning (New Harbinger Publications, 1998).

Chapter Three

Setting Ourselves in Motion

*This chapter discusses the concept of a "You Turn" or turnaround toward recovery.
It covers the importance of motivation and the obstacles to starting the recovery journey.*

Introduction

We begin this chapter by discussing motivation. Motivation is the fuel we need to move us out of our current situation and get us off to a good start. If we are to recover we have to move any inner or outer obstacles in our pathway out of the way so we can get going. As we overcome any inertia we may be feeling, that sense of not being able to move forward, we become much more active on our own behalf.

Later in the chapter we look closely at the experience of turnaround, the point at which we shift our attention from our disability to our desire for recovery. Turnaround sets us on a whole new path!

Motivation: The Fuel for the Journey

If we are unmotivated we won't get very far on the journey of recovery.

Unfortunately, many of us have lost a sense of personal motivation. Sometimes, we have had so many disappointments in our lives that we came to believe it's better not to want *anything* to protect ourselves from future losses. We can be very disheartened when the paths to our early dreams are interrupted or destroyed. We may have been told not to have any dreams, to consider ourselves completely and permanently disabled because of our diagnosis. But, recovery is all about setting goals, renewing aspirations and moving forward to realize our dreams.

What is Motivation?

Motivation is made up of all the forces acting on us or within us that initiate and direct our behavior (Petri, 1981). Motivation is the "drive" we have to act on our thoughts, ideas and intuition. The following account of one person's experience illustrates how things that exist *outside* ourselves can influence our recovery.

> *I fell into deep depression from the death of our son resulting in several hospitalizations, including ECT treatments. The experience eventually left me feeling lost, confused and unmotivated. When I was dismissed from my third hospitalization I still had a lot to do. I breed toy fox terriers, and they get me up at 7:30 every morning, and continue to push me into serving them throughout the day. I feed them, keep up with their papers and clean up their messes. I also have to put them to bed at 9:30, promptly. I believe they have literally saved my life.*
>
> *~Anonymous,*
> *Kansas Consumer*

Other people, including recovery role models, can motivate us. We may attend a recovery conference and feel very inspired by the speakers. We go home excited and begin planning our recovery. Other people can make us think more about our own motivations, they can spark or tap into our own unrealized potential. We may get going when another person says something that helps us see the motives, gifts, desires and potential that we have hidden within us. Others can give us information that changes our old ideas and reorients us toward a new way of looking at ourselves or our situations.

For those of us in recovery from psychiatric disability, as with all people, the deepest motivation must come from within. We have many dreams or needs that can help drive our recovery. Self-motivation may come from things we want to do or achieve, things that have real personal meaning for us. When we align our actions with our inner motivation, long-term change becomes a reality in our lives.

How can we find and build self- motivation? There is no such thing as a truly "unmotivated" human being. Each of us wants, and is motivated by, something. The trick is to figure out what it is we want, what it is that will motivate us.

What motivates you?

"Your distress about life might mean you have been living for the wrong reason, not that you have no reason for living."
~Tom O'Connor

MOTIVATION SELF-ASSESSMENT

☑ Use the following checklist to determine
your current level of motivation:

❑ Nothing I can do could make a difference.

❑ People around me don't expect anything of me, so I don't expect anything either.

❑ I have a slight feeling of motivation toward recovery.

❑ Sometimes I think of things that I might want to do, and get a little excited, but then I can't seem to do anything about it.

❑ I have several things I am thinking about trying and I'm thinking of moving on them soon.

❑ I have started to develop a plan of how I can get some things accomplished, and now I'm gathering ideas, supports and resources.

❑ I have definite goals for my life and a clear plan of what I want to do.

❑ I am exerting myself now and beginning to move towards what I want.

❑ I am well underway and moving firmly towards my goals.

❑ I have accomplished so much in my recovery, that I am sharing my excitement with others to motivate them.

"The secret of discipline is motivation. When a man is sufficiently motivated, discipline will take care of itself."
~Alexander Paterson

What motivates you to get out of bed and keep going?

What are some things, thoughts or feelings that motivate you to recover?

What are some other things you want, desire or seek to achieve in your life?

> "It seems to me we can never give up longing and wishing while we are alive. There are certain things we feel to be beautiful and good, and we must hunger for them."
> ~George Eliot

Taking the Driver's Seat: Self-Responsibility for Recovery

The Importance of Self-Responsibility

We have to climb into the driver's seat to make the recovery journey. We are the only person who can set goals for our life. We are the only one who can move toward our dreams.

Overcome obstacles that hold us back

If we are feeling unmotivated we have to figure out what is holding us back. Once we know what is in our way, we can begin to dismantle the barriers that block our journey. Complete the following self-assessment on motivation.

WHAT MOTIVATES ME?
A Self-Assessment

☑ (Check all that apply)

- ❑ I want to be able to climb a set of stairs without gasping for breath.
- ❑ I want to have a car so I can get around town.
- ❑ I want to keep my kids.
- ❑ I want to have a sense of meaning and purpose in my life.
- ❑ I want recognition from other people.
- ❑ I want to have something to look forward to.
- ❑ I want to feel more connected to other human beings.
- ❑ I want to make a difference.
- ❑ I want to fulfill God's purpose for me.
- ❑ I want to feel good about myself.
- ❑ I want to have a day without disturbing symptoms.
- ❑ I want to work.
- ❑ I want to feel more self-confident.
- ❑ I want to be a role model for other people in recovery.
- ❑ I want some money in the bank.
- ❑ I want to be of service to others, to give back.
- ❑ Other _____

Inertia can be the most important obstacle to taking our first steps on the journey of recovery. In the world of physics, inertia is the idea that nothing moves on its own. There is always some force that sets an object at rest into motion. The same is true for people. We do not spontaneously set ourselves into motion and suddenly change. Something has to happen inside us, or outside us, to get us moving.

"I want to do it because I want to do it!"
~Amelia Earhart

"One starts an action because one must do something."
~T. S. Eliot

Motivation for recovery can come from almost any source.

- We may quit drinking soda pop after noticing that we don't feel good after consuming a lot of sugar. Our wellness improves. Our recovery has begun.

- We may read the employment classified advertisements because our rent has gone up and we fear becoming homeless. We find a job. Our life improves. Our recovery has started!

- We may get out of bed in the morning to let the cat out, even though we're feeling very depressed, because we don't want our apartment to smell like a cat box. We keep getting up and finally we take a step out the door and begin living life again. Our recovery is underway.

List some things that have started you moving when you were feeling really stuck:

Sometimes we don't recognize the early steps on our recovery journey because they look just like everyday activities. Sometimes our first steps are invisible to anyone looking at us from the outside because they take the form of inner thoughts and feelings. Even if we just begin to *think* about getting up and letting the cat out, that is a first step in getting moving. What is important is that we recognize and encourage ourselves when we have made some small steps, and keep ourselves moving.

If we feel stalled we must try to figure out what blocks us from staying in motion. Sometimes we don't get started because we don't know we need to assume self-responsibility for our own recovery journey.

I don't have a license to drive

Empowerment is a common term in mental health circles these days. Empowerment describes our feelings of personal power and our control over important life decisions. We can lose our sense of empowerment or have it taken from us. As a result, we can feel like we do not have the right to take charge of our own recovery or that the responsibility for our recovery lies with someone else, such as our case manager or therapist.

Until very recently, many mental health systems routinely took away our sense of empowerment. Those of us who have been "in the system" for years or even decades are often left with little idea of our own power, and we can lack a sense of self-responsibility. The feeling of disempowerment can also come from relationships where we were told or felt that we were somehow worthless, or were too "sick" to know what was good for us, or when our credibility was repeatedly challenged simply because we had been given a psychiatric label.

I've never been in the driver's seat

When we begin to regain our sense of personal power, it can seem overwhelming at first. Empowerment is a wonderful thing and it is every person's right. It can also feel scary. It is normal to feel nervous and unsure with all the options open to us as part of our recovery journey. We can take time to learn and practice self-responsibility.

Why should I start out? I'll just break down!

Some of us have been told that relapse will certainly result if we make changes in our lives. We know nothing is guaranteed in moving toward recovery. We don't want to rock the boat when we have been stable for a period of time.

Do you feel any of these things or have you in the past? What are some messages that you have been given that led you to feel this way and who gave them to you?

Are there things that feel good about avoiding personal responsibility?

"To travel hopefully is a better thing than to arrive."
~Robert Louis Stevenson

Turnaround Toward Recovery

Starting the Recovery Journey: Making a "You" Turn

The beginning, or initiation, of the journey of recovery is sometimes called "turnaround." We turn away from our old way of living, our old way of seeing ourselves primarily as a person with a psychiatric disability. We set off in a new direction to reclaim a fuller, healthier, more active way of life.

We can view turnaround as a *"You Turn"* because:

- No one else can really change another person. Real change in your life is possible when *you* feel *you* want *your* life to change.

- It is an important moment when *you* firmly decide to move toward recovery. Turnaround is *your* moment, no one else's.

- No one can make you move toward recovery. Other people can inspire and encourage you, but *you* make the decision to take action on *your* own behalf.

- No one can do the work of your recovery for *you*. *You* can do the things *you* decide are important to move toward the life *you* want to have.

- In turnaround *you* realize *you* must assume primary responsibility for how *your* life is going, and *you decide to* make a commitment to *yourself* to become the person *you* want to be.

- Turnaround orients *you* to move toward *your* goals and priorities and it points *you* toward a life that honors the strengths that are uniquely *your* own. *You* can make progress on your goals!

- Once you have experienced turnaround you are heading in the direction of healing and transformation. Your life will never be the same again!

Turnaround really does change our lives!

"By turning, turning, we come round right."
~Shaker spiritual

64

What do We Know about Turnaround?

Turnaround toward recovery is a somewhat mysterious process. No one seems to be able to predict when turnaround will happen. But we do know it is possible to experience turnaround and move toward recovery even if we have had a serious psychiatric disability for ten, twenty or even thirty years!

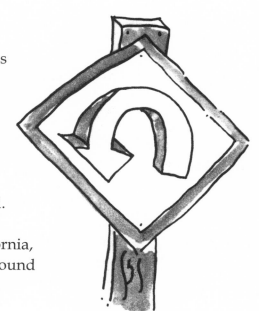

There is no "one way" or one experience of turnaround. There are many different turnaround experiences. Jay Mahler, a consumer leader from California, calls turnaround a "Eureka experience" because turnaround can be a dramatic "Ah Hah!" moment. Here is a story that represents a dramatic "Eureka" experience:

> *A friend of mine said to me one day 'You don't have to believe your diagnosis, it's only a label.' I thought I'd been given a death sentence from the medical 'experts' which I had no choice but to accept. That single moment changed my life forever...Nine years later, I'm working full time, living on my own and I'm starting my own business.*
>
> *~Consumer quoted in Kramer & Gagne (1997)*

Research on turnaround describes the importance of our attitudes, our drive to recover and our personal will in achieving recovery. At a certain point we may firmly make up our minds to do whatever it takes to change the direction of our lives.

> *I said [to myself] if I stay home and if I lay in this bed I'm going to die emotionally. My life is for all intents and purposes over if I stay in this bed and if I don't get off my butt and at least get the help. And I felt I had to get the hell out of [his mother's] house...I was like I was just... wanted to just make a step. Said what the hell. I've got nothing to lose because I'm going to die here. So I mean this is going to sound really corny to you, but I had twenty-five dollars in my pocket and I had a suitcase. This is true. Sounds like something out of a movie. And I moved into town and I never moved back.*
>
> *~"Bill" from an interview excerpt in Patricia E. Deegan's "Beyond the Coke and Smoke Syndrome"*

"The task is not to become normal. The task is to take up your journey of recovery and to become who you are called to be."
~Patricia E. Deegan, National Consumer Leader

Sometimes turnaround happens when we finally stop trying to run away from or deny the challenge of psychiatric disorder. Some of us find accepting help, getting good treatment and acknowledging we have problems are crucial turning points that ultimately lead us to recovery. This may mean finding the right medication at the right dose. Medications don't accomplish recovery. They are one tool that can help us achieve remission or reduce symptoms so that it is much more possible for us to recover. Sometimes a change in medications, especially getting off heavy drugs, can also provide an opening for recovery to begin.

Sometimes we "hit bottom" before making a turnaround. We come face to face with a loss of meaning in life, we find our isolation intolerable, or we feel death is near—our lives seem too empty or too pointless or we are too tired of suffering to go on as we have done.

> *David Reed, Kansas Consumer, experienced turnaround when he found himself in a homelessness shelter for the third time—even though he had several brothers and sisters living in the area. He decided he had to change the way he was living his life. David now works in a local Clubhouse, is on the Board of Directors of his mental health agency and is a successful Consumer as Provider program graduate.*

Turnaround can happen when we get good and angry about how we are being treated. We can use our anger as a motivating force in our recovery. We become focused on our recovery to prove to others that we are more than what they see in us.

> *Donna Story, a Kansas Consumer Provider, found her treatment team was planning to place her in a mental health nursing home for an indefinite stay. Almost by accident she found out that she could fight this decision. Her turnaround came about when she decided she did not want to enter the nursing home. She drew upon her inner and outer resources and came up with a clear alternative plan. Donna stood up for herself in court and presented the Judge with her ideas. The Judge did not commit her to the nursing home. Several months later she has become a consumer leader in her area and successfully completed the Consumer as Provider Training. Donna has set new goals based on these accomplishments. She is now earning her degree in social work in order to help others.*

We may become determined to make a turnaround when we realize that other people (or even our pets) are counting on us.

> *One Kansas consumer said she realized that she couldn't stay deeply depressed and couldn't continue to harm herself because she was a part of a family. She wanted to be a positive influence in the lives of her family members, especially her beloved grand babies. She did not want them growing up with a grandmother who was seriously disturbed or a suicide case. Thinking about how her behavior affected her family got her onto a path of recovery and keeps her focused on improving her life and mental health.*

Sometimes turnaround happens when we learn that people can and do recover — when we gain the knowledge that recovery is possible.

> *Ed Knight tells us that he was a patient in a state hospital several years ago when he attended a conference on recovery and heard about positive research findings. His turnaround came when he decided to believe the research that shows most people with prolonged and severe psychiatric disorder do recover over time, rather than believing the negative messages he had been given that he would never recover. From that point forward Ed worked toward his recovery and helped others to recover as well. He went on to direct an organization that helped found several hundred self-help groups. Ed is now a national expert on recovery, a well-regarded researcher and a renowned trainer on rehabilitation, recovery and self-help. He recently became a vice-president of a major managed care corporation and is responsible for promoting peer support and recovery.*

Sometimes we begin to move toward recovery when we find a person who becomes a role model of recovery for us.

Turnaround may also happen when we have a safe and stable environment. In one study more than half the people said they started their recovery journey once they had decent housing because having a stable living situation lessened the stress in their lives and allowed them to get organized and move forward (Coursey, et al., 1997).

Turnaround toward recovery can come when loved ones, friends, peers and mental health workers cheer us on, support us, give us hopeful messages and see and comment about the good in us, even when we are not hopeful or feeling good about ourselves.

"The best thing in life is doing things people say you can't do."
~Jennifer Moore

Chapter 3

"No one on earth can do what you alone are called to do, can give to the world what you alone were sent to give through your authentic gifts. The call may be so faint you can barely make out the message, but if you listen, you will hear it."
~Sarah Bon Breathnach

We can experience turnaround without even being conscious that we are on a recovery journey. We make some changes in our daily life, learn something new, begin participating more actively in the world, get a part time job or start volunteering or become involved in interesting relationships. We may not even know we are on a path to recovery until we are part way there! We can backtrack and see where we began to experience change and growth, but our recovery seems to have happened without our planning it!

One Kansas Consumer as Provider student didn't want to attend graduation ceremonies. She said she had never succeeded at anything and did not feel she deserved her certificate. She was somewhat surprised to realize that it was too late for her to avoid achieving a big step toward recovery. She had done very well. In fact, she had already succeeded!

What is Your Experience of Turnaround?

Was there a day when you made up your mind to work toward your recovery or was it a long process of change?

Have you experienced turnaround toward recovery? Write about your personal experience of turnaround here:

> "Once I became aware of my inner power, I became the captain of my ship so to speak, and I needed to plot a new course to discover the buried treasure...me!"
> ~Joan Lunden

> "The journey is the reward."
> ~Taoist Saying

Who or what helped sparked recovery for you?

If you haven't experienced turnaround that's O.K., you can write about your response to the idea of turnaround.

"It is good to have an end to journey toward, but it is the journey that matters in the end."
~Ursula K. LeGuin

"Let's dare to be ourselves, for we do that better than anyone else can."
~Shirley Briggs

References & Resources

References

Coursey, R. D., Alford, J. & Sajarjan, B. (1997). Significant advances in understanding and treating serious mental illness. *Professional Psychology: Research & Practice, 28*(3): 205-216.

Deegan, P. E. (1997). Recovering our sense of value after being labeled. In L. Spaniol, C. Gagne & M. Kohler (Eds.), *Psychological and Social Aspects of Psychiatric Disability* (pp. 370-376). Boston: Boston University, Center for Psychiatric Disability.

Deegan, P. E. (1999). *Beyond the Coke and Smoke Syndrome: Working with People who Appear Unmotivated.* Lawrence, MA: National Empowerment Center.

Kramer, P. J. & Gagne, C. (1997). Barriers to recovery and empowerment for people with psychiatric disabilities. In L. Spaniol, C. Gagne & M. Kohler (Eds.), *Psychological and Social Aspects of Psychiatric Disability* (pp. 467-476). Boston: Boston University, Center for Psychiatric Disability.

Landeen, J., Pawlick, J., Woodside, H., Kirkpatrick, H., & Byrne, C. (2000). Hope, quality of life, and symptom severity in individuals with schizophrenia. *Psychiatric Rehabilitation Journal, 23*(4), 364-369.

Petri, H. L. (1981). *Motivation: Theory and Research.* Belmont, CA: Wadsworth Publishing Company.

Sullivan, W. P. (1994). The long and winding road: The process of recovery from severe mental illness. *Innovations & Research, 3*(3): 19-27.

Resources

Change Your Life Without Getting Out of Bed by SARK (Simon & Schuster, 1999).

Chasing Away the Clouds by Douglas Pagels (Blue Mountain Press, 1998).

Living Juicy by SARK (Celestial Arts, 1994).

One Day My Soul Just Opened Up by Iyanla Vansant (Fireside, 1998).

Simple Abundance: A Daybook of Comfort and Joy by Sarah Ban Breathnach (WarnerBooks, 1995).

Chapter Four

Recovery is Self-Discovery:
Recognizing Our Strengths

This chapter explores initial ideas about identifying strengths and ways to make the most of personal and environmental strengths. By the end of the chapter, you will have a complete inventory of strengths that will support your personal journey of recovery.

Introduction: Exploring Our Strengths

In this chapter, we begin to carefully identify the strengths that we possess. We learn ways to make the most of our personal and environmental strengths. As we work through this process, we develop a complete inventory of our strengths that supports our personal journey of recovery.

Discovering and capitalizing on our strengths and aspirations is important, because we need to draw on both our inner and outer resources to make positive progress along our pathway to recovery. We won't be able to get far without identifying and using our strengths.

Each one of us has strengths. Sometimes we are not in touch with them, but none of us could exist if we didn't have strengths. We have always had strengths within us and around us, no matter how difficult and challenging our situation or circumstances are. One of the most important things we can do is to identify, call upon and use our unique strengths as we embark on our recovery journey.

Understanding our strengths may seem like an easy task. But, many of us find identifying and describing our strengths and capabilities is more challenging than it first appears.

My Initial Strengths List:

Take a moment and quickly jot down some of your strengths.

Was it easy for you to list your strengths? Did you find you had to stop and think about it?

"Where ever you go, go with all your heart."
~Confucius

Chapter 4

"Part of my journey to recovery was finally seeing my own strengths."
~Vicky Walter, Kansas Consumer

Did you think of one or two strengths and then get stuck? How did that feel?

If you had difficulty writing a long list, don't worry. Many people find it very difficult to identify their personal strengths off the top of their heads. The following story illustrates one person's struggle to identify her strengths:

When asked to define my strengths & how I've used them in my recovery, my first reaction was, 'Strengths! What strengths?' I have been so influenced by the medical model that I have recognized only the things about me that were deficits & that need to be changed. I did have some aspirations, well those are in the future of course, I haven't done them yet, and haven't I been trained by the trials & tribulations of life not to wish too high? Hasn't it always been stressed to me, that it would be nice to have those things, to accomplish those things, but why hope? It's never going to happen anyway. So I had one big deficit already.

Regardless of the source, the message I've gotten has been 'You are limited. You are always going to be limited. Live your life accordingly.' I listened to this for many years, and blindly obeyed. So when I had to look at my strengths, it seemed incredible that I had any strengths. But the realization also came that I must have some strengths. If I didn't, I wouldn't have survived for so long. I wouldn't have realized I had problems that needed treatment. Without strengths, I never would have gone for therapy, or been diagnosed, or put on medication. Without strengths, I would still be an alcoholic. I still would be in abusive relationships.

~Linda Endicott,
Kansas Consumer Provider

Charting Our Course Beyond a Negative Roadmap

We usually pay more attention to our problems, personal deficits and weakness than our talents and strengths. From childhood onward, we often receive the message NOT to point out our strengths. As young children learning new skills or hard at play we constantly called out for attention. Our message was, "*Look at me! Look what I can do!*" But over time our natural exuberance lessens as we are ignored or told not to call attention to ourselves.

When we seek help we are often asked "What problem brought you here today?" As we move toward recovery, we seek helpers and supporters who focus on how we can improve our wellness and mental health and support the many positive and practical things we can do for ourselves.

We are often encouraged to look at how we don't "stack up" or "don't fit in." Our culture supports a focus on pathology and problems. When we watch television talk shows we see people with the strangest problems. On the other hand, the media also floods us with images of people playing roles who are extraordinarily physically attractive and have unlimited resources (money, friends, wardrobe, luxury housing). When we compare our lives to ideals set by the media or other influences outside ourselves, it may seem hard to find personal strengths and resources in our lives.

Because we have experienced a great deal of stress and have had problems, we find it easy to dwell on past negative experiences, our personal wounds and the resources that we lack. This way of looking at things has the power to rob us of our self-esteem, harms our sense that we can achieve anything positive and lessens our commitment to a healthy lifestyle. Focusing on the negative can reduce the energy and effort we put into moving in positive directions, toward our recovery.

As adults, we may also unthinkingly recreate the kind of negative emotional environments that some of us experienced in our childhood. If we grew up in a negative environment, we often live with negative beliefs (Hay, 1984). A negative emotional atmosphere becomes normal to us. It may not be what we want, but it is what we are used to and it is what we have come to expect.

Such experiences can leave us with a "negative mental roadmap". Constantly focusing on negative expectations and problems will not take us where we want to go! In fact such a focus will take us places we don't want to go, where we find ourselves doing things we don't want to do, with people we really don't want to do them with!

Do you think you may have a negative mental roadmap? What kind of direction and experiences is the negative roadmap sending you toward?

"If you constantly think of illness, you eventually become ill; if you believe yourself to be beautiful, you become so."
~Shakti Gawain

"We are always called upon to have the courage to continue on our path toward greater and deeper feelings of self-worth."
~Sue Patton Thoele

Changing Our Orientation

Even though a negative orientation may be deeply imprinted in our thinking, it can be changed. We are not trapped in an environment of negativity! The recovery process helps us to reclaim a positive sense of self despite the challenges we have encountered. It moves us far beyond past experiences and present circumstances. We can develop a more positive inner roadmap, a more positive sense of ourselves and orient ourselves in a more positive direction!

It can be hard to move past the negatives in our lives. Things can look pretty good around us, but they could always be better. Our home could be nicer, our clothes more stylish, the weather could be better, our thighs could be slimmer, our friends more supportive...and on and on. If we are on the lookout for negative signs and experiences, they will always appear. By focusing on the negative, we remain pointed toward our _dis-abilities_. By concentrating on our strengths, we redirect ourselves towards our abilities, and this leads us on toward new possibilities.

One way we can deal with a negative mental roadmap is to acquire the tools we need to control our own thoughts, behavior and responses. We have identified and acknowledged the negative mental roadmaps that have limited us. Now is the time to shift our perspective from negativity to a strengths-recovery orientation.

Moving from a Problem Orientation to a Strengths Orientation

When we begin to move toward recovery we want to head out in the right direction. What we want to do is move away from the traditional problem focus or deficit orientation that we often have been taught and create a life that is guided by a strengths orientation. If we focus on our strengths, we have a much clearer orientation to a positive recovery. The following chart outlines the basic change we want to make in our direction or orientation.

Moving from a Problem or Deficit Orientation...	→	...to a Strengths Orientation
Instead of focusing on my problems, symptoms and deficits...	→	I am primarily concerned with what I want, desire and dream of.
I don't spotlight my pathology and difficulties...	→	I seek to understand, use and build upon my positive talents, skills, knowledge and abilities.
Rather than see myself as my diagnostic label...	→	I see myself as a unique human being, with a strong mind, body and spirit.
Instead of letting others' perspectives guide and sometimes limit my choices...	→	I honor my own standpoint, values and beliefs. I know that life holds many possibilities. I can choose a positive direction.
I don't believe that my past predicts a negative future...	→	I am concerned with the here and now and moving toward a positive future.
Rather than focusing on my functional deficits, the things I can not do...	→	I know that I have many coping skills. I've made it this far and I know I will make it in the future. I have many skills and can learn new skills if I need to.
Instead of letting professionals who know "what is best for me" control decisions in my life...	→	I have the right to explore choices and make my own decisions.
Instead of feeling that it doesn't matter if I'm irresponsible because that's part of having a psychiatric disability...	→	I take responsibility for the outcomes of my decisions. I have primary authority and ownership for my life and self-direct my recovery.
Rather than focusing on my problems so that my life seems limited and stagnant...	→	I am actively learning, growing and changing.
I don't let the people around me reinforce my limitations...	→	I seek relationships, role models and helpers who support and encourage me in my recovery journey.
I no longer see my contacts and resourcesas limited. I don't have to rely on the mental health system to meet all my needs...	→	I actively explore my community and find friendship, inspiration, help and desirable resources all around me.

Getting Going: Identifying the Sources of Our Strengths

"We have what we seek. It is there all the time, and if we give it time, it will make itself known to us."
~Thomas Merton

Let's look more closely at the sources of strengths we have within and around us.

- *For a moment, close your eyes and think about your strengths.*

- *Are you thinking of things that you have excelled in or mastered in the past? Or are you thinking of things you routinely do now?*

- *When thinking about your strengths, don't forget your unrealized potential, the abilities and interests you want to develop in the near future.*

When thinking of our strengths, we often focus on the present time. It's important to recognize and rediscover the strengths we used in the past, the "here and now" and also look forward to the dreams and aspirations we have for the future.

Almost anything imaginable can serve as a source of strength. In this section we'll explore some of the common experiences and qualities that we can discover as our strengths, competencies, talents and resources.

Strengths that Come from My Unique Knowledge

We learn as we struggle, make choices and push ourselves in new directions. Sometimes we achieve what we wish to and other times we don't achieve what we set out to do. By exploring our wants, desires or interests, we are able to continually move forward.

"If you do not ask yourself what it is you know, you will go on listening to others and change will not come because you will not hear your own truth."
~St. Bartholomew

When we think of learning, we often think of education in a formal setting such as schools, reading a thick textbook or taking a workshop or class. The truth is most learning happens in daily life in informal settings, within our family, workplace or in the community. We learn most from our first hand life experiences.

Often, learning occurs because we are curious and want to explore an interest. For example, an interest in communication leads us to play around with a computer in a library. Once we have a basic understanding, we hop on the Internet and enter an on-line chat room, and soon we have a new friend. An interest in increasing personal wellness may spark the decision to gain information on a healthy diet, or we may go in with another person to cultivate a vegetable garden in a community garden plot. We may take a yoga class offered at the local recreation department or begin collecting low fat recipes.

We also learn by struggling, experiencing dissatisfaction and taking risks. We learn a lot about ourselves through setting goals and experiencing the outcomes of our efforts. We have to stretch ourselves when trying to achieve a goal. Sometimes we don't reach the goal we have set. Taking on challenges, even if things don't always go well, teaches us about ourselves. We try to understand what would make a different outcome happen next time. We begin to ask ourselves questions like "What kinds of resources or supports would help me to achieve my goals in the future?"

The people around us also help us learn. They may provide support or have unique knowledge to share.

Think of the people around you, what kinds of knowledge do they possess? (They may know how to sketch and draw, or how to grow herbs, or they can teach you relaxation techniques, or how to make a quilt, or how to navigate through the mental health system.)

Take a moment and think about yourself, think about all the things you know. (When we stop and think about it, it is amazing all the things we are interested in and know how to do.)

Chapter 4

"To tend, unfailingly, unflinchingly, towards a goal, is the secret of success."
~Anna Pavlova

"Self-knowledge is the beginning of self-improvement."
~Spanish Proverb

EXERCISE:
Self-Reflection Around Your Knowledge

As you do this exercise, think of the things that have personal meaning to you. Go way beyond what others see on the surface; look deep within yourself. Start your list with the things you enjoy learning about or the things that you already know well. This is a beginning list, you can always come back and add to this list as you discover more about yourself and think more about your knowledge and interests.

List some of your strengths that come from what you have learned throughout your life:

Now list the things you are interested in and would like to learn more about in the near future:

Strengths that Come from the Skills and Talents I Have

People who take the time to really discover and identify their individual skills and talents are often surprised by the number of things they can do well. We may also rediscover talents and skills that we once had, but have not used lately. Skills, gifts and talents can be anything: doing funny impersonations, being able to sing on key, getting along well with people, craft-making, doing math, storytelling and understanding languages or computers.

The following account shows how one person used his unique musical talents to support his personal recovery:

I had several stays in various hospitals over the years. I had given up playing the guitar and performing for other people. I did not want to have anything to do with music, although it had been a <u>very important</u> part of my life for so long. One of the hospital staff suggested that I go to the free community concert held not too far from the hospital. On that evening, a favorite band of mine was to perform. I at first did not want to go because I knew there was going to be a large crowd in attendance and I thought that I would get very sick. A couple of other patients told me that they would go with me, so the three of us decided to go. As we were sitting on the bleachers and the crowd began to file in I began to feel like I was getting claustrophobia, but the other two kept telling me everything was going to be fine, and I continued to sit there. After awhile the band came on stage and began playing all of their hits. I noticed that I could feel my 'blood start pumping' as it did in the 'good old days' when I used to perform for other people. I started to 'feel the music'...I started to get very excited.

The next day I called a friend and I asked him to bring me my guitar. When I got my hands on the guitar I immediately started playing some of the old songs that I used to play.

Over the past ten years I have used my guitar to play at various Christmas parties, groups, churches and events throughout the city. I eventually decided to try to teach music through private lessons on piano, drums and guitar. Everything seemed to, and does to this very day, go very well. I discovered that I can teach and will continue to use my music.

~Phillip Glasgow,
Kansas Consumer

"The most difficult thing in life is to know yourself."
~Thales

"I began to have an idea of my life, not as the slow shaping of achievement to fit my preconceived purposes, but as the gradual discovery and growth of a purpose which I did not know."
~Joanna Field

EXERCISE:
Identifying Some of Your Talents and Skills

As you do this exercise, think of the things that have personal meaning to you. Go well beyond what you or others might see on the surface. Look deep into yourself. Start your list with the things you enjoy doing or the things that you do well, or the things you have an interest in and would like to develop more skills around.

List some of your talents and skills:

Now list skills and talents you would like to develop in the near future:

Strengths that I Can Draw from My Cultural Identity and Cultural Resources

Our cultural identity helps determine our lifestyle and behavior. Often we take our cultural background for granted. We may overlook the meaning our culture brings to our lives. Every culture has means of healing and making us whole again. We may find cultural strengths in many areas.

The following is a listing of a few areas of cultural identity. You may want to use this as a beginning guide and add others of your own:

- Family daily rituals (i.e. grandparents, birth family, chosen family);
- Expressions of spiritual beliefs (i.e. church/temple services, prayer, AME church);
- Ethnic roots (i.e. Asian, Irish, Latino);
- Styles of communication (i.e. chanting, storytelling, drumming);
- Ways of life (i.e. farm community, urban, rural setting);
- Generational characteristics (i.e. baby-boomer, genXer, elder);
- Cultural celebrations (i.e. Kwanzaa, Memorial Day, Hanukkah);
- Cultural values and beliefs (i.e. all my relations, do unto others as you would have them do unto you);
- Important stories of survival and resilience from your culture (i.e. Holocaust survivor, Dust Bowl, Highlands Removal, Immigration);
- Ways of healing from your culture (i.e. sweat lodge, sings, curendero);
- Comfort foods (i.e. grits and cornbread, macaroni and cheese);
- Other sources of cultural pride (i.e. knowledge about pioneer ancestors, contribution to others made by forbearers or your culture).

"The future belongs to those who live intensely in the present."
~Anonymous

"A single event can awaken within us a stranger totally unknown to us."
~Antoine de Saint-Exupery

EXERCISE:
Strengths that Come from My Cultural Identity or Cultural Resources

When listing your cultural strengths, think of the things that have personal meaning to you. Go way beyond what others see on the surface. Look deep into your heritage and culture. Start your list with the things you enjoy from your ethnicity or cultural roots or the things that strongly influence you or the things you have an interest in and would like to learn more about.

List some of the sources of your cultural identity and some of your cultural resources:

What in your culture is a special support to you?

How can you expand on your cultural identity and resources?

Community Resources that are My Strengths

Many of us have experienced mistreatment, rejection and outright discrimination when trying to access community resources. We may have learned to view ourselves as lacking power and the skills that would help us gain the resources we want and need. Counteracting powerlessness is one goal of a Strengths Recovery Approach. Gaining community resources can help us achieve our goals.

One of the key principles of recovery is "community integration." What this means is that we are full citizens and have all the rights and responsibilities that come with community membership. We can look at our community as the source of stigma, but communities are also full of wonderful resources.

We are usually aware of only a very narrow slice of what is actually available to us in our communities. Many of us see our community resource primarily as *the community mental health system*. We look for what we need from the mental health system: our leisure time means bowling with groups of consumers; learning new ways of life means daily living skills groups at day treatment; friendship means pairing up with people in a socialization club; work means a job club at the center.

Seeking resources exclusively from the mental health system greatly limits the resources for our recovery. A Strengths Recovery Approach asks us to look beyond the mental health system to the community as a whole. The more we can draw from our community, the wider our world becomes.

For example, if we want to work on our wellness, we can look to the local YMCA/YWCA or recreation department. Going to the Y will help our wellness, but we might also meet new friends with wider interests than mental health concerns. We may learn about other resources or activities that we would never have heard about at the mental health center. For example, we might learn about classes offered in our community, such as a natural foods cooking class at the health food store or a mystery book group that meets weekly at a local bookstore.

Almost all local libraries have access to the Internet or world wide web. Library cards are usually free, and the librarian can help us find books on topics related to anything, including recovery. Most libraries are a peaceful place to research information.

"We are members of one great body, planted by nature in a mutual love, and fitted for a social life. We must consider that we were born for the good of the whole."
~Seneca

"We are what we believe we are."
~B.N. Cardozo

Using naturally occurring community resources snowballs into more resources and options. The more choices and options we have to choose from in making life decisions, the more empowered we become about our life and our recovery. Try some new resources and develop new interests!

EXERCISE:
Strengths that Come from Community Resources

As you do this exercise, think of things that really interest you. Go beyond what you or others might think of on the surface. Look around your community and see what it has to offer. Start your list with the community resources you already use, then think about the kind of community resources you'd really like to become involved in.

What community resources do you currently use on a regular basis?

What community resources would you like to learn more about or try out?

Personal Qualities that are My Strengths

We all have personal qualities that serve as our strengths. We may have a sense of humor, we may be loyal to others, we may be outgoing, we may stay calm in an emergency, we may be enthusiastic, we may be detail-orientated, reliable, caring, free-spirited or a good friend. Two Kansas consumers talk about their personal qualities in the following statements:

> *I struggled for years angry, denying my illness. Finally I searched for answers to gain a better understanding and make peace with my illness. Perhaps that is when my true journey of recovery began. I have always considered my career as a personal strength. As an elementary teacher, as well as a special education teacher, I have always been able to communicate well with children and their parents. Qualities like gentleness, my abilities as a nurturer, a sense of humor, intelligence, diligence, leadership skills have always sustained me as a teacher.*
>
> *~Kathy Shinn,*
> *Kansas Consumer*

> *I love a group setting. I love to talk to all kinds of people and I try to learn from those people. I like public speaking and am good at it for the most part. I try to tell a funny story or jokes to break the ice. I am proud of who I am and my recovery. I use courage and my strengths, my final thought is:*
>
> **You can become the person you want to be!!**
>
> *~Sandy Hyde,*
> *Kansas Consumer*

"Believe in something larger than yourself. Get involved in some of the big ideas of your time."
~Barbara Bush

Chapter 4

"I accentuate my abilities. I own my excellence by concentrating on the good in myself."
~Sue Patton Thoele

EXERCISE:
Strengths that Come from My Personal Qualities

Think of some of the qualities you have that have personal meaning to you. Go well beyond what others see on the surface, really think deeply about the qualities that you have. Start your list with the things you enjoy about yourself or the traits you have that others can admire. Think about the qualities that you are interested in developing within yourself in the future.

List some of your positive personal qualities:

What are some qualities you want to cultivate within yourself?

Strengths that are Things I Have to be Proud of

People have things they can be proud of. Some people find pride in coping mechanisms they have developed. Many people find satisfaction and pride in making it through great personal challenges and barriers— this has been called "survivor's pride". Others have a high school diploma or higher education that took a lot of hard work to achieve. Some people have a child they take pride in. The things we are proud of can be a support in overcoming challenges on our pathway to recovery. Linda talks with great pride in discovering her strengths:

> *I have discovered that I have many strengths. I discovered denial was one. Without it, I doubt that I would have survived all these years. It was a coping mechanism, and a highly effective one. If not for denial I would have been crushed by my life experiences.*
>
> *I am stubborn; let's call it tenacity. I knew I had to be tenacious enough to keep going to therapy, to stay sober, even when there were setbacks, when I needed to get back on my feet and to go on. I was too stubborn to give up.*
>
> *My love of reading, writing and crocheting and my talents with them, have served me well through my recovery. Not only have they given me something to do when I was lonely or bored, they also have been ways of relieving stress. I find them relaxing, and sometimes profitable as well. I can't imagine one day going by when I don't do these things.*
>
> *My relationships with my family have been a source of strength for me. When I started my journey, it created problems with some relatives. Because of my diagnosis, I have lost relationships with some family members. But others have remained supportive. Though the process has been painful and unpleasant, it has shown me who I can truly depend on, and that knowledge is invaluable.*
>
> *I have a terrific sense of humor and that, I think, has probably helped me more than anything. It's difficult to be depressed if you can find something to laugh about. Laughter truly is the best medicine. If you have learned how to laugh at yourself, or look on your mistakes and setback with humor, you're much better off. I'm still discovering things about myself, and it will take a lifetime to do it. And I can't think of a better person to do the job than me!*
>
> *~Linda Endicott,*
> *Kansas Consumer Provider*

"I'm at peace, and with that peace, I have strength."
~Colleen Keagy, Kansas Consumer

Chapter 4

"A weakness is a strength not yet developed."
~Benjamin Franklin

EXERCISE:
Things that I am Proud of

Think of things you can be proud of. As you do, think of the things that have personal meaning to you. Go way beyond what others see on the surface, really look deep into your life experience and the experience of people you are close to. Start your list with the things you are most proud of, the things that you do well or things you have interest in and would like work toward feeling proud of in the future.

What do you feel proud of?

What strengths have made you a survivor?

What things do you want to achieve that will be sources of pride in the future?

Learning About Our Strengths from Another Person's Perspective

You have taken an important first step by doing the exercises so far in this book. By reading, thinking about and writing down your strengths you have identified important resources for your recovery journey. Now that you have identified some of your strengths, let's work to *broaden* the list of your strengths.

Getting others' perspectives about your strengths can be very helpful and eye-opening. Sometimes strengths are more apparent to other people than they are to us. You may be surprised to learn about your unique strengths that are apparent to people who are close to you, that may be hidden or closed off to you.

Gathering additional information about your strengths will help you tap into, build upon and use the unique strengths you have on your personal journey of recovery.

EXERCISE:
Strengths Others See in Me

Step 1: Gather your courage and identify someone (one person or more) whom you feel you can trust to give you honest, genuine feedback about yourself.

Make sure to ask a person whom you trust, who cares for you and who has been supportive to you in the past.

Step 2: You can have a conversation with the person, or give them the following questionnaire. Feel free to photocopy as many copies of the form as you wish.

Step 3: Ask the trusted person to identify your strengths and/or write a list of some of your strengths that they are aware of.

Step 4: Using the information gathered from your trusted friend or family member, add that information to the lists of your strengths you already made.

"The greatest good you can do for another is not just to share your riches, but to reveal to him his own self."
~Benjamin Disraeli

STRENGTHS YOU SEE IN ME:
A Questionnaire for My Allies and Supporters

I appreciate the time that you are willing to take to identify some of my strengths. The following are just a few categories that you may want to consider in listing strengths that you see in me.

What I Know/Knowledge I Have/Things I Have Learned

People are constantly learning and experiencing life. This learning can occur in a formalized setting (schools, textbooks and classes). However, the majority of learning occurs in informal settings (from family, the workplace or from our culture) especially from first-hand experience. For example, a person may understand computers, know how to take care of a baby, know how to grow geraniums, have knowledge about relaxation techniques or know how to navigate through the mental health system.

Please list below some of the knowledge you know I have:

Please list things that you believe I have an interest in learning:

The Talents and Skills I Have

Examples: being able to sing on key, solving problems, sketching and drawing, getting along well with people, gardening, reciting poetry, long distance running, crafts, baking bread.

Please list below some of the gifts, talents and skills you see in me:

My Cultural Identity and Resources

A person's cultural identity can strongly influence his or her lifestyle and behavior. Cultural strengths may include rituals, styles of communication, geographic influences, generational identity (i.e. baby-boomer), celebrations, sources of pride, cultural resources.

Please list below some of the strengths you see that I can draw from my cultural identity:

My Personal Qualities

Examples: a sense of humor, staying calm in an emergency, enthusiastic, reliable, energetic, caring, organized, free-spirited, friendly, loyal.

Please list below some of the personal qualities you see as strengths in me:

Things I Can Take Pride In

People have things to be proud of, such as attainments. One source of pride is "survivors pride" that people develop through getting through great difficulties or barriers.

Please list below some of the things you think I can take pride in:

Are there any other strengths that you see in me?

Thank You for Taking the Time to Help Me to Identify My Strengths!

Mapping Your Strengths Terrain

Now that you have identified some of your strengths and gained feedback from others about your strengths, you can add more to your personal strengths inventory by completing this exercise.

EXERCISE:
Listing More Strengths

Some of our strengths come from other people who are our allies and supporters.

Who are the people who support and encourage you?

How does each person help you? What do they do to help?

List places that you can go that support you and give you skills and encouragement: (for example: walking in a local park, attending the AME Church, fishing at Milford Lake, the consumer drop-in center, journaling at the coffee shop)

*List any **things** that support you and give you strength:* (for example: your two cats, the flower box garden you tend, your Bible)

By this point you have developed a rather long list of your strengths, gathered from your own self-reflection and from other people's perspectives about you. Please take a few minutes to read and review all the strengths you have listed.

How do you feel as you reflect on your strengths?

> "I may not have gone where I intended to go, but I think I have ended up where I intended to be."
> ~Douglas Adams

Do you see a pattern or any themes in the strengths you have identified? (For example: you may see several strengths that center around creativity and creative pursuits or several that concern relationships)

> "We all carry it within us: supreme strengths, the fullness of wisdom, unquenchable joy. It is never thwarted and cannot be destroyed."
> ~Huston Smith

After reviewing your strengths do you feel more hopeful about yourself/ your situation? Why or why not?

Do you have a stronger sense of self-esteem or a sense of pride about all the things you know and the qualities you have?

> *It's been 15 years of staying with my recovery and not giving in. I can announce with pride 'I'm not where I want to be yet, I'm not sure where I am going, but thank God I'm not where I was.'*
>
> ~Cindy,
> *Kansas Consumer*

Why are you feeling this way?

Do the resources and talents that you possess surprise you? Why?

> "To aim at the best & to remain essentially ourselves is one and the same thing."
> ~William Hazlitt

Making the Most of Our Strengths

At this point in the process of identifying your strengths, you have gathered information and listed many of your strengths. Now that you have reviewed your strengths and thought about them, let's shift into gear and use one strength to begin moving forward.

Your strengths will become the supports and guideposts for the recovery journey. If you identify and use your strengths you won't have to constantly turn to others when you are feeling empty. You can tap into what is yours—your own strengths— when you are feeling low on energy.

By returning over and over to our own strengths, we fill ourselves with the energy we need for the road to recovery that lies ahead.

> "One of the most important results you can bring into the world is the you that you really want to be."
> ~Robert Fritz

EXERCISE:
Test Driving One Strength

Scan and review the strengths you listed. Out of all the strengths that you have listed, pick <u>one</u> strength that you want to explore in more depth.

When making this decision, you may want to ask yourself some questions on which strength to pick:
- Is it a strength I have a lot of interest in?
- Is this a strength that I want to learn more about?
- Is this a strength that I can build upon?
- Is it a strength that will guide me in planning my first steps on the path of recovery?

List the one strength that you have chosen to focus on:

_____
_____

Think of the past, and ask yourself, "How did I use that strength?" (Example: "I want to be healthier, I used to take walks for over two years.")

What other things / activities / thoughts do you have that relate to the strength you have selected to work on? (Example: "I have two cookbooks and a book on low impact aerobics at my mother's house, I'm going to visit her, dig out the books and look them over.")

What activities are you doing that relate to the one strength you identified? Think about what is going on in your life *right now* rather than the past or the future. (Example: " I walk to the market every Saturday morning.")

What do you want to do in the near <u>future</u> with this strength? (Example: "I would like to find a walking partner.")

Start to set a short-term goal around the strength you have chosen.

1._____

2._____

(Do you need to gather more information about your interest in this area? Can you pick up where you left off when you used to use this strength or do you need to backtrack a bit? What small first steps can you take toward trying to use this strength more?)

What will be your very first small step?

What else will you do to build this strength? (Example: "I'd like to begin with short 5 minute walks several times a day." or "I need to save for some affordable walking shoes.")

CONGRATULATIONS!
You Have Identified Your Strengths and Begun to Take Steps on Your Journey!

It's time to celebrate the discovery of your strengths! The Strengths Recovery Approach includes rewarding yourself and celebrating all the steps you take in moving toward your goals. Here are some ideas that others have used to celebrate their progress. You may want to try some of these celebration ideas *or think of others that reflect your own interests and strengths!*

"The best bet is to bet on yourself."
~Arnold Glasow

- Play frisbee with my dog
- Go out with a friend
- Watch a community baseball game
- Treat myself to an ice cream cone
- Call a friend I haven't seen in a long time
- Sing a song
- Take a bubble bath
- Read my favorite book
- Post a list of my strengths on my refrigerator
- Listen to music at a free community concert
- Lay in the grass under a big tree and daydream

"Celebration is the recognition of a moment of joy."
~Peter Megaree Brown

What will you do to celebrate?

100

 # References & Resources

References

Copeland, M. E. (1999). *Winning Against Relapse.* Oakland, CA: New Harbinger Publications, Inc.

Eldon, K. M. (1999). *Soul Catcher.* San Francisco, CA: Chronicle Books.

Hay, L.L. (1984). *You Can Heal Your Life.* Santa Monica, CA: Hay House, Inc.

Lieberman, A. (1997). *The Social Work Out Book: Strength-Building Exercises for the Pre-Professional.* Thousand Oaks, CA: Pine Forge Press.

Rapp, Charles A. (1998). *The Strengths Model: Case Management with People Suffering from Severe and Persistent Mental Illness.* New York, NY: Oxford University Press.

Saleebey, D. (1997). *The Strengths Perspective in Social Work Practice.* White Plains, NY: Longman Publishers.

Summers, N. (2000). *Fundamentals of Case Management Practice Exercises & Readings.* Belmont, CA: Wadsworth/Brooks/Cole.

Resources

List Your Self: Listmaking as the Way to Self-Discovery by Ilene Segalove & Paul Bob Velick (Andrews & McMeel, 1996).

Ordinary People as Monks and Mystics: Lifestyles for Self-Discovery by Marsha Sinetar (Paulist Press, 1986).

Sacred Cards: The Discovery of the Self Through Native Teachings by Jamie Sams (Harper San Francisco, 1990).

Soul Mapping: An Imaginative Way to Self-Discovery by Nina H. Frost, Kenneth W. Ruge & Richard W. Shoup (Avalon Publishing Group, 2000).

The Illustrated Discovery Journal: Creating a Visual Autobiography by Sarah Ban Breathnach (Time Warner Company, 1999).

Wanting What You Have: A Self-Discovery Workbook by Timothy Miller (New Harbinger Publications, 1998).

Chapter Five

Setting a Course for the Recovery Journey

This chapter concentrates on creating a personal vision for the recovery journey and outlines methods for setting successful long-term and short-term goals.

Creating a Personal Vision of Recovery

The best journeys are made when we think ahead—this is the process of visioning. Visioning is an important part of moving from the past to a more fulfilling future. Tom Peters (1991) writes: "Visions are aesthetic and moral—as well as strategically sound. Vision comes from within—as well as from outside." Another definition of vision comes from Kouzes & Posner (1997): "Visions are statements of destination, of the ends of our labor; they are therefore future-oriented and are made real over different spans of times."

Envisioning our future is the first step in creating our future. Chris Shore, a Kansas consumer, talks about this process:

> *Everyone uses visioning without even thinking about it. If you go grocery shopping, you are using visioning techniques by the foods you buy. If you buy tomato sauce, kidney beans, hamburger, onions and peppers you probably are envisioning a hearty meal of chili.*

In a research study around vocational outcomes, Carol Mowbray (1995), a well known researcher from the University of Michigan, found that mental health consumers who could "see" themselves working were much more likely to be employed within six months. Visioning is using your imagination and creativity to project or "see" a new reality.

Vision Guideposts

Use your fundamental beliefs and values to guide your visions

Our values help shape how we see our world and ourselves. We all experience the world in a unique way. We have been raised with certain values and beliefs. We tend to look at our own life through the lenses of our early values and life experience. Sometimes we continue to filter what we want through these perspectives or viewpoints and values, even if we really don't look at life the same way anymore.

When we are creating our personal vision of recovery it's important to clarify what we really value and what we truly believe in. For many of us the first step in the visualization process is getting in touch with what our most important values and beliefs are so they can guide us.

"When there is no vision, people perish."
~Ralph Waldo Emerson

"Just because a man lacks the use of his eyes doesn't mean he lacks vision."
~Stevie Wonder

List some of your deeply held values here: (Example: "One of my strongest values is being a good parent, even though my upbringing was abusive; I believe in giving better than I had.")

Your vision should be unique to who you are

You are a unique human being, with a strong mind, body and spirit. Your preferred future should be based on your strengths, your past experiences and express who you are. Your vision should be just as unique as you are.

List some of the unique things about you:

Your vision should be guided by what you want

Your personal vision must be guided by what you want, not what someone else thinks is best for you. It may be helpful to solicit other people's ideas, but a vision has to be directed by what you want and what you envision as your preferred future. List some of what you want here:

In one month I would like to:

In one year I would like to:

Your vision should make sense to you

Your vision should be clear to you; it should not be a vague set of ideas or abstract concepts. You should be able to envision pretty clearly what your future holds if you take certain courses of action. Writing down what and how you see your future can help you clarify your vision. If you are to embark on the road to recovery you must dedicate yourself to this journey, it will help to have a vision that is unmistakable to you.

State one thing that you want. Be very precise:

Your vision must be stable, but you should remain flexible in order to flow with change

Your personal vision should have some stability at its core. But saying that doesn't mean that you will move towards recovery in a rigid step-by-step march. From first-hand accounts of recovery, we know most of us find our path often changes course, leading us in exciting and unanticipated directions.

How can you become open to mystery and new adventures?

Effective visioning is self-empowering

The act of visioning prepares you for your future. By directing your life story you are working towards a different reality. You are making choices and decisions about your future. We build self-confidence and self-esteem by making decisions, selecting from options and choices and taking responsibility to move towards our future. The process of visioning empowers us.

"The moment of enlightenment is when a person's dreams of possibilities become images of probabilities."
~Vic Braden

Chapter 5

"Everyone, regardless of their current situation or their personal characteristics, has hopes, dreams, and aspirations and may fulfill those only if they use their talents, abilities, and skills and the resources available to them."
~Alice Lieberman, social worker

You must be willing to believe in your vision and in yourself

You must be willing to make the effort to head out to achieve your personal vision of recovery. Your ability to firmly believe in your vision and in your self is important. Keep building your vision and your sense that achieving your vision is possible.

Identifying Your Preferred Future

Here is an exercise that will help clarify what you want in life. We've adapted this exercise from *The Leadership Challenge* (Kouzes & Posner, 1995). This exercise will reveal some important elements of your personal vision.

EXERCISE:
My Desired Accomplishments

Make a list of some of the things you want or want to accomplish. For each item write why you want to do this. Keep asking yourself these questions and writing your responses until you run out of reasons.

I want to: *Why?*

EXERCISE:
Building My Vision

Here are some additional questions you may want to think about and write about to extend and clarify your vision and design the map for the road ahead of you. After answering these questions, push yourself further in your thinking by asking "**WHY**?"

Why do I want to change anything at all?

What will happen if I don't do anything different?

If I could invent the future, what would it look like?

What does my ideal living environment look like?

Who would be in this environment? Why?

What do I want to prove to myself? Why?

What do I want to prove to others? Why?

Now that you have thought of what you want your future to look like, why not tap into some of your strengths and talents to help devise your very own personal vision of what your recovery will look like? Doing one or more of these exercises will create a more elaborate vision of your desired future.

SPECIAL PROJECT:
Create a Personal Vision of Recovery Collage

Gather the following supplies:

1. A piece of poster board, cardboard or large piece of paper.
2. Pictures from old magazines, calendars, newsletters, etc.
3. Favorite pictures, quotes or poems.
4. Other materials such as wrapping paper, yarn, stickers, glitter and colored markers.
5. Glue, tape or rubber cement.

Create your personal vision collage on the backing you have selected. Begin by cutting out pictures that convey what your preferred future looks like. Move the pieces around until you have created a visual image that pleases you. Add quotes or words that are positive and meaningful to you. Illustrate your vision poster by adding drawings or doodles. You may want to embellish your collage with stickers, glitter, ribbon or anything you find attractive. You can think of this project as a way to create an image of your positive future or a way to honor your resilience and power.

This may be a fun group activity to do with friends or with someone you trust who will help you strive towards creating and living your vision of recovery.

Once you complete your collage, display it in a place where you will see it to remind you of what you are striving for.

SPECIAL PROJECT:
Prepare a Visionary Speech

Think of Martin Luther King's stirring *"I Have A Dream"* speech. Dr. King's speech provided a vision for the Civil Rights movement. Try writing your own vision of recovery speech to inspire yourself.

1. Gather paper and pen.
2. Write a speech as if you were going to address a gathering of your supporters or peers.
3. Before embarking on writing a full-fledged visionary speech you may want to rapidly write down any ideas that come to you. Don't censor yourself or try to organize your thoughts. Simply list *your expectations, dreams, aspirations, hopes and struggles*.
4. Once you have your ideas written out, develop an outline describing your vision. Your outline can be a traditional writers outline (for example: A, B, C). You can also use a more informal style to organize your material.
5. A good visionary speech is future-oriented.
6. Your visionary speech should be hopeful and embrace change and optimism.
7. Try to make your visionary speech encompass what you really want to achieve.

Your visionary speech can be a source of ongoing inspiration for you. You may want to keep your vision of recovery speech around you. You could:

- Deliver your speech and record it electronically. When you feel you are straying from your goals or feeling unmotivated, turn on the video and watch yourself talk about your dream.
- Audio tape your speech and play it to encourage your motivation.
- Laminate your speech and hang it up in your home.
- Make copies of your speech and share it with trusted supporters.
- Deliver your speech at a consumer support group or conference.
- Ask to have your speech printed in a newsletter for your drop-in center, clubhouse or mental health center.

SPECIAL PROJECT:
Prepare a Formal Vision Statement

A vision statement is a short formal declarative statement that summarizes the future you'd like to achieve.

You may have seen such statements in reports of organizations and agencies. An organizational mission statement establishes and communicates the important values and main purpose of the agency.

Your statement should convey your personal vision of your recovery. Using your imagination, create a personal vision statement of recovery:

- Your vision statement should be no longer than one paragraph. Try to write your statement in two or three declarative sentences.
- A good vision statement is future-oriented.

As an example, the following statement is paraphrased from Marcia Lovejoy, an early consumer leader:

"I want to recover so I can be there for people who have never seen someone who has been there and back."

Setting a Course to Succeed: Forming Long-Term Goals

The purpose of having goals is to help us select and achieve what we desire and want in our life. There are more long-term goals than there are people because each of us has several goals. When you wrote about your vision in the previous exercise you made the first step toward setting goals.

If we follow a few specific established criteria for designing and writing goals we will have a much greater chance of achieving them. Goals that are not associated with a strong vision, goals that are not clearly stated or goals set too far into the future seldom achieve the desired effects. They won't get us where we want to go on our recovery journey!

Developing Long-Term Goals

Earlier in this chapter, you succeeded in visualizing, thinking about and writing down what your personal vision of recovery looked like. This is a big accomplishment, because it sets one or more destinations for your recovery journey. The next step is becoming clearer on what it will take to reach your desired future.

Setting out without a destination will get *us where we don't want to be*!

Our goals map a path that can be followed to achieve our dreams. Long-term goals translate our vision into statements that say where we intend to be at certain points on our journey. A long-term goal is different than a vision because it specifies the actions we will take over a limited period of time. We should be able to accomplish any long-term goal we set in three to six months.

Some of your dreams may be clear, while others need to be translated into specific things you want to achieve. Consider what it will take to make your vision and dreams a reality over the long-term.

Look over your vision statements and dreams again. As you do this, think about which goals and aspirations are most important to you. These are the ones you'll probably want to start working to achieve right away.

Everyone's vision is different. Some visions may be short, precise and attainable in three to six months, such as, "I want to spend more time with my family." Other visions may be very broad, such as, "I want to work on my recovery." If your vision is very broad, you may have to continue to explore ways of working towards your vision until you have a goal that can be accomplished in three to six months. If your vision is very broad, you will probably find that you will need to set many long-term goals in many different areas of your life. Remember that you can't do everything at once and working on many long-term goals at once can be confusing and promises less chance of success. You can continue to come back to this exercise and choose different directions to attain your vision.

> "All acts performed in the world begin in the imagination."
> ~Barbara Grizzuti Harrison

Read the following example of Jamal's vision and long-term goals to reach his vision.

Jamal's vision is: "I want to help other people with mental illness." Because Jamal's vision is rather broad and there are many ways he could accomplish the goal, he began by listing different directions he could work towards to accomplish his vision. His list consisted of: joining a self-help group, volunteering, or gaining more skills or education in order to be employed in a helping profession.

Jamal's next step was to narrow down his options into something he wanted to do and felt he could accomplish in three to six months. Jamal chose to focus on increasing his education to eventually be employed in the human service field. Though Jamal would also like to volunteer, he chose to focus on his education first and can come back to the option of doing volunteer work later.

Jamal chose his long-term goal to work on as: "In the next six months I will explore ways to increase my education in the mental health field."

Use the exercise to follow Jamal's example and look at ways to translate your vision into accomplishable, long-term goals.

Setting a Course for the Recovery Journey: Goal Chart

EXERCISE:
Develop a Long-Range Travel Plan

Complete the following questions to begin to break down your vision into accomplishable long-term goals:

Jot down a few directions you can head in to begin to accomplish your vision:

Of all the potential ways you can work towards your vision, choose a direction to head in:

Examine the method you have chosen. Is it something you are committed to? Is it something you want to do? Can it be accomplished in three to six months?

Write your long-term goal here:

_____

_____

You Have a Compass to Point the Way

You just created a prioritized list of what is most important to you. In other words, you have listed your top long-range goals! Deciding and writing down a long-term goal can be compared to having a compass that can guide you. It's great to have a long-term goal. In fact, it's awesome! This goal will help guide you on your pathway to recovery.

How will you remember the goal day-to-day? There is an old saying, "when in doubt write it out." You have just identified your most important goal. Now, find a way to keep your goal in front of you to help sustain your focus. You might want to keep your goal in a notebook, post it on your refrigerator, write about it in your journal or tape the goal on your bathroom mirror.

Later in this workbook you will create a "Personal Recovery Plan" that will include a detailed set of directions that point the way for you to achieve many of your personal goals.

What method/s will you use to remember your long-term goal?

For many of us, long-term goals are not popular. Our society is fast-paced and transient, we want immediate results, a quick turnaround, a prompt return on our investment. We want instant success (Kybartas, 1997). But we know from recovery autobiographies that recovery from psychiatric disability isn't achieved all at once, it takes time and effort and many small steps to achieve.

It takes thoughtfulness, preparation and work to achieve our goals. We need a specific plan of action. The plan of action is made up of short-term goals or action steps.

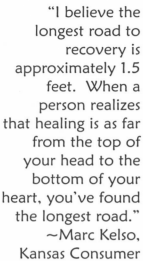

Setting Successful Short-Term Goals

Setting a Course to Succeed: The Journey is Made Step-by-Step

The next phase of the goal-setting process is to break down your long-term goals into small action steps. Short-term goals or action steps allow you to experience success along the way, as you move toward reaching your larger or longer-range goals. There are *five* important elements in writing short-term goals.

Step by step…Work to develop those activities that can help you meet your goals.

1. State your short-term goals in positive terms

You will have a much higher degree of success if you think and act on what you want versus focusing on what you shouldn't do or what you must stop doing. For example, have you ever thought about losing weight or stopping smoking? Every New Year's Eve people make resolutions to lose 10 pounds or to cut back on smoking. How often do they succeed? By February, most people have given up these ideas because they are tired of deprivation…what they can't do, what they can't have, what they *must* stop doing.

When you start to *turn around* the way you think about your goals into *what you want,* you are taking the first step in a *positive* direction. Instead of framing up your goal into what you will not do, state and write your goal in positive terms of what *you want* and <u>what you will do</u>.

Here are examples of goals that specifically state what the person wants to do:

"I want to be able to breathe better when walking up the stairs." or
"I want to have a friend I get together with every week."

Now that you know what you want and you have written it in positive terms, you can start listing small steps that begin moving you toward achieving your stated goal.

> "A goal isn't a goal until you put it down on paper, say it loud, tell others about it, learn it by heart."
> ~Judy Molnar

> "It's fun to set goals, reach goals, and reset them."
> ~Bonnie Blair

2. Choose goals that have a high probability of success

Your goal should be something that *you* really want to achieve and your short-term action steps should help in accomplishing your goal. Sometimes people around us tell us that we will never achieve our goals, that our goals are out of our reach or are too unrealistic. No one would start a recovery journey if they felt they had no chance of succeeding.

You have to decide for yourself what you want and take many small steps toward achieving your goals. When you look at what is possible, remember to take into account the strengths you have, the resources available to you and the depth of your commitment to reaching the goal when designing small short-term action steps.

It's like the kids' riddle that says: "How do you eat an elephant?" The answer is: "One bite at a time." It's amazing what we can accomplish when we put one foot in front of the other and set out towards our dreams. People have rebounded from decades of severe psychiatric disability and reclaimed full and productive lives! You can too.

One person writes about her experience with success:

> *I began with being very frightened. I was terrified of public places. I would force myself to go out every morning to a crowded restaurant, sit down and order a meal and coffee. I would eat no matter how scared I was. I would noticeably shake and tremble as I ate and drank coffee. Sometimes I would drop food and spill coffee I was shaking so. With my strengths of courage and determination, I faced my fears. It took over 2 years to control the fear and not let it control me.*
>
> *~Sandy Lewis,*
> *Kansas Consumer Provider*

When we break down our goals and write them in terms that seem realistic and achievable, we gain a sense of control over the change process.

3. Make your goals specific, small and time-limited

When writing short-term goals, try to be very, very specific about what you will be doing or what you want to accomplish. Short-term goals should be time-limited. Short-term goals should be things that can be accomplished within a period of less than months. Goals that are set far out in the future are seldom achieved. Think of what you will be doing 10 months from today. Do you have a clear plan for exactly what that will be? For most of us, it is much easier to plan our life and activities in a shorter span of time.

For example, to move toward a long-term goal of meeting new people who enjoy outdoor activities you could say:

> *"I will attend the Nature study group at the Sierra Club offices every Thursday from 7:30 to 9:00 p.m. in April."*

This goal is <u>specific,</u> because it states exactly what the person will do (attend a nature study group). It specifies a <u>small</u> segment of daily activity (Thursday evenings from 7:30 to 9:00 p.m.) and it is <u>time-limited</u> (in April).

4. Make your goals measurable and observable

We need to be able to clearly know if we have accomplished our goals. Goals should have a visible and specific end product. For this reason short-term action steps should be measurable and observable. Set some target dates to track your progress. Be specific about the steps you will take. You'll know when the short-term goal has been achieved, so you can celebrate!

Here is an example of a well-written short-term goal that is measurable and observable:

> *"I will meet Debbie for coffee on June 4, at 9:30 a.m. at the Wheatland Café."*

5. Write your short-term goals in terms that are understandable and meaningful to you

You may have the experience of working with someone who told you what you needed to do to make changes in your life. That person may have specified the goals you were expected to complete. Did you ever look at those goals and wonder what the person was talking about? What they wrote down for you to do may not sound like anything you came up with!

"Still round the corner there may wait, a new road or a secret gate."
~J.R.R.Tolkien

Here's a typical example: You have been telling the helping professional that you want to get a new apartment, you think the rent is too high, the neighborhood is dangerous and the landlord doesn't take care of the building. The worker has written your goal as: *"Maintain community tenure."* This goal has little meaning to you and really doesn't capture what you want. Goals that are not stated clearly will probably not lead to a successful outcome.

Goals must be focused on what you want and need and written in your own words. When you are breaking down your long-term goal into action steps (short-term goal steps) those actions should make sense and have meaning to you.

For example:

> *"I will take a warm bubble bath when I am having a hard time getting to sleep."*

The person who wrote this goal has found that getting out of bed when she cannot sleep, pouring bubble bath into warm water and soaking in the tub greatly relaxes her and helps her get back to sleep. That short-term goal is meaningful to her (relaxes and helps her get back to sleep) and supports her long-term goal of keeping her job.

EXERCISE:
Assessing Your Goals

Read and review these goals.

"I want to get in touch with my spirituality."
"I want to increase my energy."
"I want to be less lonely."
"I want to work on my stress."
"I will be med compliant."
"I want to feel free."
"I will avoid disagreements with others."

So what do you think?

* Are you sure *what* the person wants and why?

* Is the goal clear and measurable?

* How will you know when the person has achieved this goal?

As you can see from these *poor examples* of goals, a goal has to be *clear* and *very specific* about what the person wants.

Write a few short-term goals here that meet all the critical elements for goal-setting.

EXERCISE:
Bringing it Together:
Long-Term and Short-Term Goals

As discussed, well-defined goals will greatly increase the chances that you achieve the outcomes that you want to reach. Now that you have the all the knowledge that you need to write effective long-term and short-term goals, it is time to set some short-term goals for your long-term goal.

Write your <u>long-term</u> goal here:

Write up to five <u>short-term goals</u> that will help you work towards achieving this long-term goal:

#1

#2

#3

#4

#5

Celebrate!

In this chapter, you created a long-term vision for your recovery and learned how to set long-term and short-term goals. You selected a priority goal and have created short-term action steps that will move you forward on your journey.

You have completed a lot of work to this point in your *Pathways to Recovery* Workbook. You are to be congratulated! Your persistence in working the workbook has already given you some new views and ideas about yourself and the path toward recovery you are traveling.

It's time to honor the work you have done to identify your personal goals! Think of one of the goals that you have defined. With that goal in mind, think of a way to treat yourself to some special experience that will celebrate that goal. For example:

- If your long-term goal is to have more fun in your life, rent a goofy, rib-tickling video, make yourself some popcorn, kick back and enjoy the show!

- If your long-term goal is to get a college degree and your short-term goal is to take a class at the local community college, how about treating yourself by purchasing a 3-ring notebook with the college logo on it? You can use your notebook for gathering information and for your first class. Every time you see and use your notebook it will remind you of the goals that you have set.

- If your long-term goal is to increase your wellness, you could call a friend and take a walk around a park. When you return home take a nice warm shower to relax.

- If your long-term goal is to expand your spirituality, celebrate by finding a quote that makes you feel at peace, write it down and keep it in your wallet.

What will you do to celebrate?

"May you live all the days of your life."
~Jonathan Swift

"You will do foolish things, but do them with enthusiasm."
~Colette

References & Resources

References

Kouzes, J. & Posner, B. (1987). *Leadership Challenge: How to Get Extraordinary Things Done in Organizations.* San Francisco, CA: Jossey Bass.

Kybartas, R. (1997). *Fitness is Religion — Keeping the Faith.* New York, NY: Simon & Schuster.

Mowbray, C. T., Bybee, D., Harris, S. N., & McCrohan, N. (1995). Predictors of work status and future work orientation in people with psychiatric disability. *Psychiatric Rehabilitation Journal, 19*(2), 17-28.

Peters, T. J., & Waterman, R. H., Jr. (1982). *In Search of Excellence: Lessons from America's Best-Run Companies.* New York: Harper & Row.

Resources

Balancing Your Life: Setting Personal Goals by Paul Steven (Resource Publishing, Inc., 1996).

Life Goals: Setting and Achieving Goals to Chart the Course of Your Life by Amy E. Dean & Dan Olmos (Hay House, Inc., 1991).

Life Strategies: Doing What Works, Doing What Matters by Phillip C. McGraw (Hyperion Press, 1999).

The Four Agreements: A Practical Guide to Personal Freedom: A Toltec Wisdom Book by Don M. Ruiz & Miguel Ruiz (Amber-Allen Publishers, 1997).

The Magic Lamp: Goal Setting for People Who Hate Setting Goals by Keith Ellis (Crown Publishing Group, 1998).

Something More: Excavating Your Authentic Self by Sarah Ban Breathnach (WarnerBooks, 1998).

Unlock Your Heart: Goal Setting from the Inside Out by E. Ellen Davis (1st Books Library, 2001).

Chapter Six

Moving Forward on the Journey: Mapping Our Goals Across Major Life Domains

This chapter focuses on several major life domains and explores the directions you want to head in the future.

Introduction

Sometimes psychiatric problems take over our life. Everything about our life can come to reflect our psychiatric history. We may spend our days in mental health programs, as though having a psychiatric disability were our full-time job.

We can begin to see our lives as defined by our psychiatric label or disability and leave behind all our other social roles. We may feel like a psychiatric diagnosis spells the end of our chances for experiencing love, fun or success. We give up the things we used to enjoy. Our self-esteem suffers. We can feel trapped in a life that is very limited and become bored, depressed and end up with negative feelings about ourselves.

In recovery, we find new meaning and purpose in our life that extends well beyond our identity as a person with a disability, our psychiatric label or diagnosis, or the fact that we may be a consumer of mental health services. We move on with living and reclaim a fuller life.

Some of us may have to essentially start from scratch to rebuild a life we think is truly worthwhile. Most of us have some areas of our life that have continued to work well for us. In order to create a more meaningful and full life, we build upon the inner and outer strengths we already have and expand our horizons.

> *As I grew up, I struggled with the concept of strength. It was hard to utilize my strengths when my world was in chaos. I never quite understood what strengths were because no one explained it to me. I believe though that strengths developed within me as I matured and grew. Some strengths are not evident but waited to be developed in time of need. My time of need began early and strengths were a step forward in my journey. I may not have been conscious of the use of strengths but I think they are there for those in need.*
>
> *~Anonymous,*
> *Kansas Consumer*

In recovery, we claim or reclaim social roles that move us beyond our disability identity. We find we can work and be good employees, we can have a comfortable living situation and be good tenants, we can extend our friendship circle and have good friends. We involve ourselves in creative, fun and interesting activities, and we learn new things and grow as individuals. We also begin to claim or reclaim higher levels

"There is one thing which gives radiance to everything. It is the idea of something around the corner."
~G. K. Chesterton

Chapter 6

"The way to develop self confidence is to do the thing you fear, and get a record of successful experiences behind you."
~William Jennings Bryan

of wellness and become much healthier. Our increasing well-being extends to important areas of life such as sexuality, intimacy, parenting and spirituality that have often been ignored or actively discouraged in traditional mental health programs.

Many of us have been cautioned against taking on challenging experiences or new roles, we were told to hold off until we had our psychiatric symptoms completely in remission (symptom-free). This isn't how recovery seems to work for most of us. In fact, many of us reclaim a full and interesting life *through the process of recovery*, even while continuing to experience psychiatric symptoms. Beginning to explore areas of recovery, organizing a meaningful and well-ordered daily life, rebuilding our social support network and getting a job or finding other productive ways to spend our time actually helps many of us reduce the symptoms we experience. Sometimes our symptoms continue even as we achieve recovery. We learn to manage our symptoms so they don't stop our progress.

> *Over the years, I have found many positive assets, which have helped me through the recovery process. By focusing on my strengths, this has helped me to have a more positive self-image and realize that I am a complete person with positive and negative elements. I think focusing on the positive helps me to focus in on what I think my strengths are and what I need to work on. Life is a continual process. I think the recovery process is good because it helps me think of how far I have come as a person. I am realizing that as I continue on the path to recovery, I am getting stronger and more determined every day.*
>
> *~Sue Bennet,*
> *Kansas Consumer*

"I was raised to sense what someone wanted me to be and be that kind of person. It took me a long time not to judge myself through someone else's eyes."
~Sally Field

In recovery we don't ignore our mental health concerns. Most of us continue to use mental health services and we learn self-care techniques and wellness strategies to manage our psychiatric symptoms better. It's true that we may experience setbacks from time to time that require us to focus a great deal of our attention on our mental health. But, when we have established our recovery goals and are moving toward them, contending with a setback becomes only one challenging event in a much more interesting and rewarding life. Our work on recovery makes it easier to rebound when, and if, a setback occurs.

> *From the beginning of my illness through the journey of recovery my different forms of strengths and abilities have all played a part in my remaining well and successful.*
>
> *~Carrie Hunter,*
> *Kansas Consumer*

"Self-observation leads to making better choices."
~Les Higgins, Kansas Consumer

When we focus on our problems, deficits, symptoms and mental health issues day in and day out it gets old; we find we have very little to look forward to. Working on our recovery motivates us to get up in the morning and contend with life. Sometimes reductions in symptoms leads to interest in other areas of recovery, but working on other areas of our life can also give us reasons and ways to improve our mental health! Once we become more motivated and excited about our recovery, we find we naturally want to increase our overall wellness. We want to take care of any obstacles in the way of meeting our goals and succeeding in educational, work, recreational, social and spiritual pursuits. Many of us find we also naturally want to lessen negative behaviors, such as over-use of drugs and alcohol, that stand in our way. When we deal with such obstacles, our psychiatric symptoms frequently lessen or even disappear.

> *Accepting responsibility for my choices, knowledge of my symptoms and medication, being resilient and tenacious, being willing to ask for help, having faith and hope, being deeply committed to recovery, and having a strong determination, all were strengths that I used to keep me on the road of recovery. I am so grateful to be in the place I am, and to be working in the human services field. There is not only "light at the end of the tunnel." I am almost through the tunnel. Recovery is a wonderful process.*
>
> *~Donna R. Story,*
> *Kansas Consumer Provider*

This chapter helps us take a careful look at many areas or domains of life. We will see where we stand in each of these areas and lay out ideas about the direction we want to head in the future. The decisions we make guide us as we move toward creating a more satisfying life in areas we decide we want or need to work on.

Chapter 6

In this chapter, you will explore and set initial goals in domains concerning your living situation, learning, the assets you have, work life, leisure and recreation activities, wellness, intimacy and sexuality and spirituality. Chapter 7 centers on social relationships. As part of your recovery, you will want to explore the territory of each of these domains in some depth. This section is extensive. Take each domain one at a time and give it your full attention. Don't try to rush through this process. You may want to begin with one or two areas that seem most important to you right now to begin with, or spend time on one area after another, until you have worked through all of the domains.

- You will determine where you currently stand in each area.
- You will identify where you want to be in the future.
- You will brainstorm long-term goals for your life in each area.
- You will bring in the knowledge you have developed about your strengths to see how you can use your inner and outer resources to support your efforts in reaching the goals you want to achieve.

By the end of this chapter, you will have taken a series of steps that will give you a much more complete understanding of the kind of life you want. You will have begun to map out how to move toward achieving your desired future.

The decisions you make in this part of your recovery workbook will set the stage for developing a Personal Recovery Plan in Chapter 8.

"A preoccupation with the future not only prevents us from seeing the present as it is, but often prompts us to rearrange the past."
~Eric Hoffer

HEADING TOWARD HOME:
The Domain of Our Living Situation

Having a decent living situation is a very important support to recovery. In one study, more than half the mental health consumers surveyed said that having decent and safe housing was the factor that allowed them to make their turnaround toward recovery (Coursey, et al., 1997). Findings from studies of supported housing show safe, decent, affordable housing can cut homelessness by up to 90% and reduce the use of psychiatric hospitalization by half (Ridgway & Rapp, 1997)!

Why is having a place that feels like home so important to our positive mental health?

- First, a place to call home is a safe space. All of us need personal privacy (although the amount we need differs across ethnic and cultural groups). When we have sufficient privacy we can feel comfortable and fully relax both physically and mentally.
- We express our individuality, our interests and our cultural and family identity through the things we have around us. Our personal belongings and the way we organize our living space are extensions of who we are and help us function well. Our belongings form our "identity kit" that helps us get through the day and feel good about ourselves.
- Our living environment is the center of our own personal map of the world. If we don't have a sense of having a place that is ours, we can feel disoriented (this happens to people who have never had mental health problems).
- Our living environment is the place where we take care of our daily needs. We nourish, nurture and comfort ourselves and do our daily spiritual practices in our living situation. Daily self-care rituals help support our recovery and provide a positive structure to our day.
- Organizing or decorating our living situation, preparing and eating food to reflect the seasons of the year and celebrating important holidays gives a comforting structure to our year.
- Having a decent living situation gives us a positive social status and can help tie us into a neighborhood, town, city or region where we can begin to put down roots and feel like we belong.

"There's no place like home."
~Dorothy from
The Wizard of Oz

Chapter 6

131

Where are You in Regard to Having Decent Housing and a Sense of Home?

☑ Check all that apply

❑ I feel at home where I live.

❑ My living situation feels safe.

❑ My housing is affordable (I pay less than 30% of my income for housing).

❑ My living situation is personalized to reflect my interests and tastes.

❑ I'm living in an area where I want to live.

❑ I have enough privacy where I live.

❑ I keep my living situation up well enough based on my preferences.

❑ I have my living situation organized to support my health and well-being.

❑ I want to stay where I am.

❑ The make-up of my household (e.g. living alone or with others) is what I want.

EXERCISE:
Exploring Strengths About Housing and Home

List the housing and home strengths you <u>currently</u> have: (e.g. My apartment is OK, I have several art posters that I like, there is a big park close by that I like to walk in, the stove is big enough)

What housing and home strengths did you use in the <u>past</u>? (e.g. I had my own apartment for 5 years; I had Section 8 rental assistance; I know how to sew and once made curtains)

What housing and home goals do you want to achieve in the <u>future</u>? (e.g. I want to live closer to the bus line; I want a roommate to share expenses; I want to buy a big rocking chair (garage sale?); I want to keep my current apartment but make it safer and nicer)

Using Your Strengths to Reach Your Housing Goals

In order to reach the goals you have for your living situation you can use your unique strengths and resources: *Remember when you list your strengths, that strengths can be:*

- *Internal* (e.g. My apartment gives me a peaceful feeling; I know how to cook and can prepare nutritious meals)

- *External* (e.g. I have a big, sturdy comfortable sofa; Mike, my roommate, helps with the rent)

What naturally-occurring community resources can you draw on to reach your housing goals? (e.g. I am going to check with the gas company to see if they can help me with my heating bill)

What formal services do you want to enlist to reach your goals? (e.g. My case manager can help get flexible funds from the mental health center to have my apartment sound-proofed as a reasonable accommodation under the Americans with Disabilities Act)

Identify your feelings and attitudes around the stated goals: (e.g. I'm really excited about updating my apartment; I'm pretty scared about moving out on my own, but I feel I need to take the risk)

What are the significant barriers you may encounter as you work towards your goals? (e.g. Without a rental subsidy I may have to have a roommate; I may need to show references)

List strategies that you can use to overcome barriers in reaching your housing goals: (e.g. I'm going to apply now for a Section 8 subsidy because the waiting list is two years long)

Chapter 6

How will you chart your progress along the way as you move toward your goals? (e.g. Make a notebook of things I need to make my apartment nicer, I'll cross them off when I find each item; I'll keep a running list of apartment buildings to check out and cross them off after I see the units)

How will you celebrate when you reach your goals? (e.g. When I repaint my kitchen, I will invite my friend Sam to dinner)

LEARNING AS WE GO: The Domain of Education

Many of us first experienced psychiatric problems when we were in high school or college and this experience often disrupted our education.

Many of us have been cautioned against returning to finish up our diploma or degree because it might prove too stressful. About fifteen years ago, supported education programs were developed and the results have been incredible. Research on these programs shows most people with psychiatric disabilities can succeed in educational programs and complete college, often with very good grades (Unger, 1998; Mowbray, 2002). Some of us have already completed our education and we want to use our knowledge and skills, or we want to upgrade our knowledge and skills after a period of time.

Some people want to learn to become effective providers of mental health services. Several states have programs that teach consumers to be mental health providers. Kansas has a Consumer as Provider (CAP) program and has been graduating classes of well-trained mental health workers for some time.

Most of us automatically think of a classroom environment when we read or hear the word education. Education is much more than attending a class or getting a degree. To be successful in life and in recovery, we must become life-long learners. Our learning may occur in a classroom, but can also include the activities we do every day to learn something new. Learning can involve joining a self-help club, watching an educational television show, reading a library book, finding new information on the Internet or reading the newspaper to find out about educational activities open to the public.

Involvement in educational activities helps us to grow, to change, to expand our horizons, to extend ourselves in different directions. Educational involvement parallels recovery; both are on-going processes and both prepare us for new challenges as we travel our life's path.

"Education is our passport to the future, for tomorrow belongs to the people who prepare for it today."
~Malcolm X

"Each new step becomes a little surer, and each new grasp a little firmer."
~Sarah Ban Breathnach

> *The most marvelous mentor in my life was my Dad. He always told me that education was the one thing no one could ever take away from me. He was extremely well read and always interested in current events as well as history. He shared wonderful stories with me.*
>
> *At the present time, I don't feel that I can afford to go to college but I'm following my Dad's example: I read and learn everything I can nearly every day and it has helped me immensely. Not only do I feel like an interesting person to myself, I feel that I can be an interesting conversationalist when I am with others. This aspect of my being has been vital to my recovery because when I was very ill with my psychiatric illness, I didn't have the strength to read or learn at all. I believe that my journey of self-education will help me when I do return to college in the near future.*
>
> ~JoAnn Howley,
> Kansas Consumer

"Learning is a treasure that will follow its owner everywhere."
~Chinese Proverb

There are many reasons to get involved in educational activities. We may want to upgrade our skills to improve our chances of getting an interesting & rewarding job. We may want to explore going back to school & taking classes to finish a degree that has been on hold. We may want to learn something new to enhance our self-confidence. We may want to build a base of knowledge about ourselves & our recovery. We may just be curious about a topic and want to know more about it.

> *Even though I was moving through my journey, I struggled with flashbacks and memories many of which interfered with my life. During the rough times these flashbacks made life hell. It was so difficult in school because my mind was preoccupied with my turmoil. The present was hard to see, because my mind was filled with dark lonely thoughts. I could not concentrate when I was preoccupied with the dark gloomy scenes from the past. It took a lot of my courage to forge forward through all this turmoil and to continue.*
>
> *College, postgraduate work, and the CAP program were times for utilizing my (strengths of) intelligence and being responsible. The challenge was a good one in my life because I was developing many skills. This made me hopeful to stay on the path of a successful and pleasurable life.*
>
> ~Anonymous,
> Kansas Consumer

"Experience is a hard teacher because she gives the test first, the lesson afterward."
~Vernon Law

EXERCISE:
Exploring Educational Strengths

List your <u>current</u> educational strengths: (e.g. I watch educational TV shows about animals; I have a library card; I have 18 hours of college credit)

What educational strengths have you used in the <u>past</u>? (e.g. I successfully completed 6 hours in Art History at Colby County Community College; I used to read novels for enjoyment)

What educational goals do you want to achieve in the <u>future</u>? (e.g. I want to go back to finish my Associates Degree; I want to join a book discussion club; I want to learn how to use a computer)

Using Your Strengths To Reach Your Educational Goals

You can use internal and external resources to reach your educational goals. *Remember when you list your strengths, that strengths can be:*

- *<u>Internal</u>* (e.g. Whenever I'm learning a new subject I feel uplifted)

- *<u>External</u>* (e.g. My friend Gilbert can teach me how to repair bicycle tires)

What naturally-occurring community resources can you use to meet your educational goals? (e.g. I will use the English as a Second Language Program at the local high school to gain a better English vocabulary; I will use the computer at the local library to learn more about whales and dolphins)

What formal services and supports do you want to enlist to meet your educational goals? (e.g. I will explore supported education to have assistance in returning to school; I will try to get my tuition paid through a grant or scholarship)

Identify your attitude around your educational goals: (e.g. I'm really excited about trying to learn to sew; I'm pretty scared about what will happen if I take the risk of returning to college; I've always loved school; I'm really angry that I can't get a decent job without my high school diploma)

What are the barriers you might encounter as you work towards these goals? (e.g. I lack sufficient income to take a college class and need a scholarship; I have a hard time managing my time [*time management is the most important taking-charge skill for educational success*])

Identify how you can overcome the barriers you have listed. (e.g. I will check about scholarships or loans at the Office of Financial Aid; I will look on the Internet for funding resources; I will buy a daily planner book and make "to-do" lists; I will save up for a new pair of glasses)

How will you mark your progress along the way as you move toward your education goals? (e.g. I will use a date book and chart the time I spend practicing sign language; I will track my grade point average and maintain a B average)

How will you celebrate when you reach your goals? (e.g. I will treat myself to a cup of coffee after attending class each week)

TICKET TO RIDE:
The Domain of Assets

Most of us need to build up our assets so we have the resources we need for our journey of recovery. Not having enough money can make us feel anxious, angry and depressed. Such feelings are not symptoms, they are common emotions of people who have low incomes! Such emotions can impact our physical health and ultimately our recovery. We also know that people with low incomes and lack of insurance are nearly twice as likely to have psychiatric disorders, so low income can have a negative effect on our mental health (Henning, 2001).

Throughout this workbook we have thought and written about our personal vision of recovery, we have identified our strengths in various ways and have started to set goals. We need to gather sufficient resources to support and sustain our journey so we can reach our recovery goals.

Most of us have very limited resources. Income benefits for people with disabilities are set at such low levels that we are often forced to struggle to merely survive. Limited resources and poverty can take a toll on recovery. It's hard to even make ends meet and to stay housed with meager benefits. Some of us don't have control over our income. We may lack information on how to make decisions on spending our money or making the most of the money we do have.

Lack of assets can wear us down and keep us from doing what we'd like to do, or need to do, in all the other domains or areas of our life. For example, we could buy better food, live in a nicer apartment and afford better transportation if we had more assets. While there is no "quick fix" for building assets, we can take steps to increase our assets over time and we can improve how we use the resources we already have. Consumer leader Patricia E. Deegan has pointed out that we are often encouraged to adjust to the unnatural state of extreme poverty. *Failing to live well on a sub-poverty income is not a personal failing!*

Usually, we think of assets as cash money, but assets include more than the money we have in hand. Assets are the things we own, what we have in our personal possession. Having a skill or talent is also an asset. Having a car or our own furniture are just a few examples of assets. For this section, however, we are going to concentrate on money.

"It's good to have money and the things that money can buy, but it's good too, to check up once in a while and make sure you haven't lost the things that money can't buy."
~George Lucas Lorimer

Chapter 6

"Money, it turned out, was exactly like sex, you thought of nothing else if you didn't have it and thought of other things if you did."
~James Baldwin

In this section of the workbook, you will identify the financial resources you have as well as recognizing any financial liabilities. People who handle money as a profession (such as accountants and bankers) often create what is called a "balance sheet." A balance sheet is a tool that compares the assets on hand to the liabilities that we have, so we can see where we stand overall. After completing the first exercise, you may want to consider creating a balance sheet for yourself.

EXERCISE:
Current Assets and Those I Want or Need

Using the form on the following page, check off the assets you already have and those you need. The list is devoted to ways of keeping track of your money and other assets and getting more assets! After completing the checklist, review the list again and check off the areas that you want to focus in on.

Here are a few examples of areas that others have said they had to work on in order to move forward in recovery: help with taxes, information on using and balancing a checkbook, budgeting and money management, applying for low-income housing subsidies, low-income utility provisions, bartering for needed services/resources, becoming my own payee, insurance information, information on benefits status and the return to work.

Once you have listed your assets, list your liabilities in the next table. Once you have the two tables completed, you will be able to review the balance between your liabilities and your assets.

"To find yourself, think for yourself."
~Socrates

"Don't be run so much by what you lack as by what you have already achieved."
~Marcus Aurelius

Financial Resources and Assets	I have this	Need to get	Things I need to do to have more assets or resources
Stable monthly income			
Health insurance and/or medical card			
Affordable housing			
Transportation			
Auto Insurance			
Savings account			
Checking account/Checkbook			
Place to organize my bills			
Job/Paycheck			
Ability to make a budget			
Knowledge of how to read a bank statement			
Someone to help handle my money			
Knowledge about my credit rating			
Others owe me money			
Tax records			
Talents/skills to make extra money (list what they are and include bartering or trading)			
Benefits that I may qualify for (list what they are or may be)			
Other assets (you may want to add another sheet)			

Liabilities (Bills or Loans)	Amount Owed	What I want to do about this:
	$	
	$	
	$	
	$	
	$	
	$	
	$	
	$	
	$	
	$	
	$	
	$	
	$	
	$	
	$	
	$	
	$	
	$	

Tips and Ideas for Building Assets:

$ We don't want to constantly think "poor-me" because doing so will put us in the role of victim. We have the power to improve our financial future and build assets!

$ We need to join in coalition with other poor people to advocate for increased benefits. There are many economic human rights organizations we can join.

$ We can become a self-advocate and apply for all the programs we are eligible for.

$ Some of us say "I'm bad with money." Even if we are not skilled in money matters we can learn how to take steps to take charge of our finances or we can find others who can help us formally or informally.

$ Often money and financial matters are a reflection of how we think about ourself and our self-image. On the days we do our shopping, we can try to focus on having a positive self-image. If we are feeling bad or down, it's probably not the day to make financial decisions.

$ We can trade ideas on how to manage on extremely low income with others.

$ In good times we should avoid spending money just to spend it. Sometimes when we feel really good, we spend money as a form of recreation. This has jokingly been called "retail therapy." This type of spending seems easy and satisfying in the moment, but in the long run it can become self-defeating and a roadblock to our recovery.

$ It helps to make a monthly budget and stick to it. If we need help in learning how to budget, we can seek out an experienced friend or a no-cost credit-counseling agency (the phone book has referrals) to help us. Some of us really need, or are forced to have, another person involved in our money management. We can shop around to find a good representative payee.

"The safest way to double your money is to fold it over once and put it in your pocket."
~Frank Hubbard

Chapter 6

145

$ We shouldn't let advertisers influence our purchasing. The things that are advertised the most are often things we need the least—for example: soda pop, beer, cigarettes, candy, expensive sneakers, pre-packaged foods and fast food.

$ We can sell some of our clothes or household goods we no longer wear or use at a consignment shop. Most often we will get 50% of the selling price.

$ We can shop thrift stores. It is amazing what is available at incredibly low prices. Shopping a thrift store can be an adventure and seems to be very much in vogue. Some thrift stores have sales on top of their low prices to clearance merchandise and something new is always being added to stock. We can bring a friend and make it an adventure!

$ We can buy food in the most unprocessed state possible (for example: fruits, vegetables, rice, potatoes and meat). Prepackaged items are costly.

$ We can shop at stores that value us as a customer and show it in price, courtesy and the ability to return goods.

$ We can shop sales, have patience and make sure we really want and need the item before we purchase it.

$ We can slowly whittle down any debt we have by making small consistent payments. It may take a few years but it feels great when we can get rid of a bill.

$ We can try not to grocery shop when we are feeling hungry. It is easy to buy junk food and expensive extras on impulse.

$ For some higher price items we are considering purchasing (e.g. TV, radio, appliances), it may be helpful to take someone with us who is very knowledgeable about the item, so we can make good decisions. Consumer Reports Magazine rates many consumer goods and we can look up ratings in the library.

$ If we have to have a credit card, we should try to limit ourselves to only one. It is easy to lose track of how much we are charging when we have several cards. We should try to avoid credit cards entirely if we cannot pay off the debt every month. High credit card interest rates are a trap.

$ For anything we buy on time (like a car), we should understand the amount of interest we are paying and decide if it is worth the purchase.

$ We can avoid being a "sucker for a sad story." P.T. Barnum (of Barnum and Bailey Circus fame) has been quoted as saying, "There's a sucker born every minute." We shouldn't let others take advantage of our compassion, caring and idealism or our lack of knowledge.

$ We can shop around to try to find free checking. We can pay many of our bills automatically using electronic payment.

$ For those of us with sufficient income, it is a good idea to have a savings account with a least one-month's income saved in case of financial emergency.

$ We can find creative ways to supplement our income and look into support for a return to work.

$ If we are working, and our employer offers retirement benefits, we can try our best to fund our retirement account up to the amount matched by the employer.

$ Everyone makes bad money decisions. We can learn from our mistakes rather than dwelling on them.

$ We can become activists! Poverty needs to be addressed by all of us. We can join with others to advocate higher benefits and adequate income. The U. S. Surgeon General's report on mental health (U.S. Department of Health and Human Services, 1999) discusses the importance of mental health consumers becoming advocates in the communities where we live: "advocacy enables consumer groups to shape policy at the local level, where a direct impact can be felt." Let's also join with others on a national level to increase benefits and make a difference!

"The value of a dollar is social, as it is created by society." ~Ralph Waldo Emerson

EXERCISE:
Strengths About Assets

List the strengths you <u>currently</u> have: (e.g. I have a medical card and health insurance; I have a stable monthly income)

What are strengths you used in the <u>past</u> regarding assets? (e.g. I worked part-time and had a savings account; I paid off my health care bill over a two year period)

What goals do you want to achieve in the <u>future</u> to improve your assets? (e.g. I want to learn how to budget money better and learn how to balance a checkbook; I want to become my own payee)

Using Your Strengths to Reach Your Asset Goals

In order to reach the goals you have set you can use your unique strengths and resources. *Remember that when you list your strengths, that strengths can be:*

- <u>Internal</u> (e.g. I feel in control when I am making my own decisions about my money)

- <u>External</u> (e.g. I can go to a free Housing & Credit Counseling workshop on how to develop a budget)

What naturally-occurring community resources can you draw upon to meet your goals? (e.g. I will use the free credit counseling service at 5th and Maple Street; I will use Legal Aid to help me with my denial of benefits)

What formal services do you want to enlist to help you with assets? (e.g. I will use my case manager as an advocate to help me get my benefits and paperwork straightened out)

Describe your attitude around the goals: (e.g. I'm committed to gaining more resources; I hate always being so broke)

What barriers do you think you may encounter as you begin working towards these goals? (e.g. I don't like math, it scares me; I just don't understand the paperwork, I really need some help; I've lost all my tax forms or paperwork; I have a low level of benefits but if I make much money, my benefits drop or I have to pay for my medications)

What strategies can you use to overcome barriers as you move towards reaching these goals? (e.g. My friend Ryan used to work at a bank, maybe he can help me learn how to make a balance sheet and budget; I will begin exploring ways to work part-time; I will buy a daily planner book and make "to-do lists")

How will you mark your progress towards reaching these goals? (e.g. Keep a budget; balance my checkbook; start a savings account and track my deposits)

How will you celebrate reaching these goals? (After we create a budget together, Ryan and I will go out for coffee; I will treat myself to one small splurge that is not on my grocery list)

BUILDING A CAREER PATH:
The Vocational Domain

In the past, many of us were told to avoid working because it was considered too stressful. Research really doesn't support the idea that those of us with psychiatric disabilities cannot or should not work. In fact, many of us find working to be a powerful force for our healing and recovery, and research supports the idea that work is often beneficial. In other countries, a much higher proportion of people with psychiatric disabilities work (Ridgway & Rapp, 1999).

The Benefits of Working

Many of us find working actually benefits our mental health. Here is a paraphrased list of benefits to working that Kevin Walsh, a California consumer, describes in a "tool kit" put out by the National Association of State Mental Health Directors (1999).

- Working is healing
- Working focuses on our abilities, not our limitations
- Working improves our self-concept by overcoming the feeling we are unworthy or useless
- Working moves us into challenging relationships with others that help us grow
- Working moves us toward self-actualization (becoming the best person we can be)

Exploring the World of Work

If you are interested in going to work, there are many things you may want to consider. The most important is motivation. Ask yourself these questions.

- *Am I motivated to work?*

- *What is the source of my motivation?*

- *Does my motivation come from within me and reflect my own desires and values, or am I being encouraged or pressured by someone or something outside myself to get a job?*

"Vocation...would include fnding out the place where the need of the world coincides with your own gifts, where that which you can give is joyfully received."
~James Carroll

Motivation Assessment

☑ Check the one that comes closest to
how you feel about working

- ❑ Very highly motivated
- ❑ Highly motivated
- ❑ Somewhat motivated
- ❑ Slightly motivated
- ❑ Not motivated at this time

Motivation is important because it is the single characteristic that has been found to relate to our success at working (Ridgway & Rapp, 1999). Our motivation is more important than our work history, our treatment history, our diagnosis and the psychiatric symptoms we may have. If our motivation is high, our chances for becoming employed are high too!

How can you increase your motivation if you are not already highly motivated?

One of the most important factors in gaining employment is whether we are able to see ourselves successfully employed. One study found consumers who could see themselves working in the near future (within six months) were much more likely to go to work and hold down a job within that time period (Mowbray, et al., 1995).

Can you see yourself working? If yes, what does that look like? If not, why not?

"Blessed is he who has found his work; let him ask no other blessedness."
~Thomas Carlyle

152

If you want to work but cannot clearly visualize yourself working, what can you do to overcome obstacles so you can improve your ability to see yourself working?

Here are some ways that you can become clearer and more motivated:

- <u>Find Positive Role Models</u>—Find and talk to other consumers who are successfully working.

- <u>Use Positive Self-Talk</u>—Tell yourself over and over, "I can work. Going to work will be easier than I think. Work will be rewarding."

- <u>Conduct Informational Interviews</u>—Many workers find that exploring their interests with people who are already successful helps them build understanding. Contact someone working in a field, setting or type of job you are potentially interested in pursuing. Ask the person if you can set a time for you to talk to him or her. Ask the job holder what the job is like, what qualifications are important, how to prepare to work in the field, what working conditions are like and so on. The person will probably be flattered and you will understand much more about what it takes to be successful in that line of work.

Honor Your Interests and Aptitudes

It is important to identify areas that are interesting to you, that you would find rewarding. Research done in Kansas found that many consumers who took any kind of job just to have a job quit right away because the job did not match their interests or match other values they held (Boyd, Ridgway & Rapp, 1998). In other research, consumers who took jobs that matched their preferences and interests kept their jobs twice as long as those whose jobs did not reflect things or qualities that were important to them. We are learning not to sell ourselves short when we explore our interests. At one time we were channeled into low-level jobs and didn't know we had other options. Now we know that those of us with psychiatric disabilities can work in a whole range of jobs from consumer advocate to teacher, from waitress to executive director, from legal secretary to psychiatrist!

"To find out what one is fitted to do, and to secure an opportunity to do it, is the key to happiness."
~John Dewey

Chapter 6

153

What are your interests?

Do you have a clear idea of what kind of work you might like?

Do you know what your aptitudes are (what would you enjoy doing or be good at)?

> "In every community, there is work to be done. In every nation, there are wounds to heal. In every heart, there is a power to do it."
> ~Marianne Williamson

Review your strengths inventory. Does any area strike you as an important area to explore as a possible career interest?

Write down a list of things you know you are good at and things you are interested in:

Griff McClure, a consumer provider from Colorado who works as a vocational specialist, asks his clients this question: "What makes you feel awake and alive?" **What is your response to this question?**

Crystal shares her story of what makes her feel great:

> *When I was at the (state psychiatric hospital) I had the staff right in the palm of my hand. I knew just what behavior it took to make them SNAP! For a long time I would use this to my advantage. I had found negative attention to be very rewarding—it's the only thing I knew!*
>
> *Then I discovered a very useful and positive thing to do when I realized maybe I should try this positive attention. I would write all my feelings, whether negative or positive, instead of taking it out on staff, others or myself. I realized a lot of my writings could be called "poetry." So I became a poet. I have had nation-wide recognition for my poetry. I was even nominated as "Poet of the Year" in 2000, and my poems are in the Library of Congress. I have had poetry in the newspaper and on the radio. Every time I feel like hurting myself, I start writing.*
>
> *I am grateful. If I had my life to live over again I probably wouldn't change a thing. I have a life today. I never knew how good it was to laugh when you don't have something to laugh about. My tears today are not tears of sadness, but tears of joy, and disbelief that a person so far down, that was so negative about life, could excel as I have.*
>
> ~Crystal Dirks,
> Kansas Consumer

"Work is love made visible. "
~Kahlil Gibran

Identify What is Important in a Workplace

It is important to consider the kind of workplace environment that we want. Some of us like a busy environment while others desire a slower pace. Some of us like to work with other people, while others prefer to work alone. We should consider the physical stamina demanded in a given job and compare that with our personal level of fitness. If the job is important to us, but too physically demanding in our current state of fitness, we can decide to increase our fitness level before trying to work at such a job.

Write down characteristics of a job or workplace that are important to you:

> "True belonging is born of relationships not only to one another but to a place of shared responsibilities and benefits. We love not so much what we have acquired as what we have made and whom we have made it with."
> ~Robert Finch

Use a Wide Array of Community Resources

There are many community resources available to us as we explore the world of work and set vocational goals.

- Local Libraries have Internet access and newspaper job listings.
- Community Colleges often provide free aptitude testing.
- Adult Education Programs can help us develop basic skills such as literacy or GED.
- Job Services offer job postings and employment counseling.
- A supported employment program can help us return to work.
- Let all your supporters know you are looking for a job.

Learning About and Upholding Our Rights as Employees

When we start thinking about working, we should take the time to learn about our rights. Many people are covered by the Americans with Disabilities Act (ADA), a federal law that helps people with disabilities live, work, play and travel in the mainstream of life. All large companies must comply with the ADA. Information about the ADA is available through the Internet, a local independent living center or rights protection and advocacy agencies. Information on resources about the ADA are listed at the end of this chapter.

Disclosure of Disability to Request Reasonable Accommodations

It is up to us to decide whether or not to talk about our disability with our employers and coworkers. If we want to be protected by the American with Disabilities Act, we must tell our employer we have a disability and ask for "reasonable accommodations."

If we disclose our disability, we may be eligible for personalized workplace accommodations that can help us succeed as employees.

We have to be able to perform all the routine functions of the job, but we may need supports to succeed at the job. People with a physical disability may need a wheelchair ramp or special furniture. Those of us with psychiatric disabilities often need other types of accommodations, such as a flexible work schedule to take time for appointments, certain kinds of physical changes in the workplace, such as a cubicle to reduce noise, or certain styles of communication from supervisors.

Write down ideas about any accommodations you think you may need:

"The time is always right to do what is right."
~Martin Luther King, Jr.

Shifting Gears: When We Need to Change Our Career Path

Many of us had already established ourselves on a career path or were homemakers prior to experiencing psychiatric disability. Sometimes we lose our foothold on our career path and find our prior attainment sliding away.

This is the way Suzette Mack describes this process in her life.

Being a health professional with a mental illness caused all sorts of issues for me. First, I lost my job entirely during a severe psychotic episode. Then I realized there might be issues with my professional licensing board if they found out my psychiatric history, so I chose to not return to my field of work. This left me in a tail spin, trying to figure out what to do, where to go, how I'd ever again find viable employment that would afford me the materialistic, spiritual and professional dreams I once had. Having a mental illness has left me somewhat dependent on the system.

Thank goodness for the system…yet at the same time I curse it. Weren't independence and striving for achievement the motivating factors for much of my labors as a student and employee? What has become of that 'me' who could do it all, wanted it all, could do fifty things at once and not be overwhelmed?

Continued…

"Ain't nothin' to it but to do it."
~Maya Angelou

When you lose your ability to work because of a mental illness, it seems to be the heralded opinion to get past the grief & move on ahead — but how do you shake one identity for another when you still wear the same face, carry the same name, still bear inside what you've achieved?

I want to work again…really I do. I try, & I look for work. I tell myself that the time I've taken away from work has been time away that I genuinely needed. The wiser part of me knows that I was struggling with my work for a long, long time before I actually left my job. I've learned a lot about my mental illness — the things that trigger it, ways to accommodate my life so that its symptoms remain at a minimum. I'm ready to go back into the career force—but my resume has gaps, my confidence is shaky, I don't have good references, my medication still makes me tired, & in some ways I feel like such a failure in spite of all the positive self-talk I've learned to do.

It's going to be really important to continue to tell myself that my old ways of thinking and pressuring myself into being something 'more' are going to have to be abandoned for new ideas about vocation. I'm going to have to make a daily mental note to recognize early-on that those feelings of jealousy, competition and inadequacies I'll face, in the light of my tendency to compare myself to others of my age and educational level. I'll have to take a lot of deep breaths and practice what I know, about how it's okay to be different, to be myself through all of these occupational transitions in my life. I'll work extra hard to not see the clouds or feel the thorns, and to try to remember to laugh when I feel sadness and stress.

You have to let go of the pain and the old ideas of you, as you let in new images you have to give yourself permission to be someone different than you used to be — than maybe who you wanted to be, or could've been. You have to really dig deep — to go beyond just saying you accept others with differences, bear no prejudices, don't value people by their titles, their addresses, their lifestyles. You realize you are someone you never thought you'd be — you've been on the receiving end of those holiday fruit baskets and canned foods…you're wearing used clothing…you're lucky to be driving a car, even though it needs a lot of fixing up. You realize the barriers between the 'me' and 'them' have merged, and you are standing with your feet on both sides of the line — wondering where you fit in and if you really have to assume a whole new identity because of this thing called a mental illness.

It's really true about what they say, that it's best to take things one day at a time. It's the only way you'll work this through without hating yourself, or God, or life. It's really all you have, in spite of all the looking ahead and hoping tomorrow will somehow be different. It's hard not to compare myself with others. It's even harder to know what to focus on next, as I recover and try to figure out where to go from here. I've spent so much time being taken care of because of my illness — there wasn't much room for decisions like these because I was merely trying to survive. But now there lies ahead a whole new future for my life. I have to think about it really, really hard now…and not try to be overwhelmed by having to practically start my whole life over again, somewhere in between youth and old age.

~Suzette Mack,
Colorado Consumer & Wellness Educator

Here are Suzette's ideas about common missteps that people might make in the area of employment:

- Expecting someone else to accept responsibility for the special stresses you experience.
- Deciding not to change and being angry about what life has dealt you.
- Acting victimized and not trying.
- Trying to work by the "old rules," thinking about the way you used to be.
- Trying to over-control the situation; jobs are stressful and can't always be controlled.
- Comparing yourself to the pace set by others.
- Not having some sort of career plan.
- Picking the wrong battles.
- Trying to become best friends, or enemies, with your job; it interferes with objectivity.
- Losing track of your support.

These are Suzette's suggestions for some of the ways you might want to manage a return to work:

- Learn practical things about job accommodations and the ADA, things you can implement for your individual needs. Get help with this if necessary.
- Continue to work on having a positive, accepting attitude about the challenges in life.
- Choose to not be the victim. You are as good as, and as strong as, anyone else out there. There is no "us" versus "them"…it's all about feeling like a "we."
- Life changes; see yourself as evolving and that your job will automatically change to reflect the new you. Don't cocoon. Don't limit yourself…choose to soar!
- Learn ways to manage stress; choose to put down your anger and frustrations, and instead enjoy the work environment—even the stressful parts.
- You are yourself. Don't add pressures upon yourself that will only hurt your spirit and self-esteem. Everyone has unique gifts—find your own special niche!
- Make a plan—one month, six months, twelve months, two years, five years…it helps you find a focus and see your successes.
- Choose not to see the work field as a battleground. Learn to meditate and how to refocus energy in positive ways.

"It's easy to make a buck. It's tougher to make a difference."
~Tom Brokaw

"You must give some time to your fellow [human beings]. Even if it's a little thing, do something for others—something for which you get no pay but the privilege of doing it."
~Albert Schweitzer

159

- Learn to see your job as just one part of you. Develop hobbies over your lunch hour. Find things to work on outside of work that motivate you to look forward to the end of the workday. Make a vow to not become a workaholic.
- Keep your support system or create a new one that lets you talk about what you are dealing with at work.

Volunteerism

Volunteering is a great way to give back and help out other people in our community. It can help us, too! Scientific studies have traced a direct link between the brain and the immune system (Sobel & Ornstein, 1996). Researchers found that merely watching a film on Mother Teresa, one of the greatest role models of selfless service, strengthened the body's immune response. There truly is a healing power in helping others!

Why volunteer? The best reason for us to volunteer is a genuine desire to help others. The experience can provide us with some very substantial benefits as well. Here are some reasons why we may want to consider volunteering:

It allows us to explore career options. When we're not sure what kind of career or job we want, volunteering gives us a chance to learn more about our options before we make a commitment. It gives us a chance to research alternatives.

It's a great way to develop new skills. Volunteering can help us learn skills that employers will want us to have. Once we learn these new skills, they can easily transfer to the job of our choice.

Volunteering gives us an opportunity to gain confidence and self-esteem. The skills and benefits we gain will make a difference in how we feel about ourselves.

We meet new people. It's always a good idea to add a new friend to our support system. Volunteering can also be a good way for us to make connections for a new job or find people who can give us personal and professional references.

"You don't live in a world all your own. Your brothers are here, too."
~Albert Schweitzer

"It is expressly at those times when we feel needy that we will benefit the most from giving."
~Ruth Ross

160

We can gain valuable career-related experience. Some occupations require a certain degree or certificate, but employers also look for people who have relevant experience. Even if we have the skills and the education, volunteering can give us some up-to-date practical, "real-world" experience.

<u>We can share our knowledge and expertise with others in our community</u>. It is very rewarding to know that our education, training, experience, skills and interests are of value to others.

Volunteering is rewarding in itself. Helping others is one of the best ways for us to help ourselves. We get a healthy dose of satisfaction from volunteering.

Why would you be interested in volunteering?

What would you hope to get from the volunteer experience?

There are lots of places that welcome volunteers. Most non-profit agencies, churches and organizations need volunteers. If we are already a member of a non-profit organization or church, we can check with them to see if they can use our help. We can ask our friends or family for suggestions. Most local United Way offices keep track of volunteer opportunities in the community. We can check our local newspaper for more ideas. Career centers at local colleges also keep track of volunteer positions.

Where would you like to volunteer?

"There is a wonderful mythical law of nature that the three things we crave most in life—happiness, freedom and peace of mind—are always attained by giving them to someone else."
~Peyton Conway March

Chapter 6

"The reward for a good deed is to have done it."
~Anonymous

If there is a specific type of work that we like to do, we should go for it! If we are not sure of our interests, most organizations will be able to match us with a volunteer opportunity.

How much volunteer time should we commit to giving?

Each volunteer opportunity requires a different time commitment. Some are just a few hours each month while others may be a few hours each week up to full time. We can volunteer for a single event or make a lengthier time commitment. There are many different ways to get involved; we can find something that meets our needs and our personal schedule.

What kind of time commitment are you willing to make as a volunteer?

Why is this time commitment right for you?

Volunteering can be one of the most rewarding experiences we ever have. Even though we don't get paid in cash, the other rewards we receive are great.

No matter what you are looking for, there is a group in your community who needs YOU!

EXERCISE:
Exploring Vocational Strengths

List your <u>current</u> vocational strengths: (e.g. I have a high school diploma; I'm good at research)

What vocational strengths have you used in the <u>past</u>? (e.g. I have held part-time jobs and worked full-time for a year)

What goals around working or volunteering do you want to achieve in the <u>future</u>? (e.g. I want to hold a part-time job that pays at least $6.00 an hour)

Chapter 6

Using Your Strengths to Reach Your Goal

In order to reach your goals you can use these strengths and resources: *Remember that when you list your strengths, that strengths can be:*

- *Internal* (e.g. I know how to do crisis counseling; I am a good craftsperson; I know computer programming; I know how to work with numbers)

- *External* (e.g. My cousin George owns a company, he may give me a job)

What naturally-occurring community resources can you use to reach your vocational/volunteer goals? (e.g. I will use my local community college for free vocational aptitude testing)

List the formal services you may want to use in order to achieve your goals. (e.g. I will get involved with a supported employment program to have assistance in preparing my resume and searching for a job)

How do you feel about your vocational goals? (e.g. I'm excited about volunteering; I'm enthusiastic about returning to work)

What are the barriers that you may run into as you head towards these goals? (e.g. I need to make sure I don't lose my insurance because my meds are so expensive; I don't have a car to get to work)

List ideas and strategies that you can use to overcome the barriers to reaching these goals: (e.g. Check into having a car that is paid for through vocational rehabilitation; look on the Internet for volunteer opportunities)

How will you chart your progress along the way toward reaching your goals? (e.g. Keep track of job applications; keep a list of skills I learn as a volunteer)

How will you celebrate when you reach this goal? (e.g. I'll learn to give myself foot massages after each day I work; I'll save for a car out of each paycheck and once I have the car I will take drives into the country)

RECHARGING OUR BATTERIES:
The Domain of Leisure and Recreation

When we look at our lives and our steps towards recovery, it can seem like really serious business. As we develop and work our recovery plan, sometimes it can seem stressful or feel like too much hard work If we feel stress coming on, it's a reliable sign that it's time to recharge ourselves by engaging in leisure and recreational activities.

Leisure and recreation can be defined as involvement in activities that bring us happiness, pleasure and leave us feeling refreshed and rejuvenated.

Leisure and recreational activities are something that most people take for granted, something that they do spontaneously. Many of us who experience psychiatric disabilities forget how to relax and have fun in our lives. Planning ways to find pleasure or have fun and feel restored is an important part of the journey of recovery. We can build time into each day for having fun, taking a break or trying something new.

There are as many different kinds of recreation and leisure activities as there are people. Some of us enjoy group activities such as playing on a softball team, playing cards or joining a free book discussion group at our local library. Some of us enjoy solitary activities such as meditating, walking in nature or gardening. Listening to music and spending time with pets are leisure activities that have healing effects. The following story shows how one Kansas Consumer learned about what she enjoys.

> *I should tell you that I have always thought of myself as a simple woman, a woman who desired nothing. I always presented myself to everyone as a simple person. I used to wonder why I would portray myself that way. I was never motivated for anything. After a lifetime of severe abuse, I started feeling as though my life was coming to a standstill. I kept feeling like I never really existed. I became very bored and very lonesome. I had very little support from anyone. Everything I tried I couldn't accomplish. Everything had taken a toll out of me, my feelings, my suffering and my anger I felt within me. I lost all my self-respect. I felt nothing I did mattered. I had to find a way out of my situation.*
>
> *Continued...*

In my recovery, I had to decide what I wanted the most — my life or the will to die. It had come to that point. My two younger daughters are my life. What would happen to them if something happened to me? We had lost everything, including a place to live.

My recovery journey started with my social worker. She tried to help me create a meaningful life of my own. She involved me in classes to prepare for a job, but I was in a state of hopelessness. The hardest thing for me to accomplish was to live alone and be independent.

My social worker referred me to the mental health center for an evaluation. There I made a turnaround. They never gave up on me. I wanted to live and shout from the top of my voice that I am somebody! I wanted someone to notice me. I wanted to feel wanted. I wanted to make use of my time. In reality, I wanted to be able to trust someone. I had never had people to fuss over me like everyone did at the mental health center. I was so overwhelmed, I didn't know how to consume it all.

I started grooming myself. I started taking better care of 'me.' It was like I discovered myself all over again. I was very supportive of everyone. Through my recovery, I am able to reach out to others. I am able to have friends and don't have to isolate myself from people. In my recovery, I have become a stronger person. I have actually set goals for myself — like completing the Consumers as Providers program.

I would like to say some things about myself. I've always wanted to be a Spanish translator. I love writing poems, things about people and things that are on my mind. I am Mexican American. I love the colors blue, yellow, white and black. My favorite flowers are peonies, roses and a mixture of wild flowers. I love to wake up in the early morning and go out on the porch. While the mist is still in the air, I like to listen to the birds chirp and smell the fresh air while drinking a fresh hot cup of coffee or chocolate. In the evening, while I lie in bed near an open window, I love to gaze at the stars and dream and wonder and fantasize. I love all sorts of music and I love to dance. I enjoy bowling, volleyball and swimming. I have thoughts and possibilities. Here is a poem (Holman, 1994) that I love:

> I LOVE WHAT I SEE THERE
> I cannot love another, if I have no love to give.
> I cannot light another's way, until I learned to live.
> I cannot lend a helping hand, unless my arm is strong
> Or teach you lovely melodies, until I've learned my song.
> I cannot tell my loved ones to be strong and proud and free
> Unless I feel within my heart, that's how you fashioned me.
> I cannot touch your children, Lord, and show them that I care
> Until I look inside myself and love what I see there.
>
> ~Catherine Scruggs,
> Kansas Consumer

What kinds of leisure or recreational activities do you like to do on your own?

What kind of activities would you like to do more of on your own?

> "Slow down and enjoy life. It's not only the scenery you miss by going too fast—you also miss the sense of where you are going and why."
> ~Eddie Cantor

What kinds of leisure or recreational activities do you do with friends?

What kind of fun activities would you like to do more of with friends?

EXERCISE:
Exploring Leisure and Recreation Strengths

What recreational and leisure strengths do you <u>currently</u> have? (e.g. I have a basketball hoop that I use in my driveway; I love adventure films)

Record the strengths that you used in the <u>past</u>? (e.g. I used to knit all the time; I loved reading mysteries)

Thinking in the <u>future</u>, what recreational goals do you want to achieve? (e.g. I want to do something fun with a friend at least once a week)

Using Your Strengths to Reach Your Leisure and Recreation Goals

What strengths can you use in order to reach your goals? *Remember that when you list your strengths, that strengths can be:*

- **_Internal_** (e.g. I'm a very good swimmer)

- **_External_** (The local library has a history lecture that is free every Monday)

What naturally-occurring community resource can you use to reach your leisure and recreational goals? (e.g. I have a flair for the dramatic, I think I can contribute a lot to my local theater group)

What is your attitude about your leisure and recreational goals? (e.g. I need to begin to have some more fun in my life!)

What barriers do you think you may face as you move toward your leisure and recreational goals? (e.g. I don't know how I will get to the local theater to volunteer as an usher)

List the ways that you might overcome barriers you face as you move towards your goals. (e.g. I'll ask the volunteer coordinator about linking up for transportation)

How will you mark your progress along the way as you move towards these goals? (e.g. I'll keep a diary of the movies I see and the books I read; I'll put a sticker on my calendar every day I do something I enjoy)

How will you celebrate when you reach your leisure and recreational goals? (e.g. I'll rent a good classic video)

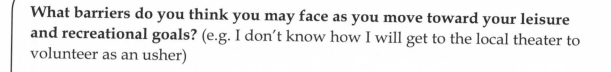

FEELING GOOD ALONG THE WAY:
The Health and Wellness Domain

Health has been described as the state of physical, mental and social well-being. Working towards a healthy lifestyle is very much the same as working towards our recovery. Wellness does not necessarily mean that we are in the prime of health; it doesn't mean we are free from illness or that we have no health challenges. John W. Travis and Regina Sarah Ryan (1988) define wellness as:

- A choice—a decision we make to move toward optimal health.

- A way of life—a lifestyle we design to achieve our highest potential for well-being.

- A process—a developing awareness that there is no end point, but that health and happiness are possible each moment, here and now.

- An efficient channeling of energy—energy received from the environment, transformed within us, and sent on to have an effect on the world outside.

- The integration of body, mind and spirit—the appreciation that everything we do, think, feel and believe has an impact on our state of health.

- The loving acceptance of our self.

Traditional medicine, including psychiatry, tends to center on pathology, diagnosis and treatment of health or mental health problems. The mere fact of a having a psychiatric diagnosis can reduce our access to health care and may even lessen the quality of care we receive from health care providers. Our physical health is often ignored.

If we have complaints, they are often seen as "all in our mind" and viewed as psychosomatic, or worse yet—as "attention seeking behavior."

We face health risks because of trauma, side effects of medications (such as weight gain) and the impact of poverty and stress on our physical health. Poor-self image from internalized stigma may lead us into high-risk behaviors such as unprotected sex or self-destructive substance abuse. Because of these problems, those of us with psychiatric disabilities have more chronic health problems and die earlier than other people do. But these effects do not have to take their toll. We can become healthier and achieve higher levels of wellness.

There is an growing interest in reclaiming wellness and well-being as a part of our recovery journey. Wellness is an important part of the process of recovery. We find that when we take steps to improve our health and wellness our mental health often improves.

Integrative Health Practices and Recovery

Many of us in recovery use a variety of integrative and complementary health practices and treatments in order to adopt healthier lifestyles. The use of alternative, complementary and holistic health approaches is generally on the upswing. Recent studies show that eight out of ten people in the general population have tried alternative treatments and most people report that alternative therapies helped their health (Bradford, 2001).

People use complementary or integrative approaches when traditional treatments fail to produce desired results or when they feel another source of support could boost their healing. Nutritionists, osteopaths, acupuncturists and other non-traditional practitioners are enlisted to provide relief or cure for chronic physical health difficulties. Many of us with psychiatric disabilities find that such approaches can improve our minds and our bodies. Such approaches can reduce symptoms and/or increase the pleasure we have in our lives.

What complementary and alternative approaches do you use?

"Human beings are bodies, minds and spirits. Health necessarily involves all of those components."
~Andrew Weil, M.D.

Chapter 6

PLEASE NOTE:

We are not promoting any specific health practice. People find many different types of health practices aid in their overall wellness and recovery. If you have interest in learning or trying alternative, complementary, holistic and/or integrative practices, it is important that you study your options.

Discuss these ideas with your current health care providers

Your physicians can provide information and monitor your treatment using conventional and/or alternative approaches. Herbs and supplements can impact your sense of well-being and mental health. Some of these natural substances can also interact with prescription medications with dramatic and sometimes dangerous effects. **Check out possible interactions before using such alternative medicine.**

Make informed choices

It's important to learn about treatments and health practices you may want to use. The following list of some integrative/alternative health practices is from *The Hamlyn Encyclopedia of Complementary Health (2001)*:

Osteopathy	Herbalism (Western or Chinese)
Relaxation	Massage
Visualization	Tai Chi
Hypnotherapy	Nutritional therapy
Yoga	Meditation
Homeopathy	Reflexology
Autogenic training	Art therapy
Aromatherapy	Cranial osteopathy

When we take positive steps to develop a healthier wellness lifestyle for ourselves we reap the rewards as we steer a course toward our recovery.

There are many areas to consider in adopting a wellness lifestyle. Rate yourself using the following self-assessment to see what kind of wellness strategies you are using now or want to bring into your life.

HEALTHY LIFESTYLE SELF-ASSESSMENT
Little Changes = Big Gains

✓ Check the answer that best fits your current approach to wellness

Do Now	Like to Try	Not for Me	Approach to Wellness	Did You Know?
			Laugh out loud; don't dwell on setbacks	People who can laugh at themselves during discouraging times have enhanced moods and lowered stress. A sense of humor helps us cope with life's stressors and crises
			Go outside	Daylight, even seeing pictures of the great outdoors, if that's the best you can do, can help you feel happier.
			Find a joyous way to move your body	A ten-minute walk in the morning can put us in a better mood for the rest of the day.
			Put your emotions on paper	We can set aside anywhere from 3-15 minutes once a day to write in our journal, create a storybook of our life, craft a love letter, write a poem or drop a note to a friend. Writing our emotions out can be a way to let out pent up feelings, as well as a vehicle for self-reflection that motivates us to make positive life changes.
			Reconnect with your spirituality	Spirituality can provide comfort and support around fears that the changes and growth associated with recovery can create.
			Engage in intimacy & safe sex practices	Involvement in an intimate relationship leads to a balance between our health and healing systems. Health and healing are enhanced when sexual hormones flow through the body.
			Eat a healthy balanced diet.	Healthful eating habits make us feel better, give us energy and provide essential nutrients to fuel our body. Healthy food choices can reduce the risks for chronic diseases such as diabetes, heart diseases, high blood pressure, stroke and cancer.

Do Now	Like to Try	Not for Me	Approach to Wellness	Did You Know?
			Pick a song that portrays your outlook towards recovery	Choose a song that is uplifting and empowering—maybe *Let the Sun Shine In, Express Yourself, Smile* or *Joy to the World*. Singing or listening to music helps to reduce stress and put us in a relaxed state that promotes wellness.
			Engage in weight bearing exercise	Exercise (e.g. walking, running, dancing) makes us stronger, builds bone, boosts our energy, tones our muscles and gets our heart and lungs in shape.
			Spend time with your friends	Having fun with friends protects our health.
			Find an exercise partner	We're more likely to stick with fitness routines when we know an exercise partner is counting on us.
			Drink plenty of water every day	Drink at least 6-8 glasses (2 quarts) of water each day. Water is necessary for all chemical reactions in our body (i.e. blood circulation, regulation of body temperature, nourishment to tissues and organs).
			Cut down or quit smoking	For every cigarette we smoke, we take 9 minutes off our life! Smoking can shorten our life 5-15 years. If we don't want to quit, we can try to smoke less.
			Get enough sleep and rest	It takes 6-8 hours of sleep to protect our health. Just relaxing for a few minutes with our eyes closed will help us make better decisions.
			Take steps to a happier lifestyle	Happy people are better equipped to fight off disease because they have more efficient immune systems than unhappy people. Anger-prone people almost triple their chances of a heart attack.

EXERCISE:
Exploring Wellness Strengths

Record your <u>current</u> wellness strengths: (e.g. I have health insurance; I have an exercise bicycle in the closet that I got at a garage sale)

What strengths did you use in the <u>past</u> to improve your wellness? (e.g. I used to do yoga for 20 minutes every morning; I know how to cook inexpensive but nutritious meals)

What health and wellness goals do you want to achieve in the <u>future</u>? (e.g. I want to cut down on smoking and ultimately quit; I will have to be fit enough to stand and walk for 8 hours so I can work as a chef; I want to be able to rollerblade for 20 minutes)

Using Your Strengths to Reach Your Wellness Goals

What strengths and resources can you use in order to reach your wellness goals? *Remember that when you list your strengths, that strengths can be:*

- <u>Internal</u> (e.g. I know I feel better when I eat lighter foods and avoid wheat; I can use my knowledge of cooking to make better meals for myself)

- <u>External</u> (e.g. I can go to the gym at my friend Mandy's apartment complex; I can go to the library and look up recipes)

What naturally-occurring community resources do you want to use to meet your health and wellness goals? (e.g. I will use the track at the local high school to do some walking in the evening, it is safe and well-lit and lots of other people my age walk or run there)

What formal resources do you want to use to meet your wellness goals? (e.g. I'm going to find a doctor who practices holistic medicine who accepts Medicaid patients)

What are your attitudes around your wellness goals? (e.g. I feel older than I am; I want some enjoyment in my life!)

What barriers do you think you may run into as you work towards your wellness goals? (e.g. I don't like exercise, and I look yucky in shorts; I don't sleep well, I'm afraid I have sleep apnea because I feel tired all the time; my current medications make me gain so much weight! It's frustrating)

What can you do to overcome these barriers? (e.g. I can get a physical at the health center; I can begin exercising at home for 10 minutes twice a day without anyone watching me)

How will you mark your progress along the way as you move toward your wellness goals? (e.g. I will make a weight chart and post it on the refrigerator and check off each pound I lose; I will keep track of how long I walk)

How will you celebrate when you reach this goal? (e.g. I will buy a new pair of earrings when I have lost one size)

PRIVATE PLEASURES:
The Domain of Intimacy and Sexuality

Intimacy and sexuality are important, but seldom discussed, areas of recovery. The National Summit of Mental Health Consumers and Survivors held in Oregon (1999) polled attendees to see what their top priorities were for supports in their recovery process. Sexuality was voted one of the most important!

However, the mention of mental health problems and sexuality in one conversation can lead to very negative reactions. Some people seem to believe those of us with psychiatric disorders should not be sexual beings. We are often socially segregated by gender and we endure lack of privacy in institutional and treatment settings. Many of us feel oppressed as sexual beings through side-effects of medications, sterilization, professionals or family members advising us against forming intimate or sexual relationships, lack of space for intimacy within residential settings and many other ways our sexuality is ignored or demeaned.

"When I get this feeling, I need sexual healing…"
~Marvin Gaye

> *The greatest and most healing service that can be offered to people with psychiatric disabilities is to treat them with respect and honor them as human beings. This means honoring us in our full humanity, including our sexuality and our desire to love and be loved.*
>
> *~Patricia E. Deegan,*
> *National Consumer Leader*

Distressed? Insecure? Embarrassed?

SEX! Just the mention of the word "sex" or "sexuality" causes most of us to have a reaction. Many of us feel uncomfortable or embarrassed by our sexuality. Why is sexuality such an uncomfortable topic? Concerns such as lack of sexual experience, the negative reactions we have felt by our family and helpers, or concerns around our sexual orientation can impede open, frank discussion about our sexuality. Sometimes we avoid discussing sex and sexuality because of our cultural heritage, religious upbringing or family taboos. If you feel uncomfortable discussing sexuality you are not alone! Most Americans find sexuality embarrassing. Embarrassment is a common experience shared by many people.

How do you feel about discussing or expressing sexuality? Why do you feel this way?

You may be asking yourself: "How do I get over negative feelings?" Here are some ideas to try:

- Seek a safe, trusting, supportive environment to discuss sexuality.
- Become informed. Having information is important to making safe and healthy sexual choices.
- Seek out someone who truly cares for you and respects your choices and decisions around sexuality to discuss this topic with.

The Impact of Trauma on Sexuality

Some of us find intimacy and sexuality very difficult and we choose to avoid it because we have experienced past trauma, sexual abuse or have memories of being involved in bad relationships. Many of us have suffered trauma and abuse, whether physical, sexual or emotional. Some of us have difficulty being present in our bodies and participating in sexual activity due to experiences of sexual abuse in our lives.

The experience of childhood sexual abuse can give rise to depression and other health and mental health problems. It is important for us to share any history of victimization with our health care providers. If you and your significant other find intimacy and sexuality difficult, you may want to seek professional counseling. It is important that we not feel ashamed of our sexuality or allow past abuse to ruin our ability to be sexual beings.

Can you identify what feels safe and what does not feel safe to you sexually, physically, emotionally and spiritually?

"If you can learn from hard knocks, you can also learn from soft touches."
~Carolyn Kenmore

Being open with our feelings and expression of our sensuality is an important part of overcoming stigma and fear about sexual experiences. Working toward healthy sexuality can be an important part of our journey of recovery. Talking with peer travelers and guides about our own experience of intimacy can also be valuable in recovery. We can learn to use our inner strengths and our values to open ourselves to experience greater intimacy and love. Being open and willing to include sensuality, intimacy and sexuality in our lives can be an important part of having a life worth living. On the other hand, some people find that sexuality is not an important aspect of recovery. Each of us has to decide how important sexuality is to us.

Sexual Expression and Psychiatric Medication

Sexual functioning, performance and fulfillment are influenced by many of the drugs used to treat psychiatric disorders. Many medications prescribed for our psychiatric symptoms (psychotropic drugs) can have serious consequences on reproductive capabilities and every stage of our sexual response (Sacks & Strain, 1982). Medications can decrease our libido (sexual drive), make it difficult for us to achieve orgasm and make us feel apathetic and disinterested in sexuality or intimacy.

"We will either find a way, or make one."
~Hannibal

Some of us feel that these common side-effects should be labeled on medications. Patricia E. Deegan invited a group of people to discuss how mental health services impact sexuality & the capacity to love. One person, discussing the side effects of medication, stated: *"I have the problem that my medication gives me which is premature ejaculation. They keep telling me, 'You have to be on this medication. There is no other medication you can be on. You have to accept this side effect.' I don't think I should have to accept this side effect. They want me to commit sexual suicide"* (Deegan, 1999).

If you are having sexual functioning or performance problems, talk with your doctor or health practitioner. Be sure to discuss your medical history and ask about possible drug interactions. Your health practitioner may suggest a different medication or treatment. You may also want to learn about alternative or integrative health approaches that may help you have a fulfilling sexual life, even with the serious impact of medications.

If you are taking medication that has a negative effect on you sexually, you may need to work harder at intimacy in your relationships than someone who does not take medication. Identifying what "turns you on" is key to sexual fulfillment and vitally important if medication hinders your sexual experiences.

Self-Pleasuring

When we think about intimacy and sexuality, most of us automatically think of coupling up with another person. Some of us choose not to have an intimate partner. Others do not know how to show our intimate partners what fulfills us sexually.

We don't just get up one morning knowing exactly what pleases and stimulates us and what doesn't. For those of us who choose to "go it alone" we can find satisfaction in releasing our sexual energy. Exploring our own bodies and our responses helps us to understand what brings us pleasure. Self-stimulation continues to be wrapped in guilt and misunderstanding. Misconceptions about self-stimulation are common. In fact, most people use self-stimulation and it is safe, healthy and can be a way of nurturing ourselves and bringing us sensual pleasure.

In the movie *Annie Hall,* Woody Allen defined self-pleasuring as "…sex with someone (you) love." Self-pleasure and sexual exploration should <u>not</u> be a shameful or guilt-producing activity. Exploration of our bodies is completely natural and healthy. Self-pleasuring is a way for us to connect and learn to love our body and ourselves. When we take care of our complex needs we are working toward our recovery.

In *The Woman's Comfort Book,* Jennifer Louden (1993) suggests gathering things that bring self-pleasure. Here are some of her ideas, along with other suggestions:
- A very private area where you will have no interruptions
- Soft sheets
- Sexual fantasies
- Erotic books or films
- Soft terry cloth towels
- A mirror to discover your intimate areas
- Soothing or stimulating music (the choice is yours)
- A sensual place to relax
- Candles or incense
- A vibrator (some experts believe they make you less sensitive, while others swear by them — the choice is yours)
- Oils (baby oil, massage oil) or lubricating jelly

"Loving self-pleasure makes us feel good about ourselves and the world."
~Jennifer Louden, *The Woman's Comfort Book*

Chapter 6

"When I think about you, I touch myself."
~song lyric by The Divinyls

183

What are your thoughts about self-pleasure?

What would you be willing to try?

What will you need?

Are there areas of your body especially sensitive to touch?

When you know what pleases you, you can tell or show an intimate partner.

Intimacy

Intimacy is connecting to another person at a far deeper level of understanding than we experience in a casual relationship. Nourishing our capacity for intimacy is a vital part of emotional and physical health. Our relationships with significant others may involve intimacy at several levels. Intimacy can be the touch of a hand or a smile that lingers. Intimacy can be sharing old photos, sharing heartfelt dreams or holding hands. Intimacy can be sipping cocoa across the table from one another and reminiscing about old times. Sharing laughter with our closest companions, seeing a shooting star with someone you care about

"Butterflies mean 'a lot' in life. Remember how they live in a cocoon before they thrive as beautiful creatures. But never forget how they feel in your stomach."
~Millie Crossland

and making a wish together, and finding an incredible feeling of joy just looking into one another's eyes—these are moments of intimacy.

Intimacy can be found in a variety of relationships, but we most often think of it when we have a sexual partner or significant other in our lives. Intimacy may involve sexuality, but not always.

Identify the ways in which you experience intimacy...

People often differ on their ideas of intimacy and sexuality. Some of us find intimacy important in a satisfying sexual experience. Others are more likely to separate the two. Intimacy lays the foundation for emotional closeness, spiritual connection and physical safety that allow us to have a positive sexual experience.

What is your own definition of intimacy?

List five things that mean intimacy to you: (e.g. touching and massage, kissing, holding hands, engaging in stimulation of areas of your body other than your genitals, sexual experiences)

1.

2.

3.

4.

5.

"Be mindful of the power...that intimacy creates."
~Daphne Rose Kingma

Chapter 6

"Love received and love given comprise the best form of therapy."
~Gordon William Allport

Are there intimate activities that you find very fulfilling?

> No one asked me about me about my partner or my sexuality. No one asked me if I had questions about sex. No one asked me if I was satisfied in my sexual relationship. Nobody seemed to care. Yet it plays a large part in my recovery. I tried to talk to my minister about it, but he said it would be better if I talked to my psychiatrist because of…you know, my mental illness.
>
> ~Anonymous,
> Kansas Consumer

"Whatever you desire, whatever change you want to occur, whatever outcome you seek, remember that it's happening now. The desire itself is already creating the outcome."
~Daphne Rose Kingma

Enhancing Sexual Partnerships

Sexuality has been defined as behavior that produces arousal and amplifies the chance of orgasm (Hyde, 1990). Human sexuality is very complex; it plays a large part in our well-being, our self-esteem and knowledge of our self. David Sobel and Robert Ornstein (1996) discuss how sexual expression contributes to positive mental health. A survey showed that people who were satisfied with their sex lives were less likely to report depression, anxiety, hostility and a variety of complaints such as fatigue and light-headedness. Sexual satisfaction may give an increased sense of control and feeling of well-being.

Healthy sex has been defined as:

- Freely chosen
- Conscious of consequences
- Respectful
- Erotic
- Playful
- A way to be closer
- An expression of love
- Caring

In our most intimate relationships, we can enhance satisfying sexual encounters through communicating to our partner what gives us pleasure and in turn asking them what pleases them. With sexuality, we often feel pressured to perform up to others' expectations. The media is a poor example for us to follow. Judging by watching cable television or spending an evening watching movies, it appears most everyone is having the sexual time of their lives. Real life sexuality is seldom like the unrealistic portrayals in the media.

The ability to perform or enjoy sex doesn't always come to us automatically. In order to nurture and further develop intimacy and sexuality with our lovers and partners, we need to gather information, be willing to try new techniques and look closely at our values, thoughts and feelings regarding sexuality. The following questions may assist in a deeper understanding:

Do you enjoy your sexual relationship with your partner? Why or Why not?

How can you help your partner know what pleases you?

What are your partner's sexual strengths?

"The mind can also be an erogenous zone."
~Racquel Welch

"Two souls with but a single thought, two hearts that beat as one."
~Maria Lovell

EXERCISE:
Intimacy and Sexuality Strengths

What strengths do you <u>currently</u> have around intimacy and sexuality? (e.g. I have a loving heart; I have one good book on intimacy)

What strengths in intimacy and sexuality did you use in the <u>past</u>? (e.g. I used to have a good sexual relationship with Sally; I value sensuality)

When you think of the <u>future</u>, what goals do you have around intimacy and sexuality? (e.g. I want to find a sexual partner; I want to explore sexuality and self-pleasuring)

Using Your Strengths to Reach Your Intimacy and Sexuality Goals

In order to reach your intimacy and sexuality goals what resources can you use? *Remember that when you list your strengths, that strengths can be:*

- *Internal* (e.g. I feel very good when I massage my own body; I can use my massage skills to give myself or my partner pleasure)

- *External* (e.g. I can go to the health clinic and get free condoms and information on safe sex practices)

What naturally-occurring community resources can you use to meet your sexual and intimacy needs? (e.g. I can get birth control information at the Womens' Community Clinic; I can meet potential partners through my church who share my values about intimacy)

List formal services you can use to reach your goals around intimacy and sexuality: (e.g. I want to get involved in a support group to work on healing my early childhood experience of sexual abuse so I can form a positive intimate relationship; I want to talk to my psychiatrist about side effects from my medications that seem to diminish my sex drive)

What is your attitude around your intimacy and sexuality goals? (e.g. I feel it's time to have some sexual pleasure in my life!; Before I get involved with anyone else I want to have some feeling of trust)

Discuss barriers that you may encounter as you work towards this goal:
(e.g. I'm 40 and still a virgin, I'm a little scared to get involved in a sexual intimate relationship; I'm very afraid of sexually transmitted diseases and HIV)

What strategies can you use to overcome barriers towards reaching your goal?
(e.g. I can get information on sexually transmitted diseases and medication or devices at the health center; I can begin by focusing on my own response to sensuality for 15 minutes a day)

How will you chart your progress along the way towards reaching this goal?
(e.g. I will keep a diary about my intimate self-pleasuring experiences)

How will you celebrate when you achieve your intimacy and sexuality goal?
(e.g. I will buy a scented candle to put near my bathtub)

FORGING A HIGHER PATH:
The Spiritual Domain

Spirituality is one of the most important dimensions of life for most people. Not surprisingly, spirituality plays an important part in our recovery journey. In fact, spirituality was rated one of the highest of all dimensions of recovery at a Mental Health Summit held in Oregon in 1999! Not all of us believe in God or a higher power. On the other hand, most of us do hold important values that can help guide our recovery journey.

This section contains food for thought about important values.

How Important is Spirituality in Your Life?

☑ Check the one closest to how you feel

- ❑ Of the highest significance
- ❑ Very important
- ❑ Somewhat important
- ❑ Not important to me at this point
- ❑ I feel completely turned off by religion & spirituality
- ❑ I have no need for spirituality in my life

What is Spirituality?

Spirituality is a term that can encompass religion but it also includes experiences that do not relate to formal spiritual traditions. Every culture and society has definitions for the experience of spirituality.

In the American Heritage Dictionary spirituality is defined as: (1) Of pertaining to, or consisting of spirit. (2) Ecclesiastical; sacred, in the definition of the word; Spirit (a) The animating or life-giving principle within a living being; soul. (b) The part of a human being associated with the mind and feelings as distinguished from the physical body. (3) The real sense or significance of something. (4) A person.

(5) A prevailing mood or attitude: A spirit of rebellion. (6) Spirit, The Holy Ghost. (verb) To carry off mysteriously or secretly.

Some of us feel damaged by our early religious experiences or by people whose very negative attitudes and behaviors were said to be based in their religious beliefs. We don't want to let the prejudiced or harmful actions of a few people keep us from exploring this domain of life!

The following questions explore spirituality. All answers are right. Be as honest as you can with your answers.

What is your personal definition of your spirituality?

> "When I do good, I feel good. When I do bad, I feel bad. That's my religion."
> ~Abraham Lincoln

Write down your view of why you are here on this earth:

If you could change something about your environment what would it be? What things in your environment would you like to keep?

Do you feel comfortable with others in your community including neighbors, friends and family? If so, in what ways do you feel comfortable? In what ways do you not feel comfortable?

How do you view or define a creator, higher power, a divine being or deity, if any?

What type of relationship do you have with any of these? Is there a being or beings or forces that are higher than humanity that you believe in?

"The lesson of the crossroads is that we cannot get off the old road and on to the new without going through this intermediate place... disintegration always precedes re-integration."
~Robert Gilman

How do define yourself? (e.g. I am a physical person with a mind and spirit or I am a spiritual being with a physical body)

What is your role spiritually?

Make a list of things you really like about yourself.

"All I have seen teaches me to trust the Creator for all that I have not seen."
~Ralph Waldo Emerson

If you could change something about yourself, what would it be? In what ways would you try to change yourself?

When do you feel most relaxed? In what ways do you find it relaxing?

What is your role in relation to spiritually? Is it structured? Is it not?

Take a moment to look at the questions and your answers. Understand your answers are based on how you see and define things now; they are your own definitions. Your answers may change through time, experiences and how you feel. There are no wrong answers. In the future, go back and answer the questions again and compare your answers to the ones you had before. Are there any changes?

The Benefits of Spirituality

There are a number of benefits that we may find in spirituality. The next segments discuss some of these benefits. In general, spirituality has been found to improve both health and mental health.

Spirituality is a source of important beliefs and values

Many of us find the basis of important values we hold and the ethical principles we believe in, in a spiritual tradition. Others of us develop values and principles for how to live our life from sources other than a formal religion. Such principles and values may include: humility, love, respect for all creation, self-respect, forgiveness, non-violence or adherence to certain guidelines for conduct.

Do you have a framework of values and ethical principles or guidelines for how to conduct your life that guide you?

What are some of the important values and principles that you hold?

"The first peace, which is the most important, is that which comes within the souls of people when they realize their relationship, their oneness with the universe and all it's powers, and when they realize at the center of the universe dwells the Great Spirit, and that this center is really everywhere, it is within each one of us."
~Black Elk

"In a dark time, the eye begins to see."
~Theodore Roethke

194

Spirituality is a source of positive relationships and builds a sense of community

Some of us find becoming involved with a group of people "of like mind" who share our spiritual beliefs and values enriches our life. We become a church member or find a faith community, a study group, a 12 step program or a group of people who are all following the same spiritual path. We may find our "spiritual support group" is the church or group we were raised in or we may feel much more comfortable in a group different from our childhood tradition.

Many of us keep in touch with our spirituality by regularly attending services at a church, synagogue or temple, while others of us do not find our spiritual connection in an organized group.

> In my personal journey of recovery I have used my spirituality strength to help me heal. I believe that my personal relationship with God has carried me a long way in my healing process. My church family members have been very supportive with me. Their love, kindness and teachings help give me the stability to stay on the right track and makes me want to stay healthy.
>
> ~Carrie Hunter,
> Kansas Consumer Provider

What places do you go to express your spirituality? How does that place or group help you? (e.g. I like to take walks through parks and visit lakes. I feel more connected to the world of nature. It relaxes me and energizes my spirit; I attend Temple Beth El, it makes me feel connected to my Jewish heritage)

Do you have a spiritual community or group you feel strongly affiliated with?

"I believe that unarmed truth and unconditional love will have the final word in reality."
~Dr. Martin Luther King, Jr.

Chapter 6

"It's not a bad thing [in life] to be serenaded by birds and church bells."
~Alexandra Stoddard

If yes, what are some of the strengths you draw from belonging to this group?

If you don't have a spiritual support group or church, do you think you would like to set a goal to find a group you want to join?

If yes, what steps do you think would help you? (e.g. read about different traditions; identify a list of local groups; attend meetings or services to "check out" how supportive and "right" the group feels)

Spiritual practices are a source of comfort and healing

Many of us find spiritual practices help us understand and accept the suffering we have experienced, and helps us feel better about ourselves, find solace or comfort or feel close to sources of spiritual support (e.g. "at one with nature," "in God's hands," "in touch with my higher power," "in the flow" or "at peace within myself.")

Have you found spiritual practices that help you achieve a sense of inner peace? (e.g. reading uplifting writing, prayer, contemplation, meditation; turning problems over to a higher power)

"Prayer is when you talk to God; meditation is when you listen to God."
~Diana Robinson

If yes, write a few sentences about the practices that are important to you.

196

If you do not use spiritual practices to support and help in your recovery, are you interested in beginning to explore such activities?

What does it mean to you to meditate or pray?

"Perhaps one of the greatest rewards of meditation and prayer is the *sense* of belonging that comes to us."
~Bill W.

What ways do you meditate or pray? How do you speak to your inner self, your creator or higher power, if any? (e.g. I like to sing and dance; I like to sit quietly and relax, talk to my Maker; I like to send positive thoughts to others; I like to contemplate my role and become more aware of myself, others, and my environment; I offer tobacco to honor the Great Spirit)

Chapter 6

How and what ways do you bring strength to your inner self? (Think of a time when you were feeling low spiritually. What brought you out of it? Is it something you can repeat?)

What ways have you found through your spiritual practices that have benefited you, and what have not? What do you like about it? What do you not like about it?

Were there times you found your spiritual beliefs or practices effective in your personal life? How? How not?

What did you find valuable in working with this practice? What did you not find valuable?

Are you interested in setting a goal to learn spiritual practices and incorporate them into your daily life?

What steps will you take to learn spiritual practices? (e.g. listen to tapes; find a book about the subject and practice on my own; attend a workshop; become involved with study group or attend religious service; find a spiritual director who can teach and guide me)

What other benefits do you find, or believe you would find, in spiritual practices?

The Experience of Spiritual Emergence/Spiritual Emergency

Some of us have very profound religious, spiritual or mystical experiences, and have entered "altered states of consciousness" or "extreme mental states" that have been labeled psychiatric symptoms. Our psychiatric emergencies seem to be tied to a difficult spiritual emergence. As one person said, this experience is like "taking a wrong exit on the spiritual path."

Often such events are very profound to those of us who experience them. Unfortunately, in our culture, such experiences are often written off as a manifestation of psychosis or delusions. Some of us feel very discouraged that our deepest spiritual experiences and insights are labeled as symptoms of a psychiatric disorder.

Not everyone views these experiences as mere symptoms. There are resources available that explore the convergence, or meeting place, of psychiatric disorder and spirituality. Some of us choose to leave our experience of intense "spiritual emergence" alone, because such experiences are very difficult to contain and seem too intense for us to handle. Others of us want to understand or learn from such experiences and seek ways to integrate these profound experiences or insights into our life.

Have you had experiences that you consider profoundly spiritual? Write about them here.

Are you interested in learning more about such experiences?

"Stand by the roads and look, and ask for the ancient paths, where the good way is; and walk in it, and find rest for your souls."
~Jeremiah 6:16

What actions do you want to take? (e.g. read what people have written about spiritual emergence; contact a member of the spiritual emergence/emergency network; share your story of spiritual emergence; explore the Internet to learn more; discuss the experience with an understanding friend or spiritual advisor)

You may want to set up a plan of action that will support you if such a state reoccurs.

The Spiritual Rewards of Psychiatric Disability

Is it possible that we can become a more spiritual person or develop positive traits out of the experience of psychiatric problems? Absolutely! Some of us find we have developed positive ethical or spiritual traits through our suffering and life challenges. One Kansas consumer recently shared such an experience at a recovery workshop. He said: *"Before my mental health problem I was a real jerk. I didn't care about anyone. Now I really care how others feel. My whole job now is to help my peers achieve a higher level of wellness."*

Have you experienced positive changes in your values or feelings for others? If you have, write about these changes here:

"Our real blessings often appear to us in the shape of pains, losses and disappointments."
~Joseph Addison

SPIRITUALITY SELF-ASSESSMENT
Spiritual Traits I Have Developed

☑ Check all that apply

☐ I feel more compassionate towards others.

☐ I care more about how others think and feel.

☐ I feel closer to God/higher power.

☐ I am a more humble person.

☐ I want to help others more.

☐ I don't want anyone else to suffer the way I have.

☐ I've developed a desire to help others.

☐ I've become a more loving person.

☐ I have the desire to give back for all the help I've received.

☐ I want to work against discrimination and improve social justice.

☐ I feel the experience of psychiatric disorder has made me a more honest and authentic person.

If you don't feel such effects, that is okay.

If you do, are there ways you could express these feelings through positive actions you want to take? What would you like to do to express your deepened humanity?

What positive steps will you take in the next few months to act on these insights, desires and feelings?

"What do we live for, if it is not to make life less difficult for each other?"
~George Eliot

EXERCISE:
Setting Goals Around Your Spirituality

The spiritual strengths you <u>currently</u> have include: (e.g. I have a church I attend; I have a deep sense of caring for others)

What types of spiritual strengths have you used in the <u>past</u>? (e.g. I have always had a strong prayer life)

What spiritual goals do you want to achieve in the <u>future</u>? (e.g. I want to feel a stronger connection to my higher power; I want to study the Bible/Koran; I want to find a church home)

Using Your Strengths to Reach Your Spiritual Goal

What strengths and resources can you use to reach your spiritual goals?
Remember that when you list your strengths, that strengths can be:

- <u>Internal</u> (e.g. I feel good when I meditate every day)

- <u>External</u> (e.g. I learn a lot by being a member of my Bible study group)

What naturally-occurring community resources can you draw upon to meet your spiritual goals? (e.g. I will attend services at three different churches to see which one feels most comfortable; I will go meditate at the Zen Center)

What formal services and supports can you draw upon to help you meet your goals? (e.g. I will begin counseling with a Christian counseling agency; I will speak at a local church on stigma-busting; I will get transportation to Temple through the consumer-run organization)

What is your attitude around your spirituality goals? (e.g. I don't feel so alone; I hope to free myself from some of the fear I feel)

What are some of the barriers that may get in the way as you move towards your spiritual goals? (e.g. I don't have any sort of relationship with God; I feel I have lost faith; Spiritual experiences scare me)

What strategies can you use to overcome the barriers you have identified? (e.g. My friend Ed has a lot of involvement with his church and feels very comfortable there, maybe I can go with him to see if I would feel comfortable at his church)

How will you record you progress along the way in trying to achieve your spiritual goals? (e.g. I will keep a diary of my prayer life; I will keep a dream journal)

How will you celebrate when you reach your spiritual goals? (e.g. I will listen to uplifting music; I will light a candle on my home altar)

CELEBRATE!

<u>You made it</u>! By going through this chapter you have reflected on the various domains that make up your life. You have decided what you desire within each domain. You have made preliminary plans about the direction you want to head toward in the future. The next chapter on social relationships represents a final domain. Once you have completed that chapter you'll be ready to pull all your goals together into practical plans for your personal journey of recovery.

We hope that the process of completing this section was enjoyable and that you learned a few new things about yourself that you may not have put such a lot of thought into before. Congratulations!

What can you do to celebrate this substantial step on your recovery journey?

"Be ye merry:
You have cause.
So have we all
of joy."
~William Shakespeare

Chapter 6

"If you're going
to dance on the
table, don't step
on my cake."
~Unknown

 References & Resources

References

Housing Domain

Coursey, R. D., Alford, J. & Sajarjan, B. (1997). Significant advances in understanding and treating serious mental illness. *Professional Psychology: Research & Practice, 28*(3): 205-216.

Kron, J. (1983). *Home-Psych: The Social Psychology of Home and Decoration.* New York, NY: Clarkson N. Potter.

Marcus, C. C. (1995). *House as Mirror of Self: Exploring the Deeper Meaning of Home.* Berkeley, CA: Conari Press.

Ridgway, P. A. (2001). *There's no place like home: Sense of home, homelessness, and challenged mental health.* Unpublished manuscript. Lawrence, KS: University of Kansas, School of Social Welfare. Office of Mental Health Research and Training.

Ridgway, P. A. & Rapp, C.A. (1997). *The Active Ingredients in Effective Supported Housing: A Research Synthesis.* Monograph. Lawrence, KS: School of Social Welfare.

Ridgway, P. A., Simpson, A., Wittman, F. D., & Wheeler, G. (1994). Home making and community-building: Notes on empowerment and place. *Journal of Mental Health Administration, 21*(4), 407-418.

Education Domain

Mowbray, C. (Ed.) (2002). *Supported Education and Psychiatric Rehabilitation: Models & Methods.* Linthicum, MD: International Association of Psychosocial Rehabilitation Services.

Unger, K. V. (1998). *Handbook on Supported Education: Providing Services for Students with Psychiatric Disabilities.* Baltimore, MA: Paul H. Brookes Publishing.

Unger, K. V. & Pardee, R. (2002). Outcome measures across program sites for postsecondary supported education programs. *Psychiatric Rehabilitation Journal, 25* (3), 299-303.

Vocational Domain

Boyd, A. S., Ridgway, P., & Rapp, C. A. (1998). *The real reasons consumers leave jobs in competitive employment: The results of a qualitative study.* Unpublished manuscript. Lawrence, KS: The University of Kansas School of Social Welfare.

Brown, E. V. (1989). Share International. *The healing power of service.* Retrieved January 25, 2001 from http://www.shareintl.org/archives/health-healing/hh_ebservice.html

Ellison, M. L., & Russinova, Z. (1997). How professionals and managers use reasonable accommodations: Highlights for a national survey. *Community Support Network News, 12*(1), 16.

Mancuso, L. L. (1990). Reasonable accommodations for workers with psychiatric disabilities. *Psychosocial Rehabilitation Journal, 14*(2), 3-19.

Mancuso, L. L., & Kotler, J. D. (Eds.) (1999). *A Technical Assistance Tool Kit on Employment for People with Psychiatric Disabilities.* Alexandria, VA: National Technical Assistance Center for State Mental Health Planning.

Mowbray, C. T., Bybee, D., Harris, S. N., & McCrohan, N. (1995). Predictors of work status and future work orientation in people with psychiatric disability. *Psychiatric Rehabilitation Journal, 19*(2), 17-28.

Peters, T. J., & Waterman, R. H., Jr. (1982). *In Search of Excellence: Lessons from America's Best-Run Companies.* New York: Harper & Row.

Ridgway, P., & Rapp, C. A. (1999). *Critical Ingredients in Achieving Competitive Employment for People with Psychiatric Disabilities: A Research Synthesis.* Lawrence, KS: The University of Kansas School of Social Welfare.

Sobel, D. S., & Ornstein, R. (1996). *The Healthy Mind Healthy Body Handbook.* New York, NY: Patient Education Media.

Walsh, K. J. (1999). Work: A Wellspring of Mental Wellness. In L. L. Mancuso, & J. D. Kotler (Eds.), *A Technical Assistance Tool Kit on Employment for People with Psychiatric Disabilities* (pp. 11-20). Alexandria, VA: National Technical Assistance Center for State Mental Health Planning.

Leisure Domain

Holman, J. L. (1994). I Love What I See There. *Christian Single Magazine*, September.

Health and Wellness Domain

Bradford, N. (2001). *The Hamlyn Encyclopedia of Complementary Health.* London, UK: Octopus Publishing Group Limited.

Chapter 6

Davis, M., Robbins Eshelman, E., & McKay, M. (1999). *The Relaxation & Stress Reduction Workbook*. Oakland, CA: New Harbinger Press.

Jaret, P. (2001). Where medicine and minds meet. *Health*, July-August.

Kybartas, R. (1997). *Fitness is Religion – Keeping the Faith*. New York, NY: Simon & Schuster.

Louden, J. (1992*). The Woman's Comfort Book : A Self-Nurturing Guide for Restoring Balance in Your Life*. San Francisco, CA: Harper.

Louden, Jennifer (1994). *The Couple's Comfort Book: A Creative Guide for Renewing Passion, Pleasure & Commitment*. San Francisco, CA: Harper.

Orem, S., & Demarest, L. (1994). *Living Simply: Timeless Thoughts for a Balanced Life*. Deerfield Beach, FL: Health Communications, Inc.

Ryan, M. J. (2000). *The Giving Heart: Unlocking the Transformative Power of Generosity in Your Life*. Berkeley, CA: Conari Press.

Travis, J. & Ryan, R. S. (1988). *The Wellness Workbook*. Berkeley, CA: Ten Speed Press.

Weil, Andrew (1997). *Eight Weeks to Optimum Health: A Proven Program for Taking Full Advantage of Your Body's Natural Healing Power*. New York, NY: Alfred A. Knopf.

Sexuality Domain

Deegan, P.E. (1999). Human sexuality and mental illness: Recovery principles and consumer viewpoints. In P. F. Buckley (Ed)., *Sexuality and Serious Mental Illness* (21-33) New York, NY: Harwood Academic Publishers.

Gochros, H. L., Gochros, J. S., & Fischer, J., (Eds.) 1986. *Helping the Sexually Oppressed*. Englewood Cliffs, NJ: Prentice Hall, Inc.

Harrison, D. F. (1986). The institutionalized mentally ill. In H. L. Gochros, J. S. Gochros & J. Fischer (Eds.) *Helping the Sexually Oppressed*. Englewood Cliffs, NJ: Prentice Hall, Inc.

Hyde, J. S. (1990*). Understanding Human Sexuality*. New York, NY: McGraw-Hill, USA.

Louden, J. (1992*). The Woman's Comfort Book : A Self-nurturing Guide for Restoring Balance in Your Life*. San Francisco, CA: Harper.

National Summit of Mental Health Consumers and Survivors. (1999, August). Retrieved November 16, 2001, from www.selfhelp.org/plank.html.

Sacks, M., & Strain, J. J. (1982). Commentary on sexual problems of patients with colostomies. *Medical Aspects of Human Sexuality,16*(6), 16GG-1611.

Sobel, D. S., & Ornstein, R.(1996). *The Healthy Mind Healthy Body Handbook.* New York: Patient Education Media, Inc.

Spirituality Domain

Clarke, L. (2001). *Psychoses and Spirituality: Exploring the New Frontier.* Philadelphia, PA: Whurr.

Dossey, L. (1993). *Healing Words: The Power of Prayer and the Practice of Medicine.* San Francisco: Harper.

Grof, S. & Grof, C. (1989). *Spiritual Emergency: When Personal Transformation Becomes a Crisis.* Los Angeles: Tarcher.

Lukoff, D., Lu, F. G., & Turner, R. (1992). Toward a more culturally sensitive DSM IV: Psychoreligious and psychospiritual problems. *Journal of Nervous and mental Disease, 180*(11), 673-682.

National Summit of Mental Health Consumers and Survivors. (1999, August). Retrieved November 16, 2001, from www.selfhelp.org/plank.html.

Nelson, J. E. (1994). *Healing the Split: Integrating Spirit into Our Understanding of the Mentally Ill.* Albany: State University of New York Press.

Sullivan, W.P. (1998). Recoiling, regrouping, and recovering: First-person accounts of the role of spirituality in the course of serious mental illness. In Roger D. Fallot (Ed.), *New Directions in Mental Health: Spirituality and Religion in Recovery from Mental Illness.* (pp. 25-33, vol. 80). San Francisco: Jossey Bass.

Tepper, L., Rogers, S. A., Coleman, E. M., & Malony, H. N. (2001). The prevalence of religious coping among persons with persistent mental illness. *Psychiatric Services, 52*(5), 660-665.

Resources

Housing Domain

Creating Community Anywhere: Finding Support and Connection in a Fragmented World by Carolyn R. Shaffer & Kristin Anundsen (Penguin USA, 1993).

Organizing from the Inside Out by Julie Mogenstern (Henry Holt & Company, Inc., 1998).

The Power of Place by Winifred Gallagher (HarperCollins, 1993).

Chapter 6

Education Domain

Cracking the GED by Geoff Martz & Laurice Pearson (Princeton Review, 2001).

How to Go to College Almost for Free: The Secrets of Winning Scholarship Money by Benjamin R. Kaplan & Ben Kaplan (HarperCollins Publishers, 2001).*How to Prepare for the GED: High School Equivalency Exam* by Murray Rockowitz, Ira K. Wolfe & Johanna Bolton (Barron's Educational Series, 2002).

Supported Education & Psychiatric Rehabilitation: Models and Methods by Carol Mowbray and others (International Association of Psychosocial Rehabilitation Services, 2002).

Websites:

www.petersons.com
Information on distance learning, colleges in the United States and career education.

www.educationindex.com
Offers links to education websites. Sorted by subject and life stage of learning including parenting, continuing education, colleges and distance learning.

Check with your local college or community college for continuing education courses. Courses can be offered in areas from computer courses to cake decorating!

Check with you local high school for information on where to take the GED and for preparation materials.

Assets Domain

How to Get Out of Debt, Stay Out of Debt and Live Prosperously by Jerrold Mundis (Bantam Doubleday Dell Publishing Group, 1990).

Nickel and Dimed: On Not Getting By in America by B. Ehrenreich (Metropolitan Books, 2001).

9 Steps to Financial Freedom by Suze Orman (Running Press Book Publishers, 2001).

Ten Minute Guide to Household Budgeting by Tracey Longo (Alpha Books, 1997).

The Complete Cheapskate: How to Break Free from Money Worries Forever, Without Sacrificing the Quality of Your Life by Mary Hunt (Broadman & Holman Publishers, 1998).

Your Money or Your Life: Transforming Your Relationship with Money and Achieving Financial Independence by Joe R. Dominguez & Vicki Robin (Penguin USA, 2000).

Websites:

www.nfcc.org
National Foundation for Credit Counseling website. You can find an agency in your area and also explore resources and assistance for dealing with financial situations. (Can be reached by phone at: 888-388-2227).

www.debtorsanonymous.org
Provides literature and information on being in debt, a 12 step program for recovery and online meetings.

www.cheapskatemonthly.com
Monthly newsletter dedicated to stretching your budget. You can explore the newsletter archives and the tiptionary. Newsletter includes ways to save money from coupons to insurance policies.

National Association of Personal Financial Advisors: 888-333-6659

Vocational Domain

A National Study on Job Accommodations for People with Psychiatric Disabilities: Final Report by Granger, Baron, & Robinson. Available from Matrix Research Institute, 6008 Wayne Avenue, Philadelphia, PA, 19144, (215)438-8200 or mri@aol.com.

Be the Difference: A Beginner's Guide to Changing the World by Danny Seo (New Society Publishers, Ltd., 2001).

EEOC Enforcement Guidance: The Americans with Disabilities Act and Psychiatric Disabilities. Available from the Equal Employment Opportunity Commission, 1801 L Street, NW, Washington, D.C., 20507, (800) 669-3362 or www.eeoc.gov.

Finding Your Perfect Work by Paul and Sarah Edwards (Putnam Book, 1996).

Let Your Life Speak: Listening for the Voice of Vocation by Parker J. Palmer (John Wiley & Sons, Inc., 1999).

The Call of Service: A Witness to Idealism by Robert Coles (Houghton Mifflin Company, 1994).

We Are All Self-employed: The New Social Contract for Working in a Changed World by Cliff Hakim (Berrett-Koehler Publishers, 1994).

Wellness at Work: Building Resilience to Job Stress by Valerie O'Hara (New Harbinger Publications, 1995).

What Color is Your Parachute? by Richard Nelson Bolles (Ten Speed Press, 2001).

Worktypes: Understand Your Work Personality — How it Helps You and Holds You back, and What You Can Do to Understand It by Jean Kummerow (Warner Books, 1997).

Websites:

www.volunteermatch.org
Search for volunteer opportunities by zip code. Provides ways to volunteer on-line.
www.unitedway.org

Find your local United Way using your zip code. Website provides information on United Way programs and ways you can get involved.

Leisure Domain

Al Roker's Big, Bad Book of Barbeque: 100 Easy Recipes for Barbeque and Grilling by Al Roker (Simon & Schuster Trade, 2002).

Bicycle Official Rules of Card Games: Over 250 Card Games by Tom Braunlich & Joli Quentin Kansil, eds. (The Unites States Playing Card Company, 2000).

No Need for Speed: A Beginner's Guide to the Joy of Running by John Bingham (Rodale Press, 2002).

The Fish's Eye: Essays about Angling and the Outdoors by Ian Frazier (Farrar, Straus & Giroux, Inc., 2002).

The Garden Primer by Barbara Damrosch (Workman Publishing Company, 1988).

Websites:

www.lovetheoutdoors.com
Provides camping tips for planning trips, outdoor cooking and information on state and national parks throughout the United States.

http://allmusic.com
Has the history of all different styles of music including influential artists and albums. Also provides history of the artists and albums with places for you to add any missing information you might know on an artist.

www.yahoo.com
You can find information on nearly any subject on this website from sports to horoscopes, from society and culture to government. Sign up for free e-mail while you're there!

www.msn.com
Gives links to different sites including maps and directions, current news and a recipe finder. Also provides free e-mail through Hotmail.

Health and Wellness Domain

8 Weeks to Optimum Health by Andrew Weil (Fawcett Book Group, 1998).

Everybody's Guide to Homeopathic Medicines: Taking Care of Yourself and Your Family with Safe and Effective Remedies by Stephen Cummings & Dana Ullman (G.P. Putnam's Sons, 1992).

Feeding the Body, Nourishing the Soul by Deborah Kesten (Conari Press, 1998).

Fitness for the Unfit by Ina Marx (Citadel, 1991).

Healthy Healings: A Guide to Self Healing for Everyone by Linda Rector-Page (Quality Books, 2000).

The American Yoga Association's Easy Does It Yoga: The Safe and Gentle Way to Health and Well-Being by A. Christenson (American Yoga Association, 1999).

The New Our Bodies, Ourselves from the Boston Women's Health Collective (Touchstone, 1992).

The Stop Smoking Workbook: Your Guide to Healthy Quitting by Anita Maximin (New Harbinger Publications, 1995).

Websites:

www.alice.columbia.edu
The Health Education and Wellness program of the Columbia University Health Service offers advice to contribute to your personal health and happiness. Includes a link to the interactive "Go Ask Alice" advice column.

www.amer-mentalhealthassoc.com
This site offers various information about schizophrenia and depression. Discussions on causes, treatment, prevention and recovery.

www.healthfinder.gov
This site created by the U.S. Department of Health and Human Services provides information and links to hundreds of related websites, including medical libraries, non-profit health organizations, support groups and more.

www.nccam.nih.gov/health
The National Center for Complementary and Alternative Medicine. Site evaluates alternative therapies and therapists.

www.stayhealthy.com
Health directory includes daily news updates, health centers ranging from diet and nutrition to mental health and a calorie counter.

<u>Sexuality Domain</u>

How to Have More Love in Your Life by Alan Epstein (Viking Penguin, 1996)

The Conscious Heart: Seven Soul-Choices that Inspire Creative Partnership by Kathlyn & Gay Hendricks (Bantam Books, 1999).

Coalition on Sexuality and Disability, Inc.
380 2nd Ave., 4th Floor, New York, N.Y., 10010
212-242-3900
Educational and advocacy organization related to sexuality and socialization for people with disabilities.

Sex Information and Education Council of the United States
32 Washington Place, New York, N.Y., 10003
Provides a library and information service on sex education. Maintains database on books and journals in human sexuality.

Spirituality Domain

Care of the Soul by Thomas Moore (HarperPerennial, 1992).

Connectedness: Some Skills for Spiritual Health by R. Bellingham, B. Cohen, T. Jones & L. Spaniol in American Journal of Health Promotion, 4(1), 1989.

Earth Wisdom: Reconnecting to Yourself Through the Power of Nature by Aubrey Wallace (Conari, 2001).

Helping People in Spiritual Emergency by E. Bragdon (Lightening Up Press, 1988).

Life's Big Questions: 200 Ways to Explore Your Spiritual Nature by Jonathan Robinson (Conari Press, 2001).

Loving Kindness: The Revolutionary Art of Happiness by S. Salzberg (Shambala, 1997).

Meditation: A Simple 8-Point Program for Translating Spiritual Ideals into Daily Life by Eknath Easwaran (Nilgiri Press, 1993).

Spiritual Literacy: Reading the Sacred in Everyday Life by Frederic & Mary Ann Brussat (Scribner, 1996).

The Call of Spiritual Emergency: From Personal Crisis to Personal Transformation by E. Bragdon (Harper & Row, 1990).

The Four Agreements by Don Miguel Ruiz (Amber-Allen Publishing, 1997).

The Invitation by Oriah Mountain Dreamer (HarperCollins, 1999).

The Way We Pray by Maggie Oman (Conari Press, 2001).

What is Spirit? Messages from the Heart by Lexie Brockway Potamkin (Hay House, Inc., 1999).

The Kundalini Experience: Psychosis or Transcendence? by L. Sanella (Integral, 1992).

Chapter Seven

Travel Companions and
Social Support for the Journey

*This chapter looks at the circle of social support and ways to nurture
and expand the supportive relationships in our lives.*

Introduction

The experience of psychiatric disability can disrupt our circle of social support, leaving us feeling alone and uncared for. We may lose much of our original circle of support from friends and family and then limit our social lives because we are afraid to open up to others. We may feel inadequate or damaged and fear rejection. Some of us have a supportive family and friendship circle, but need to put some time into healing our relationships. We may naturally want to expand our circle of support as we extend our world and the roles we play in life.

Building a strong circle of mutual supportive relationships is an important part of our recovery journey. This section of the workbook helps us:

- Understand the benefits of social support
- Assess our current circle of social support
- Identify and overcome roadblocks to building positive relationships
- Find ways to expand our circle of social support
- Nourish our support circle
- Set goals for improving or expanding supportive relationships

Social support cuts across all the other domains of life (home life, work, leisure and recreation, learning, health and wellness, sexuality and spirituality). Supportive relationships can increase our potential for a positive recovery in all of these areas. Stronger supportive relationships often grow naturally out of our recovery journey as we expand our horizons and begin to live beyond our former limitations.

Mental health services have traditionally been set up to encourage "independence." We are often discouraged from forming relationships, especially with other people with psychiatric disabilities. We are taught that being "self-sufficient" is what is important and necessary in our life.

In reality, we all need a variety of supportive relationships to survive each day. In the Strengths Recovery Approach, the focus is placed upon *mutual interdependence* rather than independence. We can strive to be as *interdependent* as possible with people, using all of our strengths and supports in a mutually beneficial way.

> "Tis the human touch in the world that counts—the touch of your hand and mine—which means far more to the sinking heart than shelter or bread or wine. For shelter is gone when the night is o'er, and bread lasts only a day. But the touch of the hand and the sound of the voice live on in the soul always."
> ~Spencer M. Free

> "Friends love the person you were and the one you've become."
> ~Anonymous

Each of us must travel our own path to recovery, but we need the help and support of guides, travel companions and allies all along the way. We need people to help speed us along our journey, people who serve as "travel agents" or who accompany us as we move forward. We also learn to balance the need for solitude and time alone with a sense of mutuality, family and community. We are not alone in our quest for recovery! We can have a sense of fellowship with others who are on the journey of healing and transformation we call recovery. We need each other and can support each other!

What is Social Support?

The term "social support" is used to describe the interactions we have with people that benefit and reassure us. Social support is the knowledge that there are people who care about us, who are concerned about us and who have a positive influence in our lives.

At the beginning of the recovery journey, many of us rely primarily on service providers such as case managers or therapists, or on family members, to give us social support and meet our needs. We often feel very vulnerable and very needy. On the other hand, we may think that we have little to offer others because we are suffering and because we have internalized the stigma associated with psychiatric problems and may consider ourselves unworthy.

As we move along through our recovery journey, we find good travel companions and broaden our circle of supportive relationships. We come to realize that true social support is a two-way street that must run in both directions. We find we naturally want to pass on the help and support that others have given to us and we find we really have a lot to offer others. Sometimes the very experience of psychiatric disorder makes us more compassionate and sensitive to those around us and these qualities allow us to provide support to other people.

There is no single word in the English language that fully explains the meaning of social support. A word in the Spanish language gives a richer picture of what social support involves. This word is *confianza*. In *Friends Can Be Good Medicine*, Marta Javier (1981) gives a definition that includes:

"We all have underlying human needs such as recognition from others, a stimulating environment, caring and affection from friends, and self acceptance."
~John Travis

218

- Social support is a symbolic understanding,
- Social support inspires trust,
- Social support makes us feel "at home" with another person,
- Social support fosters faith and loyalty,
- It involves cooperation and the ability to share,
- It includes a willingness to maintain mutual interdependency,
- Support involves circular networks of communication,
- It provides extraordinary stimulation of psychological and spiritual support for both persons.

Is there anything that you would like to add to this definition? What does social support mean to you?

What are the Benefits of Social Support?

There is a lot of research that shows social support is highly beneficial. The presence of social support reduces the severity of depression and other psychiatric symptoms. Having a life partner, spouse or someone we can share our thoughts and dreams with is connected to improved physical and mental health and a longer life-span in general. Social support also helps protect us from many illnesses such as cancer and heart disease.

The absence of social supports has been found to have negative health effects. For example, children of pregnant women who lack social support have more birth complications. Stress and resulting psychological symptoms increase if we don't have enough social support in our lives. In general, having a strong circle of social support provides us with many social, physical and psychological benefits.

Psychiatric disorders can disrupt social support and important relationships can become strained. We can lose contact with people who were important in our lives, including parents, siblings, friends, intimate partners and our children. We may find ourselves feeling isolated and alone and cut off from others, even at times when we are surrounded by people. We may give up on trying to form or maintain relationships and try to stay detached from everyone. We may avoid people to protect ourselves from emotional vulnerability and rejection. Our loneliness can be very painful.

"We must strengthen, defend, preserve and comfort each other."
~John Winthrop

Chapter 7

"Call it a clan, call it a network, call it a tribe, call it a family. Whatever you call it, whoever you are, you need one."
~Jane Howard

Have you felt any of these things? Write about your experience here:

What Do Social Supports Contribute to Our Journey of Recovery?

A group of Connecticut mental health consumers participated in a study of social support and recovery. The study found people initially relied heavily on formal helpers and family members for support.
Over time, as recovery took hold, people developed more mutual relationships that benefited their recovery in several important ways (Breier & Strauss, 1984). Here is how social relationships helped their recovery:

- Ventilation—people could express their emotions to their supporters.
- Reality testing—people could test their perceptions out with trusted people.
- Material support—people were helped with finances, housing and transportation.
- Social approval and integration—people felt acceptance and a sense of belonging.
- Constancy—people found interpersonal connections that lasted.
- Motivation—people received encouragement that motivated them.
- Modeling—people could observe and incorporate their supporter's behaviors.
- Symptom monitoring—supporters could alert them to problems.
- Problem solving—supporters acted as a sounding board and gave helpful feedback.
- Empathic understanding—people felt they were truly understood.
- Reciprocal relating—people found they could be an equal partner, both giving and receiving support.
- Insight—people gained a more complete self-understanding.

EXERCISE:
Assessing Your Circle of Support

In order to understand where you stand now in terms of having the kind of social support you want, assess your current circle of support using this exercise.

Write your name in the center of the blank circle. Each segment of the circle identifies a life domain. Identify people, pets and resources that give you support. An example of a completed assessment can be found on the next page.

Include the people who have supported you throughout your life as well as those who may have joined your circle of support recently. Include people you feel safe or comfortable with or like to talk to. Include those who you would share a meal or a cup of coffee with. Include people you can turn to for emotional support, practical help and resources, especially if you are really stuck in a jam.

Supports can be a person, place or thing. We often believe that supports only come in the form of people. You might have a great supportive "place" such as sitting under your favorite tree at the park. Examples of "things" could be spending time with a pet or reading important spiritual books. Be sure to include people, places and things that provide you with support in each domain.

Include the social support you have:

- in your living situation (neighbors you can count on, roommate, intimate partner, close family ties)
- in your learning environment (fellow learners/students, teachers and mentors)
- assets (people who help you financially and/or whom you share your resources with)
- leisure/recreation (people who you have fun with)
- workplace (co-workers, supervisors, others in the workplace, co-volunteers)
- wellness/mental health (exercise partner, gym mates, cooking club members, relaxation group members)
- intimacy and sexuality (intimate friends, sexual partners)
- spirituality (others who share your beliefs, spiritual guide/leader, people in your faith community or spiritual support group)

My Current Circle of Social Support

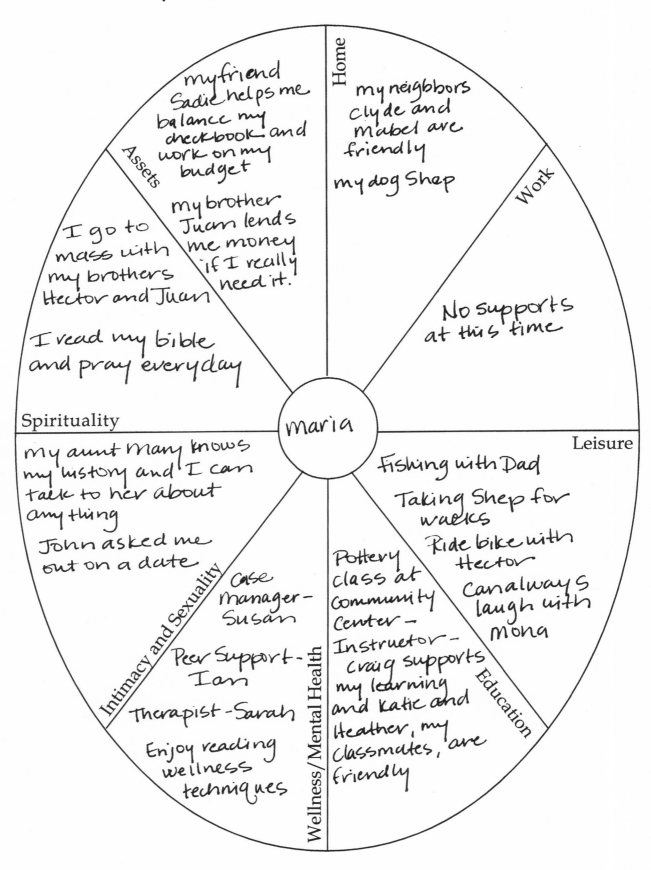

Home: my neighbors Clyde and Mabel are friendly. my dog Shep

Assets: my friend Sadie helps me balance my checkbook and work on my budget. my brother Juan lends me money if I really need it.

Work: No supports at this time

Spirituality: I go to mass with my brothers Hector and Juan. I read my bible and pray everyday

Leisure: Fishing with Dad. Taking Shep for walks. Ride bike with Hector. Can always laugh with Mona

Intimacy and Sexuality: my aunt Mary knows my history and I can talk to her about any thing. John asked me out on a date

Wellness/Mental Health: Case Manager - Susan. Peer Support - Ian. Therapist - Sarah. Enjoy reading wellness techniques

Education: Pottery class at Community Center - Instructor - Craig supports my learning and Katie and Heather, my classmates, are friendly

Maria

My Current Circle of Social Support

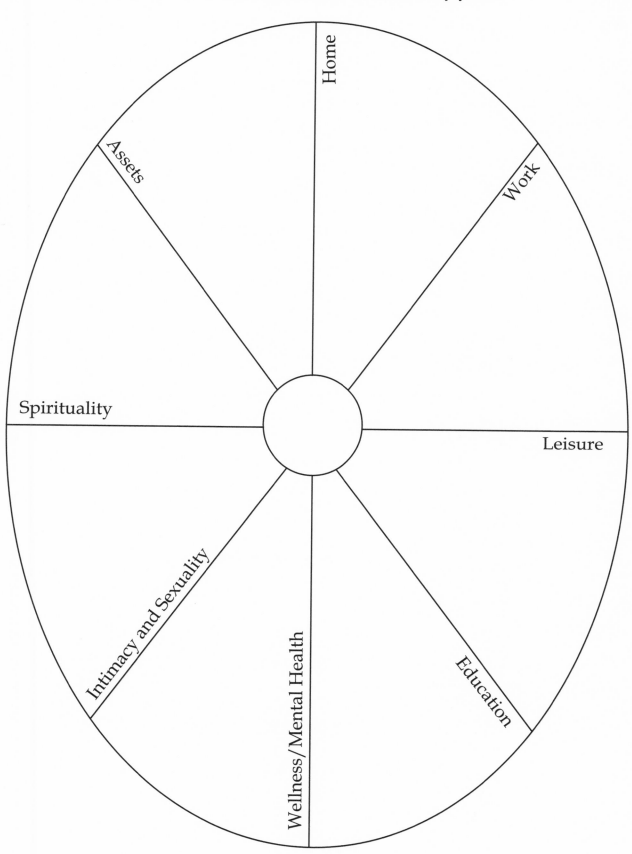

When you have finished, take a moment to look at each name and remember the kind of support you've received and/or shared with that person. Review your social support circle. Do you see any patterns?

- Do you feel very close to many people?
- Are these relationships give-and-take (mutual)?
- What does each of these relationships give you?
- Is your circle made up mostly of mental health providers and/or consumers?
- Does your circle include mostly family members?
- Is your circle very small, with few people you can really count on?
- Do you have people you see and talk with, but no one you feel really close to?
- Do all your supports cluster in a few areas, such as work, church or mental health programs, or do you have supports across many areas of your life?
- What do your supporters have in common?
- What unique qualities do these people possess?

Note any pattern/s) that you think may be important here:

How would you like to change any of the patterns you see or are you satisfied with your current social circle?

Overcoming Roadblocks to Relationships

Many people are lonely and have difficulty with finding a circle of social relationships. The experience of psychiatric disabilities can make this common human experience even more challenging for us. We may have to overcome several common roadblocks in order to build or rebuild a circle of social support.

"Nobody, but nobody can make it out here alone."
~Maya Angelou

The tendency to withdraw

Many of us find ourselves withdrawing from other people after the experience of psychiatric disorder. It's not unusual to worry about stigma, to feel like we don't fit in or seem to belong anywhere. Sometimes we don't completely withdraw, but we stay at the edge of the crowd, or sit in coffee shops or in the mall and watch others, or go to church or to programs and stay within ourselves rather than really connecting with other human beings.

Have you found yourself withdrawing from others? Write a little about your experience here:

One-way relationships

We often find ourselves in a relationship where we receive help and support, but have no opportunity to give back. We find ourselves relying on formal helpers or a few family members who can become overwhelmed with our needs. We can use mental health providers wisely and as often as necessary, but for a successful journey we must have other relationships in our lives. We should expect to get support through many relationships, not just from formal helpers or a few family members. Formal helpers cannot offer us truly mutual reciprocal relationships. We can feel frustrated, angry or dependent in relationships where we have little chance to give back the suppor receive.

Have you experienced one-way relationships? Describe your experience here:

Poor self-esteem

Poor self-esteem may leave us thinking that we don't matter to others around us.

Does poor self-esteem have an effect on your relationships? Describe that impact here:

Poverty

Lack of resources can leave us feeling like we have limited social options and choices. This situation can make us feel we are not holding up our end of a relationship.

Do you think the lack of material resources has affected your relationships? Discuss how it has here:

> "The biggest disease today is not leprosy or tuberculosis, but rather the feeling of being unwanted, uncared for, and deserted by everybody."
> ~Mother Teresa

Fear

Sometimes we are afraid to open ourselves to others because of past problems with relationships. We may fear the possibility of abuse, being taken advantage of (exploitation), rejection or betrayal. We may feel we have very little to offer others or that we will disappoint or hurt others if they care about us.

Do you have any of these fears? Write about them here:

Do roadblocks keep you from reaching out to others? What are your most important barriers and how do they impact your ability to have a circle of support?

What are some steps you can take to overcome any roadblocks you have identified to forming positive and supportive relationships?

> "There is electricity about a friendship relationship. We are both more relaxed and more sensitive, more creative and more reflective, more energetic and more casual, more excited and more serene. It is as though when we come in contact with our friend we enter into a different environment."
> ~Andrew M. Greeley

We must work to tear down roadblocks to relationships because having supporters helps us achieve recovery, helps us to enjoy and validate our progress and improves the quality of our lives. In other words, having supportive relationships is important to our recovery and is rewarding in and of itself.

Are you satisfied with the circle of supportive relationships that you have now, and the social support you both give and receive? If not, read on!

Expanding Our Circle of Support

If you are still reading, you are someone who wants to improve, deepen or expand your circle of support. This part of the recovery journey can be very challenging and takes a significant commitment. Relationships are built or repaired over a long period of time. We don't want to wait any longer; it's never too late to improve our relationships!

How Can We Build Mutual Support?

Mutual social support happens in three main ways:

Sharing information and ideas

Sharing information and ideas can include knowledge about a particular resource or suggestions that allows us to find the help we need. It might include giving and receiving advice or feedback that helps us make solid decisions. It can include sharing any kind of knowledge or idea, from our philosophy of life to how to catch the right bus.

Providing or receiving material assistance

We might get a loan from our parents to pay off a debt or our friend brings us a bag of groceries at the end of the month. We could give free baby-sitting services to a neighbor when she needs time away or we may be given the gift of a ride from a member of our church.

Social support involves providing and receiving emotional aid

Support is built on a foundation of caring, it connects us emotionally to other people and strengthens our self-esteem.

Basically there are <u>three</u> ways we can get the support we need:

1) We can wait for support to be offered or freely given

As infants and children, we waited and fussed for support. If we wait around for support to be given at this point in our lives, we remain totally dependent on others to decide when we are in need of support and companionship. We may find ourselves sitting around waiting for the phone to ring or sitting in a group of people and waiting for someone to approach us. If we wait for the phone to ring, the knock on the door or the invitation to be with others, we are not engaging ourselves in building relationships. We have to reach out to others, become vulnerable and take risks.

2) We can ask for support

This way of gaining support is harder, but much more effective. However, many of us find that asking for support is very difficult to do. Relax. Many people find it hard to ask for support from others. We may feel we have disappointed those who supported us or that we haven't lived up to their expectations. We may feel we do not deserve help and support. Some of us have had people put us down and tell us we are undeserving, worthless or will never have good relationships. We may feel we don't measure up to those who do not have to contend with a psychiatric disability or who may be further along in their recovery. Or we may think we are so far along in recovery that we are the person others come to for support. We can't show that we don't have all the answers and still need support!

We have to try to let such feelings go. We deserve support, companionship and love! We are part of the human community!

How can we cultivate the art of approaching others? We can start with small things, such as approaching someone who loves helping people (like a reference librarian). We can join a support group where giving and receiving support is a natural expectation for each member and happens all the time.

Sally Clay, a nationally known consumer leader from Florida, says that one of the main signs of a "chronically normal person" is the ability to engage in small talk or idle chatter. While Sally uses a lot of humor, there is truth in what she says. We can learn to relax and enter into casual social conversation. If we have no problem with casual communication, we can go a bit farther—we can dare to ask for support from someone! We can open up to another person about what we are thinking and feeling. If we say "yes" to the next social event that we hear about, even if part of us doesn't really want to go, we are breaking through our resistance.

What are some ways that you could ask someone for support?

"We want people to feel with us more than to act for us."
~George Eliot

Chapter 7

229

Zen masters speak of the development of plum blossom courage. The plum blossom appears soft and glowing, even when the winter winds still blow. It knows, deep in its essence, that spring is almost here...The plum blossom symbolizes the resilience of the human spirit, its ability to open again to love and to go forward into another opportunity for celebration. In close relationships we gradually develop plum-blossom courage through coming back, time and again, to fundamental skills like telling the truth, taking responsibility, and holding ourselves and our significant others in a space of loving acceptance.

~Kathlyn & Gay Hendricks

3) We can give support to someone else

Remember the old saying, "It's better to give than to receive"? This way of getting support is one of the most dependable and effective. By giving, we often feel we get more than the person who accepts our acts of kindness.

Giving support to someone else helps us to develop a greater sense of self-worth and self-esteem. We can give support to others when we are feeling the need for support ourself. We can volunteer at a local nursing home, take flowers to a neighbor or show our niece how to make scrumptious oatmeal cookies from our old family recipe. No matter what we do, if we give support to someone, chances are we'll receive more support in return.

What is one way you will give support to another person in the next week?

"It takes only a minute to get a crush on someone, an hour to like someone, and a day to love someone, but it takes a lifetime to forget someone."
~Unknown

"Help me if you can, I'm feeling down, and I do appreciate you being 'round. Help me get my feet back on the ground. Won't you please, please help me?"
~John Lennon & Paul McCartney

EXERCISE:
Exploring New Relationships

One way we can build our support circle is to look around us and identify potential friends.

- *Make a list of people you know and find interesting.*
- *Write down their phone number next to their name.* You may need to contact other people if there are phone numbers you don't know. Avoid e-mail, this is about live conversation, not written communication.
- *Write down the things you have in common with each person on the list:*

Name   **Phone #**   **What we have in common**

Pick one person each day, for a week, and call him or her. Make it a different person each day. Have a brief conversation. Base your conversation on mutual interests and a genuine desire to begin or expand a relationship with that person.

It's hard to reach out at first, but the reward is connections with people who share our interests. You may want to write down ideas to discuss or even write a short "script" as an example of what you'd like to say. Some of us are natural born communicators, but others of us are painfully shy. Having a call list and using it each week can help us begin a habit of reaching out to others, and over time we will connect with people we like and build a solid circle of supportive and interesting relationships.

Keep a Call Diary
After each call write a summary of how the call went. You can use this diary to further develop your circle of support. Write down what was positive about the call, then write about anything that did not feel as though it went as well. This will help you to determine if the call was of mutual benefit. Not everyone on our list will turn out to be a friend or supporter. Don't become discouraged! Congratulate yourself for trying to open your life to others. Over time you will succeed in creating a circle of relationships that is mutually supportive.

Deciding the Kind of Relationships We Want to Build

There are many kinds of relationships, including peer relationships, friendships, family relationships, intimate relationships and casual acquaintances. We can target the kind of relationships that we want to develop.

Peer relationships

Being able to make a connection with someone who has similar life experiences is a powerful way to help us contend with the stress and challenges we face day-to-day. As we make the recovery journey we can learn from others who are traveling a similar path. Some of us join self-help groups to increase our peer supports. If there isn't a self-help group nearby already, consider working to start a consumer-run organization or self-help group in your area.

Write the name of a peer you'd like to get to know better here:

Advisor or mentor

Whether we've just begun to work on our recovery, or have been on the road to recovery for a long time, there are people who can serve as advisors or mentors. These are the people we look to as role models. They are those who are doing things in their lives that we would like to do someday.

We may find a mentor among the leadership of our local consumer-run organizations. They may be someone who leads recovery groups or serves as consumer-providers at our local mental health center. We may find someone who speaks out about his or her experiences with psychiatric disability to reduce stigma or improve the mental health system. The strengths and passion of such role models can inspire us.

We may not find our mentor among activists or leaders, but rather we may choose someone who is doing a good job of improving his or her own wellness and making real progress on the recovery journey. We can select our role models from among people we respect, who give us hope for the future and who help us understand the struggles we face.

"Alone we can do so little; together we can do so much."
~Helen Keller

"Those whom we support hold us up in life."
~Marie von Ebner Eschenbach

232

Is there someone who stands out, someone you know who has survived challenges or adversity in his or her life who inspires you? Write the name of a potential mentor here:

Once you have identified someone you may want to have as a role model, approach them. Ask the person to tell you the story of his or her recovery. Find out what kind of things have been helpful to them and share your own story or concerns. Ask for ideas in areas where you need new thoughts or practical advice.

You may be surprised at how easily it is to get to know a potential mentor and how happy the person is to respond to your questions. You might even want to ask the person if he or she would be willing to mentor you in a more formal relationship, by meeting with you regularly to share ideas and support. If the relationship doesn't click, identify another potential mentor until you gain the knowledge and support you need. We may be able to find a mentor or role model over the internet as well.

Friends

Friendships are very special relationships. Some friendships are so strong that they last a lifetime and weather all storms. Some friendships last only a short time, but we learn so much from the experience that what we gained always stays with us.

Friends are people with whom we share common interests, experiences or activities. Friends stand up for each other and trust and support each other in times of celebration or in times of sadness or frustration. Friends are people who will help us move six times in two years, even if we always pick a third floor apartment. Friends strive to make us happy and try to see the best in us.

Do you have a "best friend," someone you feel very close to? If not, did you have a best friend in the past? Could you potentially reconnect with him or her?

"Is there anyone so wise as to learn by the experience of others?"
~Voltaire

Chapter 7

"No medicine is more valuable, none more efficacious, none better suited to the cure of all our temporal ills than a friend to whom we may turn for consolation in time of trouble, and with whom we may share our happiness in time of joy."
~Saint Ailred of Rievaulx

233

Can you identify a person you'd like to try to develop a friendship or close personal relationship with?

What things are important to you in a friend? Some of the traits you might desire are:

- Someone who keeps confidences
- Someone who is loyal
- Someone who is supportive not negative
- Someone who is honest
- A person who gives gentle feedback
- A person with a sense of humor
- Someone who is "real" and authentic, not a phony

What are some of the qualities of people you want in your life?

To what extent do you already have these important qualities?

What activities do you enjoy that might lead to meeting a person who may become a new friend?

Where do we start building friendships? Friends can be found anywhere: in self-help groups, churches, bookstore activities, intramural sports teams, women and men's groups, craft classes and other community activities. We can join the groups that interest us and engage ourselves with others.

Family

We can't choose our family members. Wouldn't that be nice? Families can be the source of our greatest joy and our deepest pain. Some of us receive most of our support from our families. Our families connect us to our cultural heritage and ethnicity and we often develop our values and ideals in family life. Families can provide guidance, unconditional love and lifelong support. They are often the people we turn to when we face adversity and when we want to celebrate good times.

Others of us have experienced family life in very different ways. We may have lost family members early in life through death, abandonment or divorce. Some of us have suffered intense emotional pain and physical or sexual abuse inflicted by members of our own family. We may also have hurt people in our family very badly. Family relationships may have suffered from the impact of our psychiatric problems and we may live apart and visits or contacts with family may be very infrequent or nonexistent.

Our painful relationships can often be healed. In other cases, we find we must protect ourselves by distancing ourselves from certain people as part of our recovery journey. In research on coping and resilience, the decision to put distance between ourselves and people who have hurt us, or who continue to abuse, misunderstand or upset us, is called "adaptive distancing."

Who in your family supports you?

Are there difficult family relationships you would like to work to heal?

"Just because someone doesn't love you the way you want them to doesn't mean they don't love you with all they have."
~Truman Capote

If yes, what steps could you take right away to heal your relationship/s? (e.g. Contact specific people, make amends, work with a mediator, talk on the telephone regularly, write letters)

Are there family relationships you feel you should pull away from, at least for now?

Some people find it is helpful to build a kind of "intentional" or "chosen family" when their own family relationships are too emotionally overwhelming, troubled, dangerous or difficult.

Do you have people in your life whom you see as your true "brothers and sisters," or those who can serve as a nurturing presence or substitute parent/aunt/uncle/grandmother/grandfather figure in your life?

Parenting

Many of us want to explore having children, have the goal of parenting, have had children and/or are actively parenting. Sometimes our parenting ability is put into question solely because we have had mental health problems. We may have custody disputes or lose custody and these events are often deeply wounding. Some of us make the turnaround toward recovery and/or work especially hard on a day-by-day basis largely because we want to be an active and responsible parent.

Some of us need to gain advocacy and legal assistance to keep an active role as parent or to reconnect with our offspring and rebuild a relationship.

In most instances, children of people with serious psychiatric diagnoses do well in their child development. Formal resources such as supported parenting, daycare, parenting groups and play groups are sometimes available for those of us who are struggling to parent well. Community settings such as schools and churches may also be a resource.

Do you have children or want children?

What are your goals and needs as a parent?

Intimate partners

We share our deepest thoughts and feelings with our intimate partners. We feel comfortable with them and allow them to see our vulnerabilities and weaknesses. We feel safe to share the unfolding of our greatest longing and potential when we are with intimates. We feel very close in intimate relationships and sense a deep connection. Sometimes we are physically close to this person. Some intimate relationships include being sexual partners as well, but sexuality is not always a part of this kind of relationship.

Think of someone you have had, or now have, an intimate relationship with. Who were/are they? What was/is your relationship with them?

"An atmosphere of trust, love, and humor can nourish extraordinary human capacity. One key is authenticity: parents acting as people, not as roles."
~Marilyn Ferguson

Chapter 7

In what ways were/are you and this person connected?

"Once the realization is accepted that even between the closest human beings infinite distances continue, a wonderful living side by side can grow if they succeed in loving the distance between them which makes it possible for each to see the other whole against the sky."
~Rainer Maria Rilke

What did/do they do to let you know they cared/care? What did/do you do for them?

What can you do that will help you find and/or enhance a relationship with an intimate partner?

Casual relationships

Casual relationships are those where we spend time with people or undertake tasks together without any deep emotional feelings or commitments. We might work together as volunteers or attend the same church; we might ride the same bus with them or see them on the street. We don't open ourselves up deeply to casual acquaintances but we do feel comforted knowing we have friendly faces around us. We might discuss shared interests with such a person or talk about impersonal topics.

How can you enhance casual relationships in your life?

Fellow community members

The members of our community can be a tremendous source of support. Whether we live in a high-rise apartment or on a rural farm, the sense and power of connecting to other people in our community can be very strong.

Have you ever heard of the idea of *"ujima"*? This is an East African term that means to share the workload of building a community. If we want a strong community, we can become more willing to take on our neighbor's concerns as our own and try to work together to resolve them. The following story is an old Nigerian folktale (Javier, 1981).

Once there was an African village where the inhabitants made their living by farming. Just beyond these fields lay a splendid river. The river was a friend to all who lived there. However, during the rainy season, the river often overflowed and the people feared its great power. The villagers had built a dam just beyond the fields that kept the water from flooding their crops.

There was a man who lived in the village named Modupe, meaning, "I am grateful." Following the death of his wife, Modupe decided to move to the top of the mountain overlooking the valley. He built a hut and planted vegetables to sustain himself. Although the people in the village rarely saw Modupe, they loved and respected him.

One year during harvest, there were very heavy rains. From his mountaintop, Modupe could see the valley. He noticed the river was so full that it was straining the dam. Modupe realized there was no time to go down the mountain to warn the villagers, it would be too late and everything would be lost. Modupe remembered his friends in the village and realized they were in great danger. He had to find a way to warn them. Suddenly, Modupe had an idea. He rushed to a pile of firewood and set it on fire. The people in the village saw the bonfire and thought their friend was in trouble. They sounded the alarm and everyone in the village came running.

The villagers were in such a hurry that they did not hear the loud noise behind them. When they reached the mountaintop, they looked down and saw that the dam had broken and the river had flooded the valley, destroying everything. The people began to cry and moan. 'Don't worry,' Modupe comforted them. 'My crops are still here and we can share them while we build a new village.' All the people began to shout and sing. They stopped to give thanks because they realized that, in coming to help their friend, they had saved themselves.

Where in your community do you go for support?

What important problems is your community faced with that you could work with others to help resolve?

Spiritual supporters

Do you have social support for your spiritual life?

We can draw on relationships for spiritual support. Social support often enhances our spiritual life and brings us comfort and peace. We can see some people as our spiritual role models or identify with how they seem to lead their lives. We may find support by visiting with clergy or spiritual leaders.

We may find attending group worship services or rituals with others is comforting and empowering. Many of us find group prayer and/or meditation or other spiritual practices to be very helpful. Finding the right spiritual community can provide us with new options for spiritual growth, along with interaction that may range from casual to the deepest spirit-enhancing relationships.

Who gives you spiritual support?

Are there forms of spiritually-oriented social support that you would like to try (study groups, services, rituals, group meditations)? List them:

Pick one to explore within the coming month. Write it here:

Pets and other supports

Pets are not human beings, but they are often very social and can be very supportive. Who will ever love us so unconditionally? Pets happily comfort us. It's easy to ask our pets for support (unless we have a cat that won't come out from under our bed).

Pets don't have to be big, expensive or difficult to maintain. Watching a few fish in a small aquarium can bring us lots of relief from stress. Taking a walk with a dog helps us get in some much needed exercise a few times a day. Many people enjoy the beauty of a parakeet or little furry guinea pigs. Having a pet will bring you lots of enjoyment and they are great mood, morale and health booster, too!

Have you had pets in your life? What pets have provided you with the most enjoyment and support?

> "Animals are such agreeable friends, they ask no questions, they pass no criticisms."
> ~George Eliot

If you can't have a pet where you live or can't afford a pet, then consider volunteering at an animal shelter, taking pets for walks, shampooing dogs or playing with cats. Many people enjoy stuffed animals—they're comforting and not just for little kids. Pouring out your feelings to a teddy bear may sound dopey but it works for many of us when we are feeling alone.

Support from the universe

We can appreciate ever more fully all the support we receive from the universe—the sun comes up each day, we turn on the taps and have clean water, the dairy farmer has gotten up at 4 a.m. every day so that we can have milk for our coffee. We feel better when we truly appreciate all the supports that we have in our lives.

If we begin to look for and trust the processes of mutual support, it becomes easier to let go of our need to control everything. Once we become more aware of the support that occurs throughout our life in small and large ways on a day-to-day basis, it is easier to "go with the flow" of life. We can cultivate the feeling that many of the most resilient people have–that the universe is supporting us; that everything happens for a reason. We can improve our sense of comfort and support and feeling of flow in our recovery journey!

> "Many times a day I realize how much my own outer and inner life is built upon the labors of my fellow men, both living and dead, and how earnestly I must exert myself in order to give in return as much as I have received."
> ~Albert Einstein

EXERCISE:
Appreciation for the Support Received

Try this. Purposefully go through a day paying attention to the support that flows to you through everything that you experience. This may take some practice. Focus on the small signs and moments of grace or support you feel. At the end of the day, return to these pages and record what you have experienced.

What surprised you the most about what you experienced?

Renewing Our Social Circle

Most of us have to make a real effort to create and nurture relationships. We need to really push ourselves to form relationships. But it's definitely worth it!

> *Sometimes I get lonely and afraid. I can tend to isolate from others. Isolation is often a warning sign for me that I am not doing as well as I could. I have to remember to call my friends, make plans on the weekends with them, and engage with my peers for my own health. Sometimes I feel unsure and not able to trust as well as I would like to. I have to remember to open my heart to others and take risks, and I have to learn to share my own uniqueness and companionship with my friends. I have strengths that I can offer in a relationship and I have to fight the feeling that I don't really matter to my friends. When I reach out and spend time with others I feel a sense of joy and pride, and my friends seem to feel pride in being with me. On my journey of recovery I have to remind myself that others do care about me and I know that by looking at their smiling faces when they are with me.*
>
> *~Julie Bayes,*
> *Kansas Consumer Provider*

"True friendship is self-love at second hand."
~William Hazlett

Look back over the diagram of your current support circle on page 225. Are there people you have listed that you really wish you were closer to? List them here:

Pick at least one name and make contact with that person this week. Write down how you will contact that person (e.g. call, send a card, e-mail, ask them out for a coffee)

List three things that you will do in the next week to nurture a relationship that you already have:

1.

2.

3.

How Well Are We Communicating?

To be a friend we must be open to friendship. We need to be as positive as possible and work to feel good about ourselves. This will make it easier to connect with other people and enlist their support. We may want or need to improve our ability to be supportive toward others. Some basic tips for good communication include:

- Use open body language. We can make eye contact, face people head on and relax our posture so we don't appear stiff or closed off.

- Listen. We can work to ignore any internal or external distractions. We can concentrate and listen actively to *what* the person is saying as well as to the *meaning* of their words. It takes practice to listen well.

- Share. We can react by sharing our own perspective, opinions, experiences and stories.

"Only connect!"
~E. M. Forster

"Listening, not imitation, may be the sincerest form of flattery."
~Dr. Joyce Brothers

- <u>Be empathetic</u>. We can learn to listen for the *feelings* that the person is describing in his or her words and then respond to those feelings. By being empathic we may share how we think we would feel if we were the other person or what we might do in a similar situation.

- <u>Grow a thicker skin</u>. Sometimes we are so sensitive that we need to be a little bit less empathic! Often we experience too much of the feelings of those around us. We can learn to buffer some of the incoming thoughts and feelings without having to shut down completely.

- <u>Use mutual interests to build relationships</u>. Be curious about those that you associate with. Ask questions and listen to the responses. What do you and your new friend have in common? What are your new friend's strengths? Are you curious about others, or are you passively watching them from a distance?

Use the six questions good journalists use — *who, what, when, where, why* and *how* — to get to know the story of someone you want as a friend. What are the person's dreams and life goals? Who have they associated with in the past? How do they manage to get through the day in a healthy way? Where do they like to go? When is the best time to get together with them?

Engage people in conversation and activities to form a mutually supportive relationship. Do you know what their favorite food, color, music, movie, sport or book is? Do they know yours? Use relationship-building questions like these to create mutual understanding.

- <u>Emphasize our strengths</u>. We may not think that we have much to contribute to a relationship, so our relationships can be lopsided. We have to build on the strengths and qualities that we have that others can benefit from.

Record why you are a valuable friend and how the strengths you have make you a good friend:

"Ideal conversation must be an exchange of thought, and not, as many of those who worry most about their shortcomings believe, an eloquent exhibition of wit or oratory."
~Emily Post

Chapter 7

Based on your strengths, what groups would you like to join to expand your circle of support?

What resources do you have available to build new relationships?

Nourishing Our Circle of Support

Once we have built our social supports we have to nourish our relationships on an on-going basis. We need to keep letting those in our circle of support know they are valued and appreciated. Some ideas for on-going nurturance include:

- Frequent communication in person, by phone and e-mail to lend an ear and share information
- Greeting cards and remembrances of special occasions
- Offers of help and practical assistance
- "Breaking bread" by sharing a meal or a snack

What are some other ideas you have for nurturing your relationships?

"Those who trust us, educate us."
~George Eliot

Building trust

We need to start to build relationships in safe way and slowly work to build trust. We can find something each day that expands our trust in others. We can find ways to explore our own trust in ourself by engaging with others. It takes a lot of effort to build new relationships.

How Do We Become Good Supporters?

How do we become a good friend? Kathlyn and Gay Hendricks are bestselling authors and experts on relationships. In their book, *The Conscious Heart* (1997), the Hendricks write about relationships as being the "greatest source of our pain," and our, "greatest source of joy." We can all probably agree with this analysis because, as much as we would like to have our relationships always be happy and growing, the truth is, they aren't.

The Hendricks have developed a list of six principles that can help nourish our relationships and take our relationships to a deeper level. We can also use these tips when our relationships get stuck or hit a roadblock.

1. <u>Make a commitment to being close; commit to clearing anything up as we go along</u>. Getting and keeping a relationship is hard work. We need to work on problems as they arise instead of holding back and sweeping things under the rug. Even though it may be easier to ignore problems at the time, we'll only have more problems later on.

2. <u>Make a commitment to developing our whole self</u>. There are two people in a relationship, two people who deserve to grow, learn and develop. We shouldn't hold ourselves back; we need to seek out opportunities that will enhance our ability to be who we are meant to be and express ourselves fully.

3. <u>Commit to helping empower those around us</u>. When we try to hold someone else back they generally become resentful. We should empower those around us to keep them in our life.

4. <u>Make a commitment to taking healthy responsibility in our relationships</u>. Sometimes we find ourselves in relationships where we spent most of our time trying to figure out who is to blame or trying to fix what is wrong with the other person. This is a waste our time. Healthy relationships require our ability—and willingness—to take responsibility for our own actions and allow others to be responsible for their own behavior.

"What one has, one ought to use; and whatever he does, he should do with all his might."
~Cicero

"You can't try to do things; You simply must do them."
~Ray Bradbury

5. <u>Make the commitment to share openly in all our relationships</u>. Hiding our thoughts and feelings won't help our relationship to blossom. This may take some time, but when we learn to develop a sense of honesty and trust, we find our relationships have more meaning.

6. <u>Commit to having a good time in our relationships</u>. We need to laugh loud and laugh often and find time to nourish our relationships with fun and humor.

When we must change our traveling companions

Everyone has watched an important relationship change over time. If we're lucky, these changes are positive ones; the relationship continues to grow and develop and flourish, becoming an even richer source of support.

Most of us have also watched an important relationship change in negative ways and become less supportive. Sometimes relationships deteriorate before our eyes. We may not hear from our friend as often or they move far away. Our personal philosophy or beliefs may change and we find we are no longer on the same wavelength. Our feelings may get hurt or there may be jealousy or resentment that spirals out of control.

Relationships can become stagnant and wither on the vine. We may have too many or too little expectations of the relationship or our expectations may change. Conflicts may arise that we are simply unable to resolve. Many relationships just dry up, as sad as this may seem. Some of the reasons relationships change we can control and some we can do nothing about.

Our circle of support often changes on the recovery journey. We may have more goals or activities and others are just not interested in our new interests. People may try to hold us back or diminish what we are doing. They may become angry because we are changing, even though we know the changes we are making are very positive and necessary. For example, we may give up partying in order to work or do well in school and our old friends just want to sit around and drink or smoke pot. We may find we need a new circle of support as our recovery journey progresses.

"There is a point at which everything becomes simple and there is no longer any question of choice, because all you have staked will be lost if you look back. Life's point of no return."
~Dag Hammerskjold

248

In what ways, if any, are your current relationships challenged by your recovery?

What have you learned about yourself and your needs that may call for some new companions?

"Treat people as if they were what they ought to be, and help them become what they are capable of being."
~Goethe

While changes in relationships are hard, we can redirect our energy toward what is positive in our life. We find we can use the changes in our relationships to help move us forward. We learn to give ourselves the opportunity to try out new connections with interesting and supportive people. We take with us all the good elements of what we learned in our relationships; we gently let go of the things that may have been painful or not supportive. We move forward, toward greater support.

Becoming a mentor to help others on their journey

We have all had people in our life who have helped us along our recovery journey. Helping others on their journey can be an exciting opportunity or role for us too. As our friends and peers learn from our life, they will naturally start sharing their own stories. We can share our experience and make it easier for others on their journey.

Mentoring another person requires responsibility. We must protect and respect the other person's story and maintain their privacy and confidentiality. We honor the people whom we mentor and respect them for who they are and for the resiliency they have.

Tips for mentoring

How can we encourage and enhance another person's recovery efforts? Here are some things we may want to keep in mind:

- Be aware of the fear that the person may have. We have to remember the fears we had as we began our journey of recovery. Others have the same concerns. We can try to find out exactly what they are afraid of and work to address those fears. We can share our own fears with them and describe how we went about overcoming them.

- Be honest. As mentors, we must challenge people to move forward on their path. We can gain other people's confidence and look for what motivates them. We can be open about what we see and what we think could help them. We can give them practical ideas and options. Providing another person with our positive ideas is one of the most powerful things we can do.

- Make specific plans with them. When we act as a mentor we should be clear about what we can do to help them. We shouldn't merely say, "Let's get together and talk." Instead, we might say (based on the individual's goals), "Let's get together on Tuesday at 2 and talk about how to look for a job." We can help the person create a Personal Recovery Plan and support them as they move through it.

- Be open about our own experiences. One of the best ways for us to learn from each other is by sharing our own stories. Sharing our experiences, both what has worked well for us and what has been difficult, provides hope and a sense of strength. Our stories help other people realize that if someone else can do well, they can too!

- Realize that mentoring is a process that will change both of us. We can't go on a recovery journey with someone else without having to look at our own trip! We come to realize that we will be changed and grow in the relationship just as the other person will. We must keep seeing ourselves as mutual learners and not assume that we have all the answers for another person. Each of us is unique and has a unique path.

EXERCISE:
Exploring Social Supports

What social supports strengths do you <u>currently</u> have? (e.g. I have a supportive mother who cares about me; I have a lot of empathy that allows me to understand what others are feeling)

What strengths in relationships have you had in the <u>past</u>? (e.g. I used to have several very good friendships; I used to be complemented on my humor and making people laugh)

What do you want to achieve in the <u>future</u> around social supports? (e.g. I want to have at least one very close friendship; I want to feel connected to my peers and work on mutual support; I want an intimate partner)

Chapter 7

Using Your Strengths to Reach Your Social Support Goals

In order to reach your goal concerning social supports what strengths can you use? *Remember that when you list your strengths, that strengths can be:*

- *Internal* (e.g. I will begin to treat myself very well and stop putting myself down)

- *External* (e.g. I can go to book discussion groups at the library and may meet other people interested in books about nature, this would give us a common interest to build a friendship around)

What naturally-occurring community resources will you use to reach this goal? (e.g. I can join a social group for unmarried members of my church that is held once a month)

What formal services do you want to enlist in order to meet this goal? (e.g. I want to go to family planning to get information on birth control and safe sex before I get involved in another intimate relationship; I want to use my counselor as a coach to help my reduce my feelings of shyness)

Discuss your attitude around this goal: (e.g. I feel like it is time to open myself up to better relationships, I'm tired of solitude!)

List barriers that you may encounter in working towards this goal: (e.g. I'm afraid if someone comes to like me they will reject me because of my mental health history)

How can you overcome barriers towards reaching your goals? (e.g. I can try to build a friendship a little at a time; I'll talk about mental health issues in general and see how the person reacts; I can begin opening up about my experience — or I can keep my history private if I choose to)

How will you record your progress along the way to reaching your relationship goals? (e.g. I will begin by noting down each time I start a conversation with another person or contribute at the self-help group)

How will you celebrate reaching your social support goal? (e.g. I will invite my new friend over for my wonderful macaroni and cheese casserole dish)

Chapter 7

Celebrating Our Supports

Relationships are one of the most important parts of our lives. We can appreciate and nurture the circles of relationships and supports in our lives, whether these connections are to kinship circles we were born into, friendships circles we develop or a band of fellow travelers on the quest to become greater than we have been. The comfort we give and receive in return is precious!

It is important to celebrate our circle of support. There are many ways can we celebrate and support the people who care for us, and who we care for. We can write a thank you note, remember a birthday, send a free e-mail greeting card, make a picnic lunch, invite someone to go for a walk, give them a flower from our yard or find a quote that they would like.

Add your ideas for celebrating your support circle here:

"People need joy quite as much as clothing...some need it far more."
~Margaret Collier Graham

"That is happiness; to be dissolved into something complete and great."
~Willa Cather

References & Resources

References

Breier, A., & Strauss, J. (1984). The role of social relationships in the recovery from psychotic disorders. *American Journal of Psychiatry, 141*(8), 949-955.

Copeland, M. E. (1994). *Living Without Depression & Manic Depression: A Workbook for Maintaining Mood Stability*. Oakland, CA: New Harbinger Publications, Inc.

Hendricks, K., & Hendricks, G. (1997). *The Conscious Heart: Seven Soul-Choices that Inspire Creative Partnership*. New York: Bantam Books.

Hopkins, E., Woods, Z., Kelley, R., Bentley, K., & Murphy, J. (1995). *Working With Groups on Spiritual Themes*. Duluth, Minnesota: Whole Person Associates.

Horton, F. (n.d.). *Eight ways to be a great mentor*. Retrieved February 6, 2001: http://ivillage.com/workingdiva/mentoring/mentor/articles/0,,54856,00.html.

Javier, M. (1981). *Friends Can be Good Medicine*. Sacramento, CA: The State of California.

Spaniol, L., Koehler, M., & Hutchinson, D. (1994). *The Recovery Workbook*. Boston, MA: Boston University, Center for Psychiatric Rehabilitation.

Resources

Animal Angels: Amazing Acts of Love and Compassion by Stephanie Laland (Conari Press, 1998).

Becoming a Wise Parent for Your Grown Child: How to Give Love and Support Without Meddling by Betty Frain & Eileen Clegg (New Harbinger Publications, 1997).

Beyond Codependency by Melody Beattie (Hazelden Information & Educational Services, 1989).

Don't Take It Personally!: The Art of Dealing with Rejection by Elaine Savage (New Harbinger Publications, 1997)

Getting Commitment by Steven Carter (M. Evans, 2000)

It's Not Okay Anymore: Your Personal Guide to Ending Abuse, Taking Charge, and Loving Yourself by Greg Enns and Jan Black (New Harbinger Publications, 1997).

50 Ways to Help Your Community: A Handbook for Change by S. Fiffer & S. S. Fiffer (Doubleday, 1994).

Kid Cooperation: How to Stop Yelling, Nagging and Pleading and Get Kids to Cooperate by Elizabeth Pantley (New Harbinger Publications, 1996).

Living in Love by Alexandra Stoddard (Avon Books, 1997).

Messages: The Communication Skills Book by Matthew McKay, Martha Davis & Patrick Fanning (New Harbinger Publications, 1995).

Reaching Across: Mental Health Clients Helping Each Other by Sally Zinman, Howie the Harp & Su Budd (eds.) (Self-Help Committee of the California Network of Mental Health Clients, 1987).

Resolving Conflict: A Guide to Resolving Your Conflicts with Others and Within Yourself by Gina Graham Savage (New Harbinger Publications, 1990).

Respect: An Exploration by Sara Lawrence Lightfoot (Perseus Publishing, 2000).

Shortcuts to Bliss: The 50 Best Ways to Improve Relationships, Connect with Spirit, and Make Dreams Come True by Jonathan Robinson (Conari Press, 2001).

Soul Moments: Marvelous Stories of Synchronicity by Phil Cousineau (Conari Press, 1997).

Stepfamily Realities: How to Overcome Difficulties and Have a Happy Family by Margaret Newman (New Harbinger Publications, 1994).

The Community of Kindness: Reconnecting to Family, Friends, and the World through the Power of Kindness by Frederick & Mary Ann Brussat (Conari Press, 1999).

The Joyful Family by John Dacey & Lynne Weygint (Conari Press, 2002).

Violent Voices: 12 Steps to Freedom from Emotional and Verbal Abuse by K. Porterfield (Health Communications, 1989).

Chapter Eight

Developing Your
Personal Recovery Plan

This section combines the vision, strengths and long-term and short-term goals to create a Personal Recovery Plan that serves as the roadmap for the recovery journey.

Introduction

We've come a long way! Thus far in the *Pathways to Recovery* workbook we have discovered our strengths in many areas. We sought feedback from trusted people in our life and gained their reflection on our strengths. We have identified important goals across our life domains, the strengths and resources that we can use to achieve them and where we want to go in the future.

Now it's time for us to take all that information and form a Personal Recovery Plan. The *Pathways to Recovery* Personal Recovery Plan will serve as our roadmap that plots out our movement toward our chosen destinations. By creating a careful step-by-step plan, the worksheet is an important tool for a successful recovery journey!

What Will Make Our Personal Recovery Plan a Success?

Don't Try to Change Every Part of Life at Once

Sometimes recovery sounds so good, we want to head off in every direction at once or change our life completely. We want to arrive at our destination right after we set out. We know from those of us who have made a successful journey that recovery usually happens in small steps over a long course of time. Use a separate Personal Recovery Plan to chart out small steps in each important area.

Set Priorities and Make Difficult Choices

We have brainstormed a whole series of long-term goals; now it's time to make some tough decisions on which directions we want to start to move toward.

Sometimes we have been forced to give up our power to make decisions to others. We may be willing to let others make decisions for us because we feel unable to make positive choices or we feel we lack real options. We have to remind ourselves that we must be in the driver's seat to be on a recovery journey. Recovery is based in self-responsibility. We need to control our own destiny as much as possible!

"Life is a process, choices are our tools."
~Alexandra Stoddard

Chapter 8

"Choice is the rudder that guides each person's destiny."
~Peter Megargee Brown

If we haven't practiced decision-making in a long time this step may feel strange, alien or scary. Nevertheless, to claim recovery we must decide what is most important to us and put our energy behind our choices. We have the power to make choices and achieve what we want. We're not giving up on our other goals, but we do need to put goals in priority order to decide which to work on first.

There are many ways to make choices and set priorities. For example, we can decide which goals seem most interesting to us, which goals most clearly reflect and uphold our values, which goals we feel the most passionate about, which reflect our greatest strengths, which will move us closer to our vision, which is easiest to achieve first or which goal just seems like the next right thing to do.

We can analyze our goals by applying some criteria we set and then rate each one using a number from one to ten. We can put our goals on little slips of paper and pick one out of a hat or toss a coin and let "fate" decide. We can use any method for selecting the goals we want to work on first.

If we haven't had much experience seeing what our options are, the process of decision-making can be rough at first. We may not feel that we can trust our decisions or our gut instincts. With practice we can learn to see our options and make decisions that move us forward. Kansas consumer Janice Driscoll recommends making decisions with the mind, the heart and our "gut feeling." The following story by Vicki Darring, a consumer from Pennsylvania, demonstrates a different perspective on decision making.

On Second Thought

As children in grade school we learn many things by rote. We memorize words, math tables, and other things to the point where we don't have to give any thought to the process; we can just spout out the answers. Well, the same kind of rote learning once governed my actions, and ultimately, my self worth. I stopped having to think through what would happen if bad events occurred in my life, because they happened so often. I learned by rote, through long years of abuse, that I was worthless, bad, and needed to be dead. I didn't have to work through any thought processes to know these facts.

I became a frequent mental hospital resident because I could become suicidal so quickly. I looked irrational, instead of being seen as the good learner that I was! Now, this may not seem like a positive strength, but being a good learner has always been one of my strengths.

One day I told my therapist that I should just go ahead and kill myself. She simply said: 'Well, that's one option...not a good one, but it's an option.' Hearing that statement out loud made me think about the potential for other options. I actually came up with several options rather quickly that had nothing to do with hurting myself! Cool!

I thought my response was a fluke at first. I decided to use that same technique on other areas of my life that were putting me in danger. I had often used a form of self-inflicted violence. Whenever I would get angry, lonely, frustrated or overly tired I would hurt myself. The next time I had the impulse to hurt myself I stopped myself and repeated the words: 'It's an option...not a good one, but an option.' I found another way to handle the feelings I had, without hurting myself. I have not used self-inflicted violence to resolve my feelings in over six years.

I committed myself to the task of examining my initial reactions to situations. I told myself that I was not to judge them, just look at them. What I discovered from this was that most of my gut reactions and responses to situations in life were 'sick' because they were based on the ingrained idea that I was worthless and bad and didn't deserve to live. In order to succeed in life I would have to instill new gut reactions.

This one moment of learning became the foundation upon which I built a history of success.

I believe the key ingredient in the new pattern was (and still is) to place NO judgment on the first thought or thing that comes to mind. This non-judgmental attitude made it so easy to forgive myself while I changed. I can actually say that in the past I did the best that I could, with what I knew. Now I <u>still</u> do the best I can with what I know. I just know more.

Continued...

> *Using another strength of mine (stubbornness), I began to create and memorize new thought patterns that led to more healthy choices. From these decisions came the new tenet that I live by: <u>Do the second thing that comes to mind</u>. Where I once used to feel I needed to commit suicide because I couldn't balance my checkbook, I followed the new pattern:*
>
> 1. *I made myself recognize the 'sick' initial reaction — that I was worthless, bad and needed to die.*
> 2. *I non-judgmentally blew the first thought off, as it represented the old pattern.*
> 3. *I thought out a few other options, such as:*
>   - *Re-check the numbers because I tend to transpose them.*
>   - *Use a calculator instead of adding and subtracting in my head.*
>   - *Ask someone else to look at the checkbook ledger to find something that I'm not seeing*
>   - *Simply accept the fact that I'm a few dollars off and leave it alone (my least likely response).*
> 4. *Choose one of the new options from the list of options I had generated.*
> 5. *Act on one of the healthy options.*
> 6. *Examine the results.*
>
> *An amazing thing happened when I did this. I discovered White Out! I also learned to have a good laugh after I found the simple mistake I had made — a mistake that previously would have lead to me becoming a danger to myself.*
>
> *~Vicki Darring,*
> *Pennsylvania Consumer Leader*

Big Sudden Changes vs. Small Steps Over Time

It is generally best to make *small steady changes* as we move towards our goals. As we break each goal down into action steps we are creating stepping stones on our pathway to recovery. Janice Driscoll puts it this way: *"I like to see my recovery in terms of many small steps. I take one step and make sure I have a firm footing, then take another one, and get my feet under me again."*

Sometimes we have to undertake a general overhaul of our entire lifestyle and there is no way that we can do it slowly or in small steps. It's difficult to make big changes, but sometimes we have no other choice. For example, if we decide to care for ourselves and we are in a situation where we are being abused, we need to leave the abusive situation right away. This may mean changing our living situation, breaking up a major relationship or losing a source of income. Some of us set career goals and then we realize that we won't succeed unless we end a habit of substance abuse. We may have to develop a whole new circle of friends and new ways of spending our free time. If we want to improve our wellness and save money and decide to quit smoking cigarettes, we may be able to cut back slowly, but most of us will have to go "cold turkey," and give up the habit entirely. Each of us has to make the decision about how we need to change our lives.

How do you see the change process occurring? Many small steps or big changes?

How can you be sure to have a firm footing as you move along?

Line Up Supports

We may think recovery is about independence, but most people going through recovery know that recovery is not done alone. Much of our success depends on what other people do and the resources we have around us. We tend to stereotype "the community" and think a lot about the social stigma that exists towards us as people with psychiatric disabilities. But, the Strengths Recovery Approach sees the community as full of naturally occurring resources. We can begin to look at our communities as a great source of strengths and resources that we can tap into in order to reach our goals. When we reach out and allow ourselves to be open to finding resources and support, it is amazing how often what we need materializes.

What kinds of things are we talking about? Want to use a computer to explore the internet, but can't afford one? Almost every library has a free Internet hookup for patrons and most library cards are free. Want to watch some videos that will really make you laugh? The library probably has some that can be borrowed for free. Need to get your G.E.D.? Most high schools have programs that cost almost nothing to prepare you. Need to deal with a bad landlord? Legal Aid is available in most areas. Want to get fit? Look around for a community recreation

Chapter 8

center or school track, they are often open and have programs for low and no cost. Feel like having a better relationship with your higher power? Look at the newspaper for the listing of churches or temples and call the pastors or rabbi to set an appointment to talk, or find a 12-step group to attend that meets your desires. Want to get away into nature? Get a community map and explore the local parks. Claim a park bench for your very own and use it as your outdoor living room. Want a new look in your bedroom? The local thrift shop may have just what you need and you may be eligible to get things for free or for a very low fee. Feeling lonely? Look on the community bulletin board, visit an Internet chat room, join the food co-op or become a church member.

We can move ourselves forward by identifying and securing the wide of range of resources and supports that can help us to achieve goals. We also need to open up and reach out and ask for support when we need it. We can form relationships that help us on our way. If we find it is difficult to create a Personal Recovery Plan and follow through on it, we can make an effort to enlist a recovery partner or support person to help us succeed.

What resources do you want to explore in your community?

Do you need a recovery partner or supporter? Who can you ask? What do you need or want from that person?

Set a Comfortable Pace

As we set out to reach our goals, we should try to set a pace that is in line with our energy and ambitions. We don't open the throttle all the way the minute we hit the road. A good steady slow pace seems to work for most people. Sometimes we feel the need to prove ourselves and we put so much pressure on ourselves that we begin to focus

"As for the future, your task is not to foresee it, but to enable it."
~St. Exupery

more on the pressure and stress we feel rather than the goal we seek to achieve. Each of us needs to find our own pace. We need to be careful not to measure our pace and progress against anyone else's experience. Our journey of recovery is unique.

What kind of pace do you want to set?

How will you know if you begin to outpace yourself?

Making a Habit Takes Energy and Time

Change is difficult and it often requires us to alter the way we look at our attitudes and behaviors. Change also takes firm commitment over a period of time. Experts differ on how long it takes to change a habit, but most seem to say that it takes up to 3 months of daily effort to form new habits and patterns that we want to bring into our lives.

This is part of the human condition; if we don't consistently move to exercise our new habit, we will revert to our old one. Ed Knight, who was once a state hospital patient and is now a national consumer leader and vice president of a large managed care corporation, tells of his efforts to move towards his recovery. At times he felt without hope, but he says he persevered by just "putting one foot in front of the other" to keep on moving.

How will you support yourself and structure your time so you can form the new habits that will make your goals a reality?

Chapter 8

265

Bringing it All Together

Now we will take several steps to create a Personal Recovery Plan.

Step 1. Review your goals

Go back over chapters six and seven. Review the goals you have for the **eight domains** plus **social supports.** Look at those areas you would like to gain additional information on or actively work toward achieving.

As you look over the domains, pick **one high priority goal** from each domain. Decide which goal holds the **most interest** for you in that domain or which seems **most important.**

Step 2. List the areas you want to work on

On the following list write **your number one or highest priority goal** for each domain:

Housing   I want to:_____

Education   I want to:_____

Assets   I want to:_____

Vocation   I want to:_____

Leisure   I want to:_____

Health   I want to:_____

Sexuality   I want to:_____

Spirituality   I want to:_____

Social Supports I want to:_____

"If a man can keep alert & imaginative, an error is a possiblity, a chance at something new; to him, wandering and wondering are part of the same process and he is most mistaken, most in error, whenever he quits exploring."
~William Least Heat Moon

Step 3. Select one area to work on first

Review the list of "wants" that you have written. From the list that you have created, **pick out one area that seems most important to you and your recovery at this point in time**.

Make sure the domain you want to work on and your stated goal or desire is something that *you* want to do and *you* want to work on. Don't pick an area that others think you need to work on...the area you pick should be **one that is your own personal priority**.

My top priority goal:

_____
_____
_____

Step 4. Clearly state your long-term and short-term goals

Good work! Now that you have picked your top priority goal, it's time to <u>put your priority and your strengths together</u> to proceed on the journey. Write down the *long-term goal* that you will start to work with on your Personal Recovery Plan. You may want to go back and review ways to formulate long-term goals. Also keep in mind the ways to write effective short-term goals:

- They are stated in positive terms
- They have a high probability of success
- They are measurable and observable
- They are specific, small and time-limited
- They are understandable and meaningful to you

My long-term goal is:

_____
_____
_____
_____

My short-term goals to reach the long-term goal are:

_____
_____
_____
_____

"A goal is a dream that has an ending."
~Duke Ellington

"The tragedy of life doesn't lie in not reaching your goal. The tragedy lies in having no goal to reach."
~Benjamin Mays

Chapter 8

Step 5. Identify the resources and supports you'll want to draw on to put the plan into operation

It is important to clearly state who will be responsible for each step and the resources needed to make the action step happen. This includes the steps you will take, and the steps you need support on and the people you want to involve in making your goals a reality.

The resources and supports I need include:

_____

_____

_____

_____

Design a Plan to Make the Goal a Reality

The following is an example of one person's approach to developing and working on a *Pathways to Recovery* Personal Recovery Plan.

Jim is a talented artist. He has always enjoyed sketching and drawing. He received recognition for his artwork from an early age. In fifth grade, he won a prize for a charcoal sketch of a stallion in a school art contest. After Jim graduated from high school, he went on to a local college near his home where he finished his first semester of general studies. He planned to enter the art program.

In the first few weeks of his second semester of college, Jim started losing his motivation. He would often stay up all night, go to bars and stay until closing. When he returned to his dorm room Jim would spend hours in chat rooms on the Internet, he would drink massive amounts of coffee and soda and eat doughnuts and chips. Jim lost a lot of sleep and when he finally went to bed he had a hard time getting up to attend classes. He began experiencing periods of extreme highs and lows.

After several weeks, Jim dropped out of school hoping to explore other parts of the country. He packed up his belongings and headed out on a cross-country adventure. Jim found he could go several days at a time without sleeping, but his thinking became confused. He ended up in jail after being arrested for disorderly conduct and vagrancy. In jail he was clearly hallucinating, which led to his admission to a psychiatric unit.

"Having the world's best idea will do you no good unless you act on it. People who want milk shouldn't sit on a stool in the middle of a field in hopes that a cow will back up to them."
~Curtis Grant

After three years in the mental health system, Jim had the opportunity to attend an art show by consumers of mental health services. A spark ignited within him and he had a strong desire to do artwork again.

Jim bought a sketch pad and sketched often. His specialty was drawing wildlife. He produced pictures of mustangs, geese, elk and other wildlife. Jim would often give away his artwork as presents to friends. In the past year, Jim's reputation for artistic talent was recognized by the mental health center when he was asked to illustrate the cover of the center's annual report. Jim talked to his good friend Antonio about his love of art and his desire to someday be a professional artist. Jim has a good feeling about himself in terms of his artistic talent and Antonio encouraged him to reach out for his dream.

Jim made the decision to return to college to get his degree in fine arts in order to attain his long-term goal of becoming a professional artist.

The following page shows the Personal Recovery Plan that Jim created to move towards his vision of becoming a professional artist. Jim's long-term goal for this part of his vision is: "To take one class in fine arts at the local community college."

"The victory of success is half won when one gains the habit of setting goals and achieving them. Even the most tedious chore will become endurable as you parade through each day convinced that every task, no matter how menial or boring, brings you closer to fulfilling your dreams."
~Og Mandino

PERSONAL RECOVERY PLAN

For: _____Jim_____

My Vision: _"I want to go back to college and get a bachelor's degree in fine arts."_

My Long-Term Goal (3-6 months): _"To take one class in fine arts at the local college."_

Short-term goals or action steps that will help me reach my goal:

#	Short Term Action Steps	Responsibility	Date to accomplish this step by	Comments	Date Step Completed
1	Call Prairie College to request application and catalog	Jim	June 3	Hope there are some classes that will interest me!	June 2
2	Review catalog for classes of interest	Jim	When I receive catalog in the may. (By June 30)	There is an introductory drawing class (on Wednesday) that I would like.	June 9 (day I received catalog)
3	Talk to vocational counselor (Maria) if funding is available	Jim and Maria	June 14	We already had an appointment to meet—this is working out!	June 14
4	Fill our paperwork for educational funding and return to Maria	Jim	June 20	The paperwork is confusing. I need help.	_____
5	Call Maria to ask how to fill out educational paperwork	Jim and Maria	June 20	She helped get me through it...whew! I wasn't as bad as I thought!	June 20
6	Fill out and send in college application	Jim	June 25	Accomplished	June 24
7	Go with Anton io to walk around campus and check out Fine Arts Department	Jim and Antonio	June 28	We went to the Student Union and had ice cream. It felt great to be on campus, but a little scary.	June 28
8	Enroll to Take BFA #102 Introduction to Drawing	Jim	July 15	I was accepted! Taking this course is moving me toward getting my degree! I can do this!	July 13
9	(Next steps yet to be decided...				

As you can see from this example, a Personal Recovery Plan serves many functions:

1. <u>The Personal Recovery Plan helps you set the course of your recovery journey</u>. An effective plan helps you accomplish your goals and answers the questions: "Who will do what, by when?"

Go back and look at Jim's Personal Recovery Plan. Can you tell exactly *who* is going to do *what* by *when*? Jim's plan answers that question very specifically. Your Personal Recovery Plan should also answer the *"who will do what by when"* question.

2. <u>The Personal Recovery Plan is a "to-do" list</u>. The more **specific** you can be about what you and other people need to do to accomplish your short-term goal the better. Look at Jim's plan. Are the short-term action steps written clearly? Remember your short-term action plan must be written in a way that has personal meaning to you.

3. Notice Jim has listed only one thing (taking one class) on the line that states his long-term goal. **To be most effective, you should create a different Personal Recovery Plan for each one of your long-term goals**. Only you can decide how much change you want to make in your life at any given time. Most people find that trying to work more than 2 or 3 major long-term goals at a time requires too much juggling and can be exhausting and overwhelming.

4. When you work towards your long-term goals it can seem like you are making little progress. <u>The Personal Recovery Plan serves as a **list of all you have accomplished**</u>. Look over Jim's plan again; note all the things Jim accomplished in a short period of time. Jim's Personal Recovery Plan marks his progress towards his goal as he makes strides step-by-step. You can simply review your Personal Recovery Plans to see how much you are actually accomplishing and how reaching your goal is becoming very "do-able."

5. <u>It's important to **celebrate the steps** you make towards your goals</u>. On Jim's Personal Recovery Plan the progress he is making is terrific!

6. **Barriers can be noted** on the worksheet. What barriers are identified on Jim's Personal Recovery Plan? Jim was able to address the barrier of confusing paperwork for educational funding by writing it down and coming up with an **alternative plan** to address this problem (calling

> "Even if you are on the right track, you will get run over if you just sit there."
> ~Will Rogers

Maria for some assistance). Not everything we want to accomplish will go the way we plan. When this happens, don't feel bad, just form a new short-term goal to address the change in course.

Setting a Personal Recovery Plan for Exploring New Territory on the Journey

In Jim's Personal Recovery Plan, his goal is very clear as are the steps he is taking. But many of us are not at a place where we are certain of what we want to do. In fact, some of us aren't sure what our goals are. This is completely okay. Many of us missed out on some of the typical search for ideals, vocation, favorite ways of spending time or the developments of relationships because we were contending with psychiatric problems in our early adult years. We need to give ourselves the time to explore and discover who we are, what we like and what we want in our lives! Taking the time for exploration can help us become more certain about what it is we want to achieve.

If you are unsure of what you want and how to proceed, you can use the Personal Recovery Plan format as a way to explore your interests.

An example of one person's exploratory Plan follows. In the last few months, Pam made the decision to rent an apartment without roommates. She has been living in her own apartment for over three months and has found that she often feels lonely late in the evening. When Pam starts to feel lonely she usually telephones her former roommate and friend, Tannisha. However, Pam has been thinking about the possibility of getting a pet for companionship. In developing her Personal Recovery Plan, Pam is exploring <u>choices</u> and <u>possibilities</u>.

On the pages following Pam's sample Plan you will find two blank Personal Recovery Plans. Feel free to make as many copies of the Personal Recovery Plan as you want. You'll need to make several copies because you will have more than one goal and your recovery goals will change over time. Fill in all the information you have decided on. Enlist the people you need to support or advance your actions steps.

"I am not the smartest person or most talented person in the world, but I succeeded because I keep going, and going, and going."
~Sylvester Stallone

272

PERSONAL RECOVERY PLAN

For: _Pam_

My Vision: _"To have companionship in the evening."_

My Long-Term Goal (3-6 months) : _"To check out the possibility of getting a pet."_

Short-term goals or action steps that will help me reach my goal:

#	Short Term Action Steps	Responsibility	Date to accomplish this step by	Comments	Date Step Completed
1	Check with my landlord if I can have pets (when I pay rent	Pam	April 30	I asked her if I can have pets and what kind of pets I can have. (It's okay.)	May 1
2	Ask friends who have pets how much they spend to keep their pet each month.	Pam	May 3	Ask Tannisha and Sarah. They say a dog is about $20 a month and a cat about $15	May 5
3	Review my budget to see how much money I can spend on a pet	Pam and Miguel	May 6	Ask Miguel to help me with budget review.	May 6
4	I may want a dog. I'm going to check this out. I'll volunteer at an animal shelter to walk dogs.	Pam	May 7	The dogs were too aggressive. I don't want a dog.	May 8
5	I may want a bird. Visit neighbor and ask questions about her parrot.	Pam	May 10	Birds are too expensive and dirty. Ugh!	May 11
6	Look in the newspaper under the "free column for pets.	Pam	May 13	I can read the paper for free at the library	May 13
7	I may want a cat. I'll check out books about cat care at the library.	Pam	May 13	I've decided to look for a kitty.	May 13
8	Call "No Kill Shelter for Cats" about their program to help with pet adoptions	Pam	May 16	This was a great idea from Sarah!	May 17
9	Go to the local shelters and look at cats and kittens.	Pam and Tannisha	May 20	Tannisha will drive us on Saturday. This is going to be fun!	May 24
10	(Next steps yet to be decided...)				

PERSONAL RECOVERY PLAN

For: _____

My Vision: _____

My Long-Term Goal (3-6 months): _____

Short-term goals or action steps that will help me reach my goal:

#	Short Term Action Steps	Responsibility	Date to accomplish this step by	Comments	Date Step Completed
1					
2					
3					
4					
5					
6					
7					
8					
9					

PERSONAL RECOVERY PLAN

For: _____

My Vision: _____

My Long-Term Goal (3-6 months): _____

Short-term goals or action steps that will help me reach my goal:

#	Short Term Action Steps	Responsibility	Date to accomplish this step by	Comments	Date Step Completed
1					
2					
3					
4					
5					
6					
7					
8					
9					

Get the Rubber on the Road

Now that you have created a Personal Recovery Plan for your future, it's time to put your plan into action. This is where the "rubber hits the road." Head out on your journey taking each step day-by-day.

Remain Flexible

When we start out on our journey of recovery, sooner or later we run up against roadblocks and our plans will break down. When this happens we may feel like giving up or that we have blown our chances. The following chapter provides details on common detours and strategies to overcome them. It's important to be flexible. Don't give up! Stick to your vision. Be willing to make changes to your travel plan. Forge new pathways. Find new and alternative routes. But most of all, stay on the road to recovery!

Shirley Pilger, one of the consumer advisors to the *Pathways to Recovery* project, pointed out that *most* self-help books tell you to "do this... do that...do this...and then you will succeed." When you follow the directions and you don't succeed, you can feel like you are a complete failure. It is important to remember that everyone learns by *trial and error* and not *trial and success*!

No one can tell you what to do to achieve recovery and no one can give you a surefire roadmap with clear directions! Most of us traveling on the path toward recovery find that the journey is long, winding and bumpy. We have to be willing to change our course and try many alternative routes to get where we want to go. We need to try new things. We can revise our Personal Recovery Plan often and begin rewriting our short-term goals as soon as we find that they aren't working for us or moving us toward where we want to be.

> "Every thought you think, builds your character. Just as bricks are laid, one on top of another, to build a house, so do your thoughts build on each other, moment by moment. The person you become, the things you accomplish, the joy and fulfillment you find, all depend on the thoughts you use to build your life."
> ~Ralph S. Marston, Jr.

Celebrate!

Most of the steps we plan work out! Don't forget to celebrate all the steps you make as you move forward. Sometimes we are so focused upon the work of recovery we forget to include celebrations as part of the journey.

How about treating yourself to something special when you complete each action step? When you have help taking a step you can write a thank you to the people who helped you. When you hit a dead end and have to backtrack, celebrate the fact that you are learning what works and what doesn't work for you! Throw yourself a party to thank the universe for your 4,000th second chance!

What can you do to celebrate your progress thus far?

"Great things are not done by impulse but by a series of small things brought together."
~Vincent Van Gogh

Chapter 8

 # References & Resources

Resources

Changing for Good by James Prochaska, John Norcross & Carlos Diclemente (Morrow, William & Co., 1995).

Life Strategies: Doing What Works, Doing What Matters by Phillip C. McGraw (Hyperion Press, 2000).

Self Matters: Creating Your Life from the Inside Out by Phillip C. McGraw (Simon & Schuster Trade, 2001).

Self-Nurture: Learning to Care for Yourself as Effectively as Your Care for Everyone Else by Alice D. Domar & Henry Dreher (Penguin USA, 2001).

Take Time for Your Life by Cheryl Richardson & Lauren Marino (eds.) (Bantam Books, 1999).

The Circle: How the Power of a Single Wish Can Change Your Life by Laura Day (Putnam Publishing, 2001).

The Seven Habits of Highly Effective People: Powerful Lessons in Personal Change by Stephen R. Covey (Simon & Schuster, 1990).

Transitions: Making Sense of Life's Changes by William P. Bridges (Perseus Publishing, 1980).

You Can Heal Your Life and *You Can Heal Your Life: Companion Book* by Louise L. Hay (Hay House, Inc., 2002).

Chapter Nine

Making it Past
Detours and Roadblocks

This chapter explores common detours and roadblocks that can stall or block the journey of recovery and how to navigate past these barriers.

Introduction: Common Pitfalls, Detours and Roadblocks on the Journey of Recovery

The following poem by Portia Nelson (1994) is often used to show how we can run up against many pitfalls as we change and grow.

I walk down the street. There is a deep hole in the sidewalk. I fall in. I am lost...I am helpless. It isn't my fault. It takes forever to find a way out.

I walk down the street. There is a deep hole in the sidewalk. I pretend that I don't see it. I fall in again. I can't believe I am in this same place. But it isn't my fault. It still takes a long time to get out.

I walk down the same street. There is a deep hole in the sidewalk. I see it is there. I still fall in...it's a habit...but, my eyes are open. I know where I am. It is my fault. I get out immediately.

I walk down the same street. There is a deep hole in the sidewalk. I walk around it.

I walk down another street.

The journey of recovery from psychiatric disability doesn't usually follow a straight or smooth course. We find unexpected twists and turns in the process of recovery. This chapter covers some of the common potholes, detours, ruts and roadblocks we face. While it is not possible to avoid all detours or barriers, we can navigate our way through them and learn from them. By joining with others we can also work together to remove some of the major structural roadblocks that stand in our way.

Awareness of the challenges ahead keeps us focused on success. By having strategies to contend with challenges and knowing what we can do when we encounter roadblocks, we can continue to move toward our goals.

By understanding what others have faced, we may be less likely to encounter these roadblocks and better able to avoid their negative impact. Sometimes just knowing that other people fall into the same ruts we

> "If we only dwell on the problems we have, we can never create the future we need."
> ~Anonymous

do and face the same barriers we face helps us to keep going. We find we can get through these experiences and keep moving. Sometimes the roadblocks we encounter become our teachers. We learn a great deal when we are open and allow ourselves to risk, and don't succeed, but try again.

It's important to keep in mind that most of us eventually find our way over, under, around and through the barriers we encounter on our journey and successfully recover. By persevering, or continuing on, in times of difficulty, we can make many positive changes in our lives. The best directions we can get for the recovery journey are keep trying new routes and _never, never give up_!

Driving Using the Rearview Mirror: Trying to Head "Back to the Past"

Many of us wish that we could return to a time in our lives before we began to experience psychiatric problems. Some of us take off on our recovery journey and try to head "back to the past!"

Some of us think that the idea of recovery is to return to the life we once had. One consumer lamented that she could not return to the person she was prior to having psychiatric problems, because she had "no before" — she had always had symptoms as long as she could remember. Many of us had goals, relationships, careers, good times and roles that were taken from us as mental health problems claimed more of our lives.

What we find over time as we recover, is that we are simply not the same person we were earlier in our lives. We have changed, other people have changed, time has gone by, circumstances have altered and a return to the past is impossible.

"Fall seven times, stand up eight."
~Japanese Proverb

Pat Risser, a consumer leader from Oregon, shared part of his recovery story at a conference. He spent 10 years bitterly trying, without success, to reclaim the life he had before he experienced psychiatric problems. Ultimately, he found he had to let go of his past. When he released his dream of reclaiming the life he had before, he found _a new life_ by working on his recovery step-by-step. What really surprised him is that he went further than he ever had before and created a much more interesting and satisfying life than he could ever have anticipated!

It's not that we must forget our past and our interests and former achievements. Many of the inner and outer strengths and resources that we thought we left behind *can* be reclaimed and put to good use as we shape a new future.

What are some of the positive experiences, relationships, dreams and memories you would like to be sure to reclaim and/or hold onto from earlier periods of your life?

How do We Handle Our Psychiatric History?

As we recover, some of us feel the need to "seal off" our experience and attempt to forget that we ever had mental health problems. We try to move on with our lives and stop ourselves from dwelling on the past. We do not share our history with people we meet or work with.

Others of us find that all of our life experiences, even the most challenging, the roughest times and the storms of extreme mental states we pass through, are important in our personal development. We come to accept our experiences and see that all we have been though is a part of who we are today and has formed us into a deeply unique human being.

Some of us do not want to deny or hide our experiences of psychiatric disorder. We want to embrace and even celebrate our experiences! We can point to the fact that people with visionary experiences or unusual states of consciousness are respected, even honored or seen as healers, shamans or mystics in some cultures. We may feel a sense of "survivor pride" for having made it through so much adversity in our lives. Some of us come to view our psychiatric symptoms as part of the creative potential of the mind. For example, we may feel our ability to disassociate protected us and permitted us to adapt to impossible circumstances. We believe our "psychiatric symptoms" allowed us to survive the experience of very intense traumatic events.

Chapter 9

"A gem cannot be polished without friction, nor people perfected without trials."
~Chinese Proverb

How do you see your psychiatric history? Do you want to embrace your experience, integrate your experience or seal over your experience of mental health problems?

Heading in Someone Else's Direction

We often measure our recovery by someone else's expectations. All of us are motivated to some degree by how others view us. We may begin our recovery journey largely to please our spouse, therapist, children, parents, peers, or to meet the expectations of our mental health program or fit within the standard for functioning within our culture.

Our journey can become misguided when it is largely about pleasing other people or doing what we believe they want us to do. If we are motivated by what others want, we can make decisions and compromises that throw us far off course. We find ourselves doing things that do not reflect our own strengths, values, who we really are or what we really want out of life. We may find we are not behind the wheel guiding our own recovery journey, we are just taking directions, moving along a track that someone else has laid out for us to follow.

Our parents may have career or educational goals for us or may expect us to be like our brothers and sisters. Our culture has many expectations, such as when we should be married and how we should spend our days. Maybe we have not been able to work full time, or to work at all, and our family and friends don't understand why. In addition, there is the inescapable fact that many demands are placed on us by a variety of roles and environments that we participate in every day. We may also look at our peers who are on a journey of recovery and think we *should* be having the same experiences they are having.

If we find we are not in the driver's seat of our own recovery, we can try to return again and again to a position of self-responsibility and self-determination. We want to have a strong sense of personal authority over our life and try to achieve an even better sense of our own desires, goals and needs.

"You must know for which harbor you are headed if you are to catch the right winds to take you there."
~Seneca

284

We can learn to actively determine which steps to take to move toward our *self-selected* goals. We can learn to be stronger in our commitment to ourselves and what we want out of life. It's very difficult to arrive at our own self-determined destinations by following any other person's roadmap. We have to set our direction using our own inner compass, not one that belongs to someone else.

I am 42 years old and have spent most of my life living by someone else's expectations. I've tried to be what my parents, my partners, my children & my friends wanted me to be. Each time I tried to recover by their guidelines, I failed. I used drugs & alcohol to ease the pain I felt. When my partner said she'd take the kids & leave me, I molded myself into what she wanted me to be, by trying to stay clean & sober. I pushed myself to recover on her terms. Several times I cleaned up, got a job, dieted severely to lose weight & ignored my mental health issues to keep peace in our family. Each time I relapsed into mental illness because I was trying to live up to someone else's expectations, which set me up for failure.

My partner eventually left me & I sunk into a severe depression, wanting to end my life & attempting suicide several times. I started using drugs & alcohol again & my only goal in life was to die. I felt like I could never live up to other's expectations & I felt worthless.

But I learned something valuable...if I were going to clean up & try to recover again I was going to have to do it on my own terms, not because someone else was telling me I had to. My therapists repeatedly encouraged me to change my life and I rebelled, saying that I wasn't going to change for someone else again, because it didn't work.

I started seeing that I needed to change <u>for me</u>. Some deep-seeded voice way inside of me began to emerge, began to care that I lived. There was some hidden motivation inside of me that began to bring me into emotional recovery for what seemed like the hundredth time...but this time it was different. I was choosing recovery for me, not for someone else, and it was the strongest desire I had ever had to recover. It felt real & alive, unstoppable & honest. For the first time, I was changing because I wanted to. I was drawing on my own inner strengths. I had failed before because I was living for someone else. I quit living my life for my parents, my partner, my children or my therapist & I feel stronger in recovery than I ever have. This time I'm doing it for me & because of that, I will not fail.

~Julie Bayes,
Kansas Consumer

Chapter 9

Self-Assessment: Off-Course/On-Course

Look back over your lists of goals and strengths. Your challenge is to determine your own course, based on ideas you have come up with.

How much of what you have mapped out for your recovery is based on your own ideas, intuition and personal desires?

How much of it reflects your own strengths and deeply held values?

"Never give up, for that is just the place and time that the tide will turn."
~Harriet Beecher Stowe

How much of the journey you've planned is really based on what others expect of you?

Do you have any heavy expectations that you have picked up from others that seem to be loading you down? What do you want to do with them? Are there expectations and goals that you don't want to carry that you can release alongside the road to recovery?

By answering the following questions you may be better able to set your own course. You'll want to map out what your personal wants and expectations are for your recovery journey, versus ideas and goals that are based mostly in other people's desires or expectations.

You may find a pattern of compliance or compromise of your personal goals. That's OK, because you are taking the time now to recognize this pattern. By resetting your course now, you will avoid wasting a lot of time moving in a direction that will not lead you where you truly want to be. Take some time to answer the following questions thoroughly, based on past and present expectations.

My parents have always wanted me to...

My friends always say that I should...

My therapist thinks that I am...

My culture tells me that I should...

My children need me to...

"Take your life in
your own hands and
what happens?
A terrible thing:
no one to blame."
~Erica Jong

My significant other expects me to...

I want and need to...

If your goals have not been your own, review what you wish to achieve in your own recovery and reset your goals if necessary.

What We Want for Our Own Recovery is Most Important!

In a Strengths Recovery Approach, the focus is upon self-direction or self-determination *NOT* doing what you are told, or "compliance." The true compass for determining the direction of our recovery lies within each of us. We are the only person who can identify and work toward our personal dreams and goals. The quest begins with developing <u>our own roadmap</u> and heading towards *our* destination. After all, whose life are we living?

We have goals that are uniquely ours. All of our major goals should reflect *what we want*, not what we think others want for us or expect of us or what someone else desires in his or her recovery. True change occurs when we are clear about what *we want and why we want it!*

If we have people in our life who have goals for us, it may be helpful to listen to them, to try to understand their point of view, to know why they are encouraging us to move in a certain direction. Ultimately the goals they may have for us are *their* goals and *their* concerns, not ours.

As a traveler on the pathway of recovery, our recognition and identification of *our* dreams must direct and guide the course of our journey.

Driving Ourselves Day and Night: Falling Into the Speed Trap

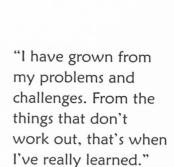

Sometimes we are so excited about the potential for recovery and so concerned with making up for lost time, that we want to make the entire journey in a day and a half. We put ourselves into overdrive and rush off and take a job, move out of where we are living, drop out of programs, decide we really didn't need the people who are trying to be our supporters after all. We may suddenly stop taking psychiatric medications rather than cut back slowly under medical supervision. We may feel we need to take on tasks that are genuinely beyond our capabilities or take on burdens that we are unprepared for, just to show ourselves or others how far we've come. We pour on the energy and relentlessly drive ourselves to do better, to do more, to show "them."

We take a job and we work so very hard to be a super employee. When our supervisor asks us to work more hours because we are such a good employee, we agree. We work 10, then 20, then 30, then 50 hours a week, then we take a second job.

Hey, we're recovered! We have it made! Then we wake up one day thoroughly depleted and exhausted, without the energy to go on, or we wobble off into the breakdown lane and lose much of the ground we have covered. When this kind of "crash" happens we may think "they" were right, we really can't cope with the demands of life. We don't recognize that we just tried to do more than is humanly possible just to prove ourselves capable!

Every person has vulnerabilities and limitations. We may not know what they are until we bump up against them. We have to pace ourselves and be gentle towards ourselves to gain a firm foothold on the path to recovery. We learn about ourselves, in part, through finding our limits.

We can also begin to see that we have nothing to prove to anyone else, really we don't. We don't need to change everything in our lives all at once, we don't need to be the super top employee and overwork ourselves beyond our energy reserves. We don't need to ignore the basic human needs for support or rest. We don't need to cut off all help from everyone around us just to prove we are independent.

> "I have grown from my problems and challenges. From the things that don't work out, that's when I've really learned."
> ~Carol Burnett

Chapter 9

Even without intensely over-working ourselves we can sometimes become exhausted on our recovery journey and lose the motivation we need to continue. We may feel ourselves running out of gas or going flat. We may not have learned to pace ourselves and may not recognize when it's time to slow down, rest and regain energy. Being on the wrong medication or being over-medicated can also lead to the feeling of exhaustion when we are striving very hard to recover.

SELF-ASSESSMENT:
Setting a Pace for Change

Each of us on a journey of recovery needs to shift into the gear that is comfortable for us as an individual.

☑ Do I want or need: (check all that apply)

- ❏ Lots of stimulation around me
- ❏ A very fast-paced life
- ❏ Trying something new every day
- ❏ A busy environment with lots of stimulation
- ❏ A moderate pace of life
- ❏ Taking on new challenges that allow me to stretch frequently
- ❏ Growing at a slow but steady pace
- ❏ A very ordered environment
- ❏ Regular habits and a set schedule
- ❏ Making small changes and seeing how that feels, before making any more changes in my life
- ❏ Quiet/peaceful environment with low demands

What pace do you want to set for your recovery?

How much stamina, or energy, do you have right now? How can you build your stamina if your energy reserves are low and your goals are high?

Have you out-paced your ability to contend with challenge in the past and found yourself in a danger zone? Describe what was that like.

What can you learn about your wants or needs from those experiences in order to nurture yourself and make your recovery a better experience in the future?

"Asking me to 'accept my limitations' is like asking me to stand in an open field and imagine high brick walls all around me with no way out. If I had 'accepted my limitations' there is no way I would be where I am now."
~Randy Johnson, Kansas Consumer Affairs Officer

Slowed by the Drag of Low Expectations/ Held Back by Self-Stigma

Some of us start out on our recovery journey but find ourselves being dragged backwards by the fears or negative attitudes of others. Sometimes our peers, friends, intimate partners or family members ask us to step on the brakes; they try to get us to back off on the changes we are making in our lives. They may become very upset or negative and "freak out" when we begin moving forward in our lives.

They may be afraid of being left behind or fearful about our changing relationship.

Sometimes people steer us toward experiences that do not respect our true strengths and capabilities (like having us work as a janitor when we already have a Masters degree). They may focus largely on our vulnerabilities, skill deficits and limitations. They ask us to avoid challenging ourselves to avoid stress that could lead to relapse.

When we are repeatedly told we must not do too much, or expect too much out of life, it sounds like people want to help us avoid potential problems. But constantly dwelling on our problems or symptoms really takes energy away from the recovery journey and makes us feel like we are "running out of gas." When we repeatedly receive negative messages, we may feel ourselves begin to shut down. We may become deeply demoralized and depressed and we may pull over to the sidelines of life and just give up.

We often pick up negative messages about our potential from the media or culture. Many people continue to have wrong assumptions about people with psychiatric disabilities—they may hold negative attitudes and beliefs, such as the idea that we are less intelligent, unable to work, dangerous, unworthy of friendship and incapable of having intimate relationships. Sometimes we even find these attitudes among the staff of mental health agencies who are there to help us!

Some consumer rights leaders have called the discrimination, stereotyping and prejudice we face "mentalism." Mentalism is like racism, sexism, homophobia and all the other limiting and oppressive ways of clumping people together and discounting them based on false or prejudiced ideas about their social group or status.

Self-Stigma

Self-stigma may result when we begin to see ourselves in a negative way based on social stigma, oppressive attitudes and the stories we have been told. Limiting and negative ideas based on stigma can become so ingrained in our minds that we simply see them as the truth about us.

Once we have bought negative messages about ourselves and our potential, self-limiting thoughts arise within us without question. Stigmatizing ideas can have a very negative impact on us, even though they are not in alignment with our values or with our personal strengths and the resources we have in our lives.

We can become our own worst enemy when we internalize, or take in, false ideas about our deficits and ignore our very real strengths. Once we accept limited ideas about who we are, it's like setting our auto-pilot on a very slow speed; our progress is self-limited, even without the direct drag of other people's negativity. Self-stigma can sideline us and interrupt our recovery journey.

Self-Stigma Self-Assessment

Self-stigma includes feelings of unworthiness, negative self-talk and discouraging beliefs we have about ourselves based in social stigma associated with psychiatric disorders. Do you think your recovery may be limited by self-stigma? If you have a feeling this may be true, conduct the following self-stigma check-up.

> Note: This self-assessment may bring up feelings, memories or thoughts that are difficult to deal with. You may feel sadness, anger or emotional pain. You may want to have someone who supports your recovery journey available to talk with to vent about how you are feeling as you answer these questions.

Remember, the purpose of this self-assessment is to identify self-stigma so you can begin to **heal and release it**. This assessment is intended to help drain off some of the old gunk we carry around in our system and release the brakes we may put on ourselves so we can move as rapidly as possible toward a positive future.

Write down any negative descriptions about yourself that you were given by members of your family, peers, friends, treatment providers or other individuals that have had an enduring affect on you.

"It's not who you are that holds you back, it's who you think you're not."
~Unknown

Chapter 9

293

Describe any negative assessments that you or others made of your ability, skills, knowledge, creativity, intelligence or worthiness that you came to believe to be true.

> "There is nothing either good or bad, but thinking makes it so."
> ~William Shakespeare

Write down any negative stories about any of your past actions that you continue to run over in your mind that negatively influence your motivation or behavior.

Write about any feelings of guilt, unworthiness or shame that you may have for your behavior from real events in the past or events you imagine may happen in the future.

> "No pessimist ever discovered the secrets of stars, or sailed to an uncharted land, or opened a new heaven to the human spirit."
> ~Helen Keller

Record any negative predictions that you or others may have made about your future or your potential for success in life.

Exploring the Impact of Self-Stigma

What kind of impact has self-stigma had on your life and your recovery journey? Examine the following results of self-stigma and assess whether self-stigma may be causing any of these negative consequences in your life. Are any of the following factors slowing you down or holding you back?

Lack of self-esteem and low self-worth. Do you find you have an inability to believe in yourself or to see that your life has value? Do you have a diminished self-image? Are you unable to believe that you could be successful? *Write down such feelings here...*

Over-dependence on the opinions and approval of others. Do you find yourself needing a tremendous amount of approval from others outside yourself for who you are and what you do? Do you feel unable to be nice to yourself, care for yourself or give yourself rewards or a pat on the back for something you did well? *Write about it here...*

A negative or pessimistic view of the world. If you have a negative view of yourself, you may also have a negative view of your entire world. Pessimism can make you see the world in terms of gloom and doom. *Write any pessimistic ideas you have about the world and the people in it here...*

"He who has so little knowledge of human nature as to seek happiness by changing anything but his own disposition will waste his life away in fruitless efforts."
~Samuel Johnson

"I have learned from experience that the greater part of our happiness or misery depends on our dispositions and not on our circumstances."
~Martha Washington

Chapter 9

Self-pity. Do you find yourself spending a lot of the day feeling sorry for yourself and how you have been treated in life? Do you feel unable to view yourself in any role other than that of victim? *Write about how self-pity is affecting your life here...*

Cynicism. Do you have a "yes, but" way of looking at life? Do you doubt the sincerity of others who are trying to help and support you? Do you find yourself blocking the support of family or friends, convincing yourself that they don't really care about you? Do you mistrust opportunities, thinking they won't really lead you anywhere? *Write about how this affects you...*

"We don't see things as they are, we see them as we are."
~Anais Nin

Self-fulfilling negative prophecies. What we believe often has an effect on what happens to us. *Has self-stigma led you to experience further failure, rejection or resulted in a pattern of self-destructive behavior?*

Immobilization. Does self-stigma cause you to be unable to act, make changes or take risks, leaving you feeling stuck and unable to move in a more positive direction? *Write about it here...*

Healing Self-Stigma

How can we begin to let go of self-stigma?

In discussing his personal struggle with self-stigma, New York consumer Michael Spennato, provides this advice: *"We need to give ourselves a chance to grow and develop into the meaningful person we were meant to be,"* he says. *"Think well of ourselves. Believe in a god. Speak and cry out, 'I am human.'"*

It takes time and effort to heal self-stigma. If you know self-stigma is slowing you down, you might want to try some of the following activities:

Read the stories of people who have recovered/ Spend time with recovery role models

We can learn from other people who struggled with self-stigma and overcame it. By spending time with people who have grown beyond self-stigma we can find it is possible to heal such feelings in our life.

Join self-help and disability rights groups

Self-help groups can help us through "consciousness raising" activities that make us aware of the *external* oppression that lead to *internalized* oppression and self-stigma. When we share our experiences and hope we can begin to understand that we are not alone—we come to know why we feel as we do and how we can overcome internalized oppression. We can begin to work with others to change public attitudes. We feel empowered instead of disempowered.

Make amends to anyone you have hurt or harmed/ Practice forgiveness toward self and others

Ed Knight, a leading consumer recovery educator who lives in Colorado, has pointed out that we may believe we have a "no fault biological brain disorder" that covers us for any action we take when we are psychotic. But Ed points out that we often carry around the burden of unhealed guilt and shame because we have not taken responsibility for our own actions. He recommends healing these feelings by making amends, whenever possible, for any behavior that has caused harm or distress to another human being.

"No one can make you feel inferior without your consent."
~Eleanor Roosevelt

"If you're going to hold someone down you're going to have to hold on to the other end of the chain. You are confined by your own repression."
~Toni Morrison

Chapter 9

297

We may be holding onto terrible feelings about the harm others have done to us. Learning to forgive others can help free us and heal our emotional wounds. Forgiveness does not mean forgetting our experiences or allowing anyone to continue to abuse us. It does mean letting go of the ongoing anger and constant thoughts of revenge, hurt or victimization.

Sometimes we have to let go of the idea that we can heal the relationship that caused us pain or trauma. We may have to accept that we will never achieve a sense of justice or peace in that relationship. We may need to work on a larger scale to end abuse or mistreatment as a way of healing our world and ourselves. We may achieve peace of mind or increase social justice by working to end abuse or support other people who have been victims of abuse.

We may also need to work to forgive and accept ourselves as part of our healing. We can come to love and respect ourselves as imperfect, but striving and growing, human beings.

Use cognitive techniques/Positive self-talk to challenge negativity

We may need to work hard to reject the negative thoughts that grew from stigma that now slow or block our progress in recovery. We can use cognitive techniques that have proven to be effective in healing negativity and depression. These involve "thought stopping" and "thought substitution."

> "Although the connections are not always obvious, personal change is inseparable from social and political change."
> ~Harriet Lerner

When you become aware of having a negative thought that arises from self-stigma, silently say: "STOP!!!"

Use visualization (i.e. make a picture in your mind) to make this challenge to your negative thought very dramatic. You may want to visualize a stop light, a warning sign or a knight with shining armor blocking the path of the negative thought. Create your own personal symbol. Immediately after blocking the negative thought, substitute a different thought, one that is much more positive and self-supporting.

For example, if you often think: "I'm a loser," visualize a "STOP" sign and substitute a positive thought such as "I can succeed!" *The more your thinking includes strong inner feelings the better this technique will work.*

It can take a lot of effort and time to change negative thought patterns. Over time, as we change our thinking, we will find that we feel better about ourselves and better about the people around us. We will find we have more energy for our recovery journey. We begin to appreciate the positive opportunities and resources around us much more clearly!

Undertake self-advocacy

Some major roadblocks to recovery have been built on a foundation of social stigma. There are many barriers built into policies and systems that slow our ability to achieve full recovery. These include disincentives or loss of benefits for going to work, workplace discrimination against people with disabilities, the high costs for medications that bump up against the limits of the medical benefits that we have, the lack of housing subsidies and many others.

It is important for us to get to know our rights under the law and to become increasingly assertive in expressing our rights. It is also important to join with others to change attitudes and laws through self-advocacy. We can work together to break down the major barriers that have been erected which put roadblocks in our way.

Driving in Circles: Having an Unclear Destination or Few Clear Goals

We may be so clouded by concerns and expectations that we cannot see our own goals clearly. We can become overwhelmed if we have inaccessible goals or try to achieve too many things at once. Sometimes we have set our goals so far out in the future that we can't see a clear path toward achieving them. Having too many destinations on a trip can also leave us with our travel plans confused.

To address these pitfalls, identify a few very clear goals and take them on one-by-one. For some of us, getting out of bed in the morning is where our goals must begin. Once we are successfully doing that, we can continue with new short-term goals, one small practical step after another, to improve our daily lives.

Having a clear roadmap for the journey is important. Remember our goals need to be specific, achievable, meaningful to us, and have realistic time frames. Overstating what we can reasonably achieve in the near future can cause us to hit a wall of self-defeat. **If you don't seem to be getting anywhere, check your goals. If they are overwhelming or**

"Often we allow ourselves to be upset by small things we should despise and forget. We lose many irreplaceable hours brooding over grievances that, in a year's time, will be forgotten by us and by everybody. No, let us devote our life to worthwhile actions and feelings, to great thoughts, real affections and enduring undertakings."
~Andre Maurois

Chapter 9

299

confusing, reset them so they are specific and realistic and reflect your current needs and abilities.

When we are doing well we may feel we can take on the world, but it's best to break each day down into a structured set of tasks to be accomplished and progress one step at a time.

It is often worthwhile to keep to-do lists and a daily journal of the things we want to accomplish and cross each activity off the list when we achieve them. Many of us have found that creating a positive structure and a schedule for our day really supports our recovery.

If some item on your list of goals and action steps keeps getting moved to the next day, and then the day after that, it may not be the right goal to work on at this time. If so, you can take that goal off your to-do list for now and come back to it later when you feel you can meet the challenge. You may decide you want to keep the goal. Break it down into smaller short-term goals and action steps that you know you can accomplish at this time.

Even though we may set long-term goals or destinations far in the future, we have to use the time and energy that we have right now to get to the "next place" on our journey. We come to appreciate and enjoy the process of recovery itself.

We can find ways to enjoy the place we are at in our life right now, the moment in time we are living. Over time, we eventually get to our greater far-off destinations. Our need to make progress doesn't have to stop us from enjoying where we are. We don't want to feel we must wait until we achieve our long-term goals to begin to have a good life.

Thrown Off-Track by Symptoms

While this workbook doesn't focus on mental health problems, it's true that symptoms can come up from time to time that throw us off-course. By attending to self-care and self-managing our psychiatric symptoms we can continue on our journey without getting completely derailed.

> "Be patient toward all that is unresolved in your heart and try to love the questions themselves like locked rooms or books written in a foreign tongue. Live the questions now. Perhaps you will then gradually without noticing it live your way some distant day into the answers."
> ~Rainer Maria Rilke

There are several processes that can help us avoid severe symptoms. One is WRAP, the *Wellness Recovery Action Plan* developed by consumer recovery educator Mary Ellen Copeland (1997). Her work shows us that the best way to manage symptoms is to contend with them *before* they become a serious pitfall. We can make plans to maintain personal wellness on a day-to-day basis and actively contending with triggers and early warning signs before things start breaking down. If we plan ahead of time for what we want to happen, we can stay in the driver's seat even in crisis. We can guide the help, treatment and support that we receive even when experiencing serious mental health problems.

We can teach ourselves to monitor our own emotions and thinking in order to identify when we are under stress. When symptoms come into play, we can develop personalized strategies to contend with them. For example, we can learn to rebalance and slow racing or disorganized thoughts by doing things like focusing on our breathing. We can actively change rapid thoughts and negative self-talk.

> "Love yourself first and everything else falls into line. You really have to love yourself to get anything done in this world."
> ~Lucille Ball

EXERCISE:
Thought Journal

You can record your negative thoughts in a journal. Start with your most prevalent repetitive thought. Once you are aware of your thoughts you can practice countering them with more productive or positive thoughts. Record those, too. We can do a lot to change the quality of our thinking! Here are some examples:

Racing thought:	Countering thought:
"I can't go on anymore."	"I only have to get through this one moment."
"I'm no use to anyone."	"I am a valuable and worthwhile person and my friends and family really do need me."
"I'll never be well."	"I have made a lot of progress toward recovery."
"I'm out of control."	"I can remain in this moment and I can calm myself."

> # EXERCISE:
> ## Positive Thought Collage
>
> You may want to create one or more positive thought posters or collages that you can hang up around your home where you can see them every day. To make such a poster, cut positive phrases and images out of magazines and paste or glue them on a piece of poster board or cardboard along with positive images.
>
> Reading positive statements about yourself on a daily basis will help you to feel better and can eventually end negative ideas that many of us have so often.

Reframe relapse

OK, so sometimes we lose it. Is it the end of the road? We can choose to view relapse *as a part of the process of recovery*. The idea is to learn more about ourselves and our needs and vulnerabilities in the process. We should never view relapse as a failure or the end of the recovery journey!

> *[In my recovery] progress did not come easy, by any means. Often it was a matter of reminding myself that three steps forward and two steps back, is still progress. Other times, it has been necessary to try to conceive of the fact that three steps forward and five steps back, is still progress... Relapse is a part of recovery. It is not a failure.*
>
> *~Donna Orrin,*
> *Michigan Consumer and President of Creative Connections*

Riding the Brake Pedal: Fear of Failure and Fear of Success

Both fears of failure and fears of success can inhibit our progress. Recognizing the reasoning behind our fears is the first step in learning to no longer be afraid. Knowing exactly what we are afraid of can help us calm ourselves and overcome our fears. We can forge ahead, even when recovery seems risky.

SELF-ASSESSMENT:
☑What Do I Fear?

- ❏ I'm afraid someone will laugh at me or think less of me.
- ❏ My parents always said I would fail. It will make what they said true.
- ❏ It will mean I am not worthy.
- ❏ I'm afraid I'm just going to fall on my face.
- ❏ I'm afraid of taking too much on, because I might become ill.
- ❏ I will feel ashamed of myself if I blow this opportunity.
- ❏ Other fears:

What is the worst thing that has happened to you when you felt like you failed at something?

What can you learn from that experience? Can you see the experience differently now?

What inner and outer strengths did you use to rebound from that experience?

We will experience some disappointment and failure if we try anything at all. Pulling the covers up over our heads will not save us. Unfortunately, we often remember our failures more than our successes. We can make an effort to remember our successes and learn from the things that didn't work out in our lives. In fact, we often learn a great deal from things that don't work out. We can't let our fears stop our recovery.

SELF-ASSESSMENT:
Assess the Fear of Success

Identify what it is about succeeding that scares you.

☑Check all that apply

❑ If I succeed people will expect more of me.
❑ When I succeed I always push myself to outdo myself and end up exhausted.
❑ I feel like an imposter when I succeed, like I'm fooling everyone.
❑ I'm afraid my success will ultimately end and I'll crash.
❑ I'm afraid of losing supports and benefits.
❑ I'll end up looking like a fool.
❑ I don't deserve to succeed.
❑ Other fears:

How can you deal with the fear of success?

A good way to counteract fears is by keeping a record of our thoughts. We can begin to challenge these fearful statements with strength-based statements of our own. For example, if we hear ourselves say "I don't deserve to succeed," we can repeat a more positive thought to our self like, "I have the right to be happy," or "I can do this!"

We all deserve to have success in our lives. We can start allowing positive things into our lives and embrace the small successes that we have. It is important to reward ourselves and celebrate even the smallest positive movement and changes in our lives.

The following is a list of the kinds of things that could be celebrated each day. If we start celebrating small things, we will learn to accept and celebrate the bigger successes in our life!

"We should not let our fears hold us back from pursuing our hopes."
~John F. Kennedy

My Daily Successes

☑ Today I successfully:

- ❑ Got up on time
- ❑ Took a shower
- ❑ Walked my dog or played with my pet
- ❑ Kept an appointment
- ❑ Ate well-balanced meals
- ❑ Attended school, work or other commitments
- ❑ Got enough sleep
- ❑ Made a phone call I needed to make
- ❑ Talked to a friend
- ❑ Cleaned my apartment
- ❑ Finished a project I've been working on
- ❑ Worked on my Personal Recovery Plan
- ❑ Paid my bills
- ❑ Watered my house plants
- ❑ Studied for my class
- ❑ Had lunch with a friend
- ❑ Washed the dishes
- ❑ Flossed my teeth
- ❑ Called my brother
- ❑ Read my Bible
- ❑ Meditated
- ❑ Went outside in the sunshine

"Grab the broom of anger and drive off the beast of fear."
~Nora Zeale Hurston

Chapter 9

The important thing is not to check off everything on this list, the important thing is to **make your own list** of things you know you can successfully complete. Then you can begin adding items to your list that may be a bit more challenging and use your strengths to accomplish them. Take it slow, take it moment by moment, and celebrate every step of the way!

When the Going Gets Boring

Okay, so we have our list of short-term goals and it seems to go on forever, leaving us feeling tired and a little overwhelmed. Or we've made a little progress but it doesn't seem that great, in fact we are feeling a little bored. We may have been working, working, working on our recovery journey and it is starting to feel less like an adventure and more like a demanding business trip. The day-by-day grind of working on our recovery may be getting a little stale.

We are the master of our own dreams and desires! If we are bored on the recovery journey, we can open ourselves up to new possibilities, route out a new adventure or create a new point of interest. We can spice up our journey by stopping at unique little road-side attractions. We never know what may come our way if we take a few risks. Risk-taking is key to over-coming the doldrums. If we find our goals are a little too boring, we can find ways to improve them and make them more exciting. This is our journey to recovery and it can include a lot of fun!

We can put some more enjoyable activities into our short-term goals and then celebrate our new experience! Some fun things to add to a journey might include:

- Finding a bargain outfit at the thrift store
- Climbing the rock face at the new sporting goods store
- Watching a ball game and cheering your team
- Taking a ride in the country or a walk in nature
- Watching a favorite old movie and eating popcorn
- Inviting a new friend to go for a walk or a cup of coffee
- Giving yourself a foot massage
- Going to the lake and watching the sailboats
- Attending an art show or exploring a museum
- Dancing to oldies in the living room
- Flying a kite

- Lying in the grass at night and watching the moon and stars
- Volunteering at the animal shelter and walking big, furry dogs
- Starting to sketch or paint
- Joining a club or getting involved in community projects

The list can go on and on. It doesn't take a lot of money to have more enjoyment in our lives if we are creative.

Write some new ideas for spicing up your journey here:

Feeling Lost

Sometimes we leave our map at home when we start out on our journey. We need to pull over, make a U-turn and go back to the house and get it. We need it! After all the careful planning we have done, we have to apply our ideas to our daily life. Our recovery journey doesn't happen in our minds or on a piece of paper, it takes shape and is tested in our daily lives. We have to put the rubber to the road or "walk the talk." We can keep our lists of strengths and goals handy and available for reference. We can tell others about our plans and the steps we are taking on our journey. We can ask trusted people to give us useful directions when we are feeling a little lost. We can post reminders around our house to remember our desired destinations and pin up affirmations about our goals.

It takes many weeks of effort for any of us to change a habit. In the beginning it is probably a good idea to plan a structure for our day that helps us to accomplish the short-term goals we have set. Until a new activity becomes a habit it can easily drop away and our old habits will return. People in sports and music know the key to success is practice, practice, practice and the same is true for the journey.

Recovery is made up of hundreds of small changes made day-by-day. We don't want to begin a big recovery adventure and then find in a month or two that we are back in bed or sitting in the recliner, in front of the TV, smoking cigarettes, drinking a soft drink and longing for a fuller life.

"Live life to the fullest. You have to color outside the lines once in a while if you want to make your life a masterpiece. Laugh some every day, keep growing, keep dreaming, keep following your heart. The important thing is not to stop questioning."
~Albert Einstein

Chapter 9

"The man who moved a mountain was the one who began by carrying away small stones."
~Chinese Proverb

Celebrate!!

When we make it through a roadblock, take charge of our life, begin making decisions and change our opinion of ourselves and our potential, it's time to CELEBRATE! How about doing a ritual of writing the negative thoughts we have had about ourselves on slips of paper and burning them up in a barbeque at the park? How about sending a love letter to ourself saying how amazing it is that we have been through so much and are still beautiful people? How about joining in solidarity with a few others and having a speak-out about claiming recovery? How about ending the sharing with a candlelight ceremony that honors our resilience, or the ability to "hang in there," and keep bouncing back?

How will you celebrate?

"A light heart
lives long!"
~William Shakespeare

"Anticipate the
good so that
you may enjoy it."
~Ethiopian Proverb

References & Resources

References

Deegan, P. (1996). Recovery as a journey of the heart. *Psychiatric Rehabilitation Journal, 9*(3), 91-97.

Copeland, M. E. (1997). Wellness Recovery Action Plan. West Dummerston, VT: Peach Press.

Copeland, M. E. (1998). Winning Against Relapse. Oakland, CA: New Harbinger Publications.

Kramer, P.M. & Gagne, C. (1997). Barriers to recovery and empowerment for people with psychiatric disabilities. In Spaniol, L., Gagne, C. & Koehler, M. (Eds.), *Psychological and Social Aspects of Psychiatric Disability*. Boston, MA: Boston University, Center for Psychiatric Rehabilitation.

Nelson, Portia (1994). *There's a Hole in My Sidewalk: The Romance of Self-Discovery.* Hillsboro, OR: Beyond Words Publishing, Inc.

Orrin, D. (1997). Struggles of mental illness, toward the development of quality lives. In L. Spaniol, C. Gagne & M. Koehler (Eds.), *Psychological and Social Aspects of Psychiatric Disability* (pp. 138-155). Boston, MA: Boston University, Center for Psychiatric Rehabilitation.

Spennato, M. G. (November/December, 1997). *Through the eyes of a stranger: part 1.* New York City Voices. Retrieved January 25, 2001 from: http://www.newyorkcityvoices.org/nov97c.html.

Stone, H. & Winkelman, S. (1993). *Embracing Your Inner Critic: Turning Self-Criticism into a Creative Asset.* San Francisco, CA: Harper.

Resources

Chasing Away the Clouds by Douglas Pages (Blue Mountain Press, 1998).

Clear Your Past, Change Your Future: Proven Techniques for Inner Explorations and Healing by Lynne D. Finney (New Harbinger Publications, 1997).

Talking to Yourself: Learning the Language of Support by Pamela E. Butler (Harper San Francisco, 1983).

The Dance of Connection: How to Talk to Someone When You're Mad, Hurt, Scared, Frustrated, Insulted, Betrayed, or Desperate by Harriet Lerner (HarperCollins, 2001).

Chapter Ten

Rest Stops and Travel Tips

This chapter explores the need for breaks and rest stops during the recovery journey. It also provides suggestions for ways to tune-up recovery and avoid burn out.

The Need for Tune-Ups and Rest Stops

The journey of recovery is a long and winding road. We've gone to the mountaintop to gain a long-range vision. We've made a turnaround and started our recovery journey. We may have attempted to drive straight through from one destination to the next. We may have experienced quiet, calm periods that seem like country roads and periods of rapid change that feel like speedy expressways. We can be intensely challenged by the recovery process and feel like we are hanging onto the side of cliff by our fingernails or trying to make our way through the dark shadows of a narrow canyon.

Sometimes our recovery journey goes well and we feel like we are finely tuned and running flawlessly. At other times we sputter along on two cylinders. Sometimes we feel like the changes we've made have taken us beyond the capacity of the shock absorbers in our system. After doing so much good work we may simply feel a little burned out and low on energy.

In any long journey, there's a need for revitalization, tune-ups and rest stops!

It may be time for us to take a break. We need periods when we intensively nurture ourselves and relax in order to rejuvenate our mind, body and spirit. By taking frequent tune-ups and rest stops we relax, rebalance and celebrate our accomplishments. So, pull over for a moment. Get out and stretch your legs.

This chapter supports our need for rest stops and tune-ups that refuel and refresh us. If we undertake self-care and bring more balance into our lives *before* we find ourselves in a danger zone, it's easier to keep going. If we slow down and celebrate each step we take, we find the daily work of recovery is much easier to sustain.

AHHHH...Letting Go of Stress

Let's acknowledge something straight out—many of us have a vulnerability to stress. We don't do all that well under very stressful conditions.

"Only those who are able to relax can create, and then ideas reach the mind like lightening."
~Cicero

Does this mean we must wait for a stress-free time before moving out on our journey of recovery? No! Stress-free times don't exist. If we try to pull back from life, and avoid challenging experience we feel very stressed. In fact, living a life of disability and facing each day without hope or meaningful activity is often more stressful than taking active steps to improve our lives. We may think we can hide from stress, but it turns out that under-stimulation, social isolation and inactivity are some of the most stressful things we can experience as human beings!

Let's acknowledge something else. The process of recovery does include experiences that are stressful, because <u>we are moving beyond what we thought of as our limits</u>. There is no doubt that going through the day-to-day challenges and changes associated with recovery can add stress to our lives. Stress even comes along with positive life changes and pleasurable experiences.

We accept stress as a part of life. Stress is inevitable and can even be desirable. A certain level of stress motivates us; without some stress we wouldn't accomplish anything. But, too much stress can have serious consequences. We can learn to anticipate stress and take action before we feel unhappy or find ourselves, or our relationships, in trouble.

What do we feel under conditions of stress? We may be constantly on guard and feel exhausted. We may worry a lot and have difficulty shutting off our racing thoughts. We may feel like our stomach is in knots or our mind is in a blur, and we may be unable to think straight or concentrate. Feeling anxious and stressed is not a state of well-being. On the other hand, most people have experienced such feelings under conditions of stress; these are common human experiences, not symptoms of a psychiatric disorder. Fortunately, there are some very simple ways we can relax and overcome any anxiety we may be feeling.

We can begin to notice the effects of stress. Our muscles may feel tight and our breathing may become shallow and fast. Our blood pressure and heart rate may increase and we may have headaches or feel "butterflies" or sick to our stomach. We may lack energy, have difficulty concentrating and experience poor memory. High levels of stress can leave us feeling irritable and drained.

What specific sensations do you experience when you are feeling a lot of stress?

If we anticipate stress we can develop certain attitudes and behaviors that help us contend well with it, or we can decide to temporarily reduce the amount of stress in our life if we find ourselves becoming overwhelmed. The key to managing stress is to recognize it and deal with it effectively. We need to have several tools ready to use to work on the stress and tension we will naturally feel in our lives as we set goals, challenge ourselves and take on new roles.

This section includes several techniques that help us feel calm in times of stress. The techniques are simple, take just a few minutes and require no equipment. Most of these tools can be used anywhere, anytime.

Pick a technique and try it. Learn more about it; give it a chance. We shouldn't give up or try to *force* ourselves to relax. We just let it happen. Relaxation is a natural process, although it takes practice until it becomes a comfortable routine.

> "Drop the idea that you are Atlas carrying the world on your shoulders. The world would goon even without you.
> Don't take yourself so seriously."
> ~Norman Vincent Peale

EXERCISE:
Following the Breath For Relaxation

Get into a comfortable position in a chair with your feet planted squarely on the floor. Close your eyes, or half close them and fix your eyes on one place without looking around. Concentrate on your breath. For a few moments just feel your breath as you inhale and exhale. Don't try to change how you are breathing. If you are not doing so already, begin to breath in through your nostrils, and breath out through your nostrils or your mouth.

Follow your breath down your airway into the center of your body. Feel your abdomen rise as you breathe in and your chest settle as you breathe out. You may notice that your breathing becomes deeper than normal. Begin to lengthen each breath. Breathe in while counting from 1 to 10, and breathe out while counting backwards from 9 to 1. When you take your next breath in start with number 2, 3, 4, 5, 6, 7, 8, 9, 10. When you breath out start with 9, 8, 7, 6, 5, 4, 3, 2, 1, then in— 2, 3, 4, 5, 6,7, 8, 9, 10, out 9, 8, 7, 6, 5, 4, 3, 2, 1.

If you cannot take such long breaths, just try to take your breath to the count you can comfortably reach. Don't force your breath, or hold it too long.

Continue this breathing exercise for three to five minutes, or as long as you can focus on your breath and counting your breaths. When you are done slowly open your eyes and begin to come back into awareness. You may feel a little light-headed. Most of us are used to breathing very shallowly. It's OK, that sensation will pass. Just don't get up too fast!

More Breath Work Exercises

Breathing has a strong effect on our mind, body and moods. By simply paying attention to our breathing, without making any changes whatsoever, we move toward relaxation. Here are a few more simple breathing exercises that can help us relax quickly.

Method 1. This is an old <u>yoga technique</u> suggested by the wellness expert, Dr. Andrew Weil.

First, sit with your back straight. Place the tip of your tongue next to the ridge just behind your upper front teeth. You will be exhaling out of your mouth and around your tongue. Purse your lips a little bit if this feels awkward.

Exhale totally through your mouth, making a "whoosh" sound.

Next close your mouth and inhale quietly through your nose to a count of four (don't count out loud, just in your mind).

Hold your breath for a count of seven.

Exhale completely through your mouth, making the whoosh sound as you count to eight.

This cycle is one breath. Inhale again and repeat the sequence three more times for a total of four breaths. Do this at least twice a day.

This technique works like a natural tranquilizer. Use it whenever anything upsetting happens to you or when you are aware of tension in your body.

Method 2. This is a very simple <u>two-step breath</u> exercise.

Sit straight. Inhale, filling the bottom of your lungs first, then add more air to top off the top of your lungs as you breathe in through your nose. Then breathe out slowly. Visualize the tension flowing out of your body as you breathe out. Repeat 3 to 5 times.

This exercise is an easy one to perform, especially if you are feeling extremely anxious. The focus on the breath will help you refocus any negative emotion or energy.

Take a few moments and try one of these techniques. How did it make you feel? Are you more relaxed?

"Stress is basically a disconnection from the earth, a forgetting of the breath. It believes everything is an emergency. Nothing is that important. Just lie down."
~Natalie Goldberg

"I breathe in the fullness and richness of life."
~Louise L. Hay

Chapter 10

Simple exercises like this one can relax us and help lessen any anxiety that we are feeling. There are many breathing and stress reduction exercises available. Being aware of our own breath is a valuable tool in lessening stress and it takes just a few minutes of our time to start feeling better!

Muscle Relaxation Techniques

Here are three methods for relaxing muscular tension and releasing the stuck energy we have stored in our tight, sore muscles.

Method 1. Tense/Relax. Tighten any muscle that you want to relax, such as your back muscles. Focus on and feel the tension where you are tightening. Now let the muscle become loose and limp. Feel the relaxation flow into the sore muscle. Do this 5-6 times or until you can feel that the muscle is really relaxed.

Method 2. Body scan. In your mind, briefly scan every muscle in your body from the tips of your toes to the top of your head (be sure to include your scalp and jaw). When you reach a muscle that feels tight, use your thought process to let it become limp and relaxed. This technique takes some practice but can be very effective. Remember, don't force yourself to relax, just let it happen.

Method 3: Limp rag doll. Do a short breathing exercise (like the 2-step breath described earlier). With your mind, imagine that you are a limp rag doll. Feel your mind and body become limp and relaxed. You may use whatever image you like that works for you (how about a cat lounging in the sun or warm butter melting into a biscuit). Become physically limp as your mind moves you through each muscle of your body.

Pick one of these techniques and try it. Were you able to relax any muscle tension? How did it feel?

"If you take muddy water and still it, it gradually becomes clear. If you bring something to rest in order to move it, it gradually comes alive."
~Lao-Tzu

There are many methods that can be used to promote relaxation. Some of them include massage, biofeedback, aromatherapy, self-hypnosis, taking calcium supplements or bubble baths! There is no one method that works for everyone. Try several approaches and see what works best for you.

Doing relaxation exercises once or twice won't have much of an effect on stress, but as we take time to learn to relax and practice these techniques our bodies and minds begin to remember the state of relaxation more deeply. We can build relaxation into our everyday life and get support when we need it.

What are some techniques that you currently use to help you relax? How do they help you?

Rebalancing Ourselves When We are Out of Alignment

How can we find balance in our life? Finding the proper balance and maintaining a high level of well-being are key to developing a meaningful and satisfying life. We cannot assume we are in a natural state of balance; it is something we may have to work to achieve and maintain. Many times we ignore our own needs and our life becomes unstable and our health and/or mental health suffers. A big part of the journey of recovery is about understanding and honoring our own needs and creating a more balanced life.

What do you do to realign yourself and achieve balance if you find your life is too full of stress and out of balance?

One of the major balance points in life is the balance between being focused on others and taking time for ourselves. Most of us have a lot of demands placed on us. Family, friends, church, work, school or other social groups are important and make life richer, but it is equally important to balance social time with time for ourselves. We may be doing a lot for other people but neglecting self-care.

On the other hand, we may be too withdrawn and need to balance our solitude with positive relationships and shared activities. If we spend too much time on our own, even if it is time spent in positive self-care, we can feel lonely and empty. Giving too much of our time to others can leave us feeling tired and drained.

How is the balance in your life around taking time for yourself and spending time with others?

> "No one is in control of your happiness but you; therefore, you have the power to change anything about yourself or your life that you want to change."
> ~Barbara De Angelis

What is one thing you will do to improve or maintain that balance?

We may need to build a positive lifestyle that includes plenty of self-care and avoid certain activities that make stress worse. Positive lifestyle changes can allow us to go further on the path of recovery. The following assessment can help you determine how stress-resistant your life is.

> "What we put into every moment is all we have."
> ~Gilda Radner

SELF-ASSESSMENT:
Stress and Lifestyle

☑ Take a look at your life. How well are you taking care of yourself? Check all that apply.

- ❑ I eat healthy meals three times a day.
- ❑ I avoid smoking.
- ❑ I avoid caffeine.
- ❑ I exercise regularly.
- ❑ I set aside time each day for myself, to meditate, be creative or pray.
- ❑ I take time to enjoy nature or my pets.
- ❑ I spend time being with supportive people.
- ❑ I do something to help others.
- ❑ I listen to music that I enjoy.
- ❑ I get all the sleep I need.

All of these activities have been found to help people manage stress levels better and allow a greater sense of balance in one's life.

Spending all our time in a state of misalignment isn't much fun. If we are out of touch with our needs we feel out of sorts. It is important to keep our life in perspective. We are not perfect. All that is required of us is to try to do our best, given everything that life has thrown at us.

What do you want to do to start taking care of yourself a little better?

"Very often a change of self is needed more than a change of scene."
~A.C. Benson

"When you have two pennies left in the world, buy a loaf of bread with one, and a lily with the other."
~Chinese Proverb

Chapter 10

EXERCISE:
Finding Balance

We all need to work on achieving balance. But how do we know when we are there? Here's a simple exercise to find out where our life may be out of balance.

Envision your typical week. Think about all the activities you carry out, all the roles you play, what your responsibilities are and what you enjoy doing that *gives* you a lot of energy. Consider those tasks or relationships that are demanding and *take* a lot of your energy. Which of these are absolutely necessary? Envision yourself in each of these activities, paying particular attention to the amount of time and importance you give each activity and how the activity makes you feel.

Make a chart or map of how you spend each week including the different periods of activity. Draw a large circle or square on a piece of paper. Divide the shape into sections that represent all of the activities, roles, responsibilities, and fun things you give time to. Try to make each section represent the amount of time that you give to that activity by making a larger or smaller size. You may want to use color or design to characterize each kind of activity. Label each section with the name of the activity. Sit back and study the map you've created of your current life. Ask yourself the following questions:

Is there anything about your life that you would like to change?

Is there anything that you'd like to begin to limit or cut out completely?

Do you have a balance across the different areas of you life or are there big differences with some areas receiving a lot of you time and energy and others receiving little or no time and attention? Is any domain or area of life totally lacking attention? (Remember the domains include: having a home, assets, working or other productive activity, learning, social relationships, intimacy and sexuality, recreation and leisure, wellness and spirituality)

Now take a second piece of paper and make a map of how you would like your life to look, using the same process. Look at both of the maps together. Do they look different? Seeing your life laid out visually can help you look carefully at how balanced or unbalanced your life actually is and how you can make changes that incorporate the things you really would like to have in your life.

Think about your new life map. Take a close look at what you would really like to change. What are these changes? Why are they important to you?

How can you go about reorganizing your day or week to reflect your new priorities? What specific changes will you make over the next few days?

The next few months?

The next year?

Make sure the goals and plans you've developed fit with the new map you want for your life. Set new goals to match your ideas for gaining better balance in life.

Spend Time Reflecting on and Enjoying the Present Moment

There isn't much encouragement in our culture to enjoy what is happening <u>right now</u>. We are bombarded with television messages about what we *should* buy and what we *must* have in order to be happy. We know the standard of living we see in the media is unattainable to most people, but we always have desires and want more than we have in our lives.

It is also natural for us to dwell on what's happened in the past and the losses we have experienced, even though there isn't anything we can do to change what we've already been through. On the other hand, we may look forward so much, and be living for the future attainment of our goals, that we miss the sweetness that we can experience right now.

Thornton Wilder, author of the popular play *Our Town,* once said, "Enjoy your ice cream while it is on your plate." We can make the decision to savor what's on our plate or we can let it melt while we wait for a better flavor to come along.

Living in the moment and enjoying what we have can give us a greater sense of peace over our past and create a base of enjoyment that allows us to appreciate what happens in our lives in the future. We don't want to miss the opportunities we have to enjoy the goodness available in the life we are living in the present.

What are you enjoying around you right now? Describe its message to you.

"Why are we here? We're here to feel the joy of life pulsing in us now."
~Joyce Carol Oates

"If you never change your mind, why have one?"
~Edward De Bono

324

Remember the old adage: "Take time to stop and smell the roses"? Our five senses can play a role in our happiness in recovery. We can become more mindful of the beauty around us. We can look at a single flower, observe its beauty, notice its fragrance and touch its silky petals. It's surprising how such a small thing can soothe us and bring us enjoyment.

We may recall the smell of fresh baked cookies our mother or grandmother made us. We can remember the warm feeling we had when we smelled the scent of these delicious concoctions. We can bake ourselves a batch of cookies using our old family recipe. We can remember the fun times we had in our life and get involved in similar activities today. If we liked to swim in a pond, we can walk to a pond or public pool close by and enjoy the light dancing on the surface of the water. If we want to, we can bring a suit and jump in!

Maybe we have a pet that we love to play with or talk to. The sense of touch can bring pleasure to us as we feel the wonderful soft fur of our dog or cat, and listening to the sound of our cat purring can be soothing and bring a smile to our face.

What comforting memories do you have that are brought back by a scent or smell? How can you use your senses to comfort yourself?

"Everyday...look at a beautiful poem, listen to some beautiful music, and if possible, say some reasonable thing..."
~Goethe

"Once in a while you can get shown the light in the strangest of places if you look at it right."
~Jerry Garcia

Chapter 10

325

EXERCISE:
Using the Five Senses to Achieve Enjoyment

By becoming more aware of sights, sounds, fragrances, sensations and tastes we can bring more joy into our journey of recovery.

List things you see, hear, touch, taste and smell that bring you pleasure:

How can you bring more simple enjoyments into your life?

Just being aware of the people, places and events that bring pleasure to your life can add joy to your recovery journey. Do you enjoy sporting events, movies, long walks, music or dance, hanging out with friends, eating your favorite foods or doing crafts or hobbies?

List one or two things that you really enjoyed in the past, and things that you would like to try in the future. Then make a plan of how you can incorporate them into your life today. Maybe you have enjoyed watching baseball on television and always wished you could join in on the fun and excitement. Can you find a softball team in your area and become a member? Think of all the possibilities that you can, based on your strengths and interests.

What have you enjoyed in the past?

What are some of the things you would like to try in the future?

What steps can you take to begin having more fun in your life?

What resources can you use to accomplish these things? (Example: Is there a parks and recreation listing in your community that you could access to find out information on activities?)

Create a Wellness-Oriented "Comfort Container" or Toolbox

We can gather wellness objects that support and comfort us and put them in a handy "comfort container." The comfort toolbox is a place (a shoe box, a dresser drawer, a backpack, a basket, an old suitcase or some other container) that holds items that have special meaning to us and bring a sense of comfort to our recovery. A comfort container or wellness toolbox holds items as varied as the people who gathered them. The following list is a *sample* of items that can be found in a comfort container:

Tapes of favorite music	Self-help or relaxation tapes
Photos of family and friends	Workout equipment
Affirmations	Poetry
Rocks or Crystals	Candles
Puzzles	Yoga book
Stuffed animals or toys	Hobby materials
Lotion or massage oils	Hot cocoa mix
Markers and tablet	Spiritual books
Old letters	Colorful paper and scissors
Personal journal and pens	Fuzzy socks
Peanut butter and crackers	Sunglasses and sun block lotion
Favorite quotations	Herbal tea
Magazine articles	Herbs or supplements
Drum or other rhythm instrument	Aromatherapy oils

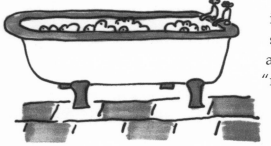

The list can go on and on. The point is to gather those items that are of comfort *to you*. Your comfort container should be unique to the person you are, what you value and what you believe. For example, one person wanted to "nurture and pamper" herself. In order to do so, she decided to create her own *home spa*. She filled a large wicker basket with fluffy towels, bath salts, her favorite shampoo and a net sponge. She added bath oils and candles she received as gifts during Kwanzaa celebration to her home spa comfort container. When she felt the desire to be pampered, her home spa comfort container was ready and available.

When you feel especially tired you can go to your personal comfort container and get an item that will lift your spirits and make you feel better.

What do you want to gather to create your own comfort container?

What do these items mean to you? Why do you want them?

Travel Tips

Travel Tip 1:

Stay flexible, change your plans and goals as you learn, grow and come to understand yourself

A successful recovery journey requires many mid-course corrections. We have to be open to change and stay flexible along the way.

We can change our goals, Personal Recovery Plan or the particular steps we are taking whenever we need, or want, to alter our course. Our goals change over time. Being rigid about what we must accomplish will not help us. We have to become willing to flow with change and be open to new challenges and opportunities. We learn to develop a "Plan B" or an alternate route if our initial roadmap fails. We correct our course as needed.

Even though we set our course based on our personal strengths and interests, we must keep our eyes out for new, wonderful, unexpected places to explore! Many of us have found our recovery journey opens up when surprising things happen to us that we could never have planned.

"Although our inattention can contribute to our lack of total well-being, we also have the power to choose positive behaviors and responses.
In that we change our every experience of life."
~Greg Anderson

Chapter 10

Travel Tip 2:

Embrace change, recovery is a life-long journey not a destination

Most people come to accept that recovery is a life-long process of change and transformation. We have goals that we want to meet, but these goals open us to new processes of change. Our healing journey is on-going.

The Greek philosopher, Heraclitus, stated, "there is nothing permanent except change." Change is going on constantly around us, yet change is one of the things that we naturally resist most. If we are to live a more balanced life, it is important that we learn how to become comfortable with the experience of change.

What kinds of changes seem to be easy for you to accept?

What kinds of changes do you find are most difficult to adjust to?

To become more open to change we can explore new things. We can develop new skills. We can go home and move our furniture around. We can go new places and interact with new people. By embracing change we become more adaptable.

What is one change that you have wanted to explore but have not? Why?

> "Certainly, travel is more than the seeing of sights; it is a change that goes on, deep and permanent, in the ideas of the living."
> ~Miriam Beard

> "My fear of change caused me a lot of anguish & heartache until I learned to accept some simple facts of life: change is the only constant—the trick is to learn to see it as just another opportunity to grow, a chance to transform yourself from the person you are into the person you want to be. When you fear it, you fight it. And when you fight it, you block the blessing."
> ~Patti Labelle

What can you to do to encourage yourself to embrace this change?

"Don't be discouraged. It's often the last key in the bunch that opens the lock."
~Anonymous

"Standing is still going."
~Swahili Proverb

Travel Tip 3:

Don't give up—build your endurance and keep on keeping on. Persistence will get you where you want to go

Keep moving forward! Sometimes we feel tired, we lose steam and run out of gas. Sometimes the potholes along the road seem to be so large they will knock us off course. The secret of a successful journey is to keep on keeping on.

> *I go along pretty well when I start a new job or new project because my success at my new endeavor brings praise from my peers or coworkers. But as with anything new, the "new" wears off and I am just another cog, like everyone else. But I don't see it that way. I lose some of my confidence and self-esteem when the praise is no longer pouring in. It is hard for me to give myself the praise I need to keep going and I even start feeling paranoid about the job I am doing. Am I not good enough anymore? Am I not important anymore? I feel like I'm failing and often I quit. What I have learned this time around in my recovery is that I have to pat myself on the back, to praise my own importance and know that I'm doing okay whether I'm getting kudos from others or not. So every evening when my day is over I reflect on what I have accomplished throughout the day and give myself credit for a job well done. I also reward myself in small ways every week for my accomplishments. I reward myself for just being me.*
>
> *~Julie Bayes,*
> *Kansas Consumer Provider*

Chapter 10

Recognizing the strengths you have that can help you endure the rough times and persist is key in your journey of recovery.

Think about the strengths and tools that you use to keep going even when you'd like to give up. Do you call others for support? Do you take a break, a mental health day, and nurture yourself? Recognizing what you need to stay on track is the first step to staying focused on recovery.

What strengths do you have that you can draw upon to keep moving and build endurance on your journey?

Recovery isn't an easy journey. We need to keep focused and use our inner strengths and resources. Remember, even if you are feeling stuck or stalled on your journey, never, never give up. Never, never quit! It gets better!

What supports and tools can you use to help keep going when you feel like you want to give up?

Travel Tip 4:

Don't compare your journey with anyone elses'—your goals and your path are uniquely your own

The recovery journey is different for each person. Don't look at another person's recovery experiences and expect your life to be just like theirs. Look at your own life, set your own goals, go at your own pace. Learn from others, but mind your own recovery process.

Travel Tip 5:

Don't attempt to travel alone—get plenty of support and find good travel companions

The ability to be able to bounce back and recover happens in relationships with others. Things don't go as well if we try to go it alone. Even though each of our journeys of recovery is unique, we can learn a lot and get much out of having traveling companions who are struggling with the same things we are and making recovery discoveries. Find great people to walk the journey with.

Travel Tip 6:

Celebrate every step of the way!

Everyone needs an occasional pat on the back to keep motivation and self-esteem up, but we will find times when our strengths may not be readily recognized.

What are the strengths you have that you can pat yourself on the back for daily? (Remember, sometimes just getting up and facing the day is a strength)

What are some simple ways you can reward yourself for small accomplishments?

What small things can you do to celebrate your achievements?
(For example: fix your favorite snack, take a relaxing nature walk, read a trashy novel, spend time with your loved ones, call a friend you haven't seen for awhile)

"Celebrate anything you want. Celebrate the start of something, the end of something. Dance and sing, give speeches, take pictures, finger-paint... squeeze your own lemonade and bake a pie. Celebrate early, celebrate late, and celebrate often. Celebrate."
~Rachel Snyder

Chapter 10

 References & Resources

References

Copeland, M. E. (1997). *Wellness Recovery Action Plan*. West Dummerston, VT: Peach Press.

Kirsta, A. (1986). *The Book of Stress Survival: Identifying and Reducing the Stresses in Your Life*. New York, NY: Simon & Schuster.

Sultanoff, B. & Zalaquett, C. (2000). Relaxation therapies. In D. Novey (Ed.), *Clinician's Complete Reference to Complementary & Alternative Medicine* (pp. 114-129). New York: Mosby.

Weil, A. (n.d.). *Relaxation*. Retrieved January 25, 2001 from: http://www.drweil.com/database/display/0,1412,100,00.html.

Resources

Breathing: Expanding Your Power and Energy by Michael Sky (Bear and Company, 1991).

Creating Extraordinary Joy by Chris Alexander (Hunter House Publishers, 2001).

Expect Miracles: Inspiring Stories of the Miraculous in Everyday Life by Mary Ellen Angelscribe (Conari Press, 2000).

Five Weeks to Healing Stress: The Wellness Option by Valeria O'Hara (New Harbinger Publications, 1996).

Living in Balance by Joel & Michelle Levey (Conari Press, 1998).

Living Simply: Timeless Thoughts for a Balanced Life by Sara Orem & Larry Demarest (Health Communications, 1994).

Something Good for a Change: Random Notes on Peace Thru Living by Wavy Gravy (St. Martin's Press, 1992).

The Daily Relaxer by Matthew McKay & Patrick Fanning (New Harbinger Publications, 1997).

Visualization for Change by Patrick Fanning (New Harbinger Publications, 1994).

Chapter Eleven

Supercharging the Recovery Journey

*This chapter highlights some ways to "supercharge" the recovery process.
These supercharging strategies fill the recovery journey with creativity,
gratitude, positive energy, humor and celebration!*

Introduction

We want our journey of recovery to go as smoothly as possible. How can we keep friction to a minimum and generate as much positive energy and well-being as we can along the way? How can we get ourselves into high gear so our experience of recovery is really great? This section of *Pathways to Recovery* highlights some ways to "supercharge" our recovery process. These strategies can make our journey one filled with creativity, gratitude, positive energy, humor and celebration!

Supercharging Strategy # 1: Using Creative Potentials to Explore New Paths

Most of us are trying to reclaim or develop parts of our identity that extend far beyond being recipients of mental health services. All of us are making the recovery journey without having a clear map to follow. The possibilities of recovery are vast, largely unexplored territories and each one of our journeys is unique. We must break new ground and use creative potentials to explore our capabilities.

In order to advance rapidly, we have to look at ourselves, our supporters, our communities and the resources around us in new ways. We find innovative ways to go beyond the challenges we face and make peace with the fact that not every new avenue we explore will be right for us. To venture onward with vitality we must view recovery as a creative act.

What is Creativity?

There are many definitions of creativity. Essentially, creativity involves taking existing ideas or images and combining them in different ways to create something new — a new idea, a new way of doing things, new ways of thinking or talking about something or a creative product or process.

All of us have creative urges that want to be expressed. When we create something new, we take a step into the unknown and allow our unique viewpoint to take form. We get involved in creative activities and gain new energy; we feel more confident about moving forward. Creative activities are often very pleasurable. We may even enter a state that has

"Be brave enough to live life creatively. The creative is the place where no one else has ever been. You have to leave the city of your comfort and go into the wilderness of your intuition. You can't get there by bus, only by hard work and risk and by not quite knowing what you're doing. What you'll discover will be wonderful. What you'll discover will be yourself."
~Alan Alda

been called "flow" by the psychologist Mihaly Csikszenthmihaly (1997). When we are in flow, we become so absorbed in the creative process that we feel we have gone beyond time and experienced a sense of oneness and peace.

Have you ever experienced the sense of "flow"? What were you doing when you felt you were in "flow?" Write about your experience here:

Many of us believe creativity is only for artists, writers and actors, but creativity goes well beyond art and music. We are all creative beings in different ways and to different degrees. Some of us tap into our creative spirit and use it often. Many of us pay attention to creative urges only occasionally, but don't fully use our creative capacities. Some of us are out of touch with our creative potential.

Curiosity and creativity come naturally to us when we are young, but we can lose touch with these qualities over time. Most of us have had our creative nature shot down by others. As youngsters we were having fun with crayons when the teacher told us we had to always color _inside_ the lines. We played in a stream for hours and then found ourselves in trouble for being late and muddy. By the time we reach adulthood, many of us believe we have lost our potential for creativity.

How creative do you consider yourself to be now? Why?

We can look back at creative things that we did in our lives and reconnect with our abilities. Most of us have some joyful memories of times that we used our creativity.

Describe a few times when you felt creative in your life:

"Creativity can be described as letting go of uncertanties."
~Gail Sheehy

"Do not be too timid & squeamish about your actions... What if you fail and get fairly rolled in the dirt once or twice? Up again: you shall never be so afraid to tumble."
~Ralph Waldo Emerson

338

Why is it Important to Nurture Creativity?

Creativity can heal and transform us, enrich our lives, give us new options and amuse and entertain us. We can use our creative potential to design our goals, teach a class, plan a party, write a grant, conduct advocacy or support a friend. Creativity takes our unique talents, gifts and visions to a new level. We go beyond having good ideas and turn our creative thoughts into a form that can be shared with others.

In her book, *The Creative Journal*, author Lucia Capacchione (1989) lists several reasons for developing and celebrating the creative process in our lives:

- Creativity can help us express thoughts or feelings that have been long buried.

- Creativity gives us a way of sorting out the seemingly random experiences that we have undergone, giving us a clearer picture of the possibilities in our life.

- Creativity gives us the ability to make meaningful experiences so we can understand them and put them in context.

- Creativity can help us deal with negative behavior patterns or thoughts, turning our energy into positive experiences. It can help us make more conscious and healthier choices.

- Creativity can help us define and implement the goals we have and give a sense of deeper meaning to our life.

> "The artist is not a different kind of person, but every person is a different kind of artist."
> ~Eric Gill

How Can Creativity Contribute to Recovery?

Creativity allows us to get out of the ruts we have been in. We can use our creativity to find new ways of solving problems and using our strengths to address all of the things we face.

> "If you would create something, you must be something."
> ~Goethe

Many of us find involvement in creative pursuits to be very healing. Poetry, artwork and even doodling, can have a positive influence on our outlook and well-being. More than half the mental health consumers responding to a survey conducted by consumer-researcher Jean Campbell and her colleague Schraiber said creative pursuits contributed to their well-being (1989).

Creativity can be a lifesaver. Kansan Elizabeth "Grandma" Layton had experienced severe depression and many periods of psychiatric hospitalization for 35 years. She was contemplating suicide at age 68 after the death of her son. Layton took a single art class and studied "contour drawing." She said she achieved recovery from depression through her artistic expression. Over the course of her 15-year career as an artist, Grandma Layton produced thousands of highly original drawings. Many of them concerned social issues such as aging and mortality, women's rights, prejudice, world peace and loving relationships. Her drawings have been shown in more than 200 art museums in the USA and France, and in *People*, *Life* and *Parade* magazines.

How Can We Nurture and Develop Our Creativity?

Creativity is a fundamental human capacity, but nurturing our capacities takes time and effort. We can begin to open ourselves to new ideas and different solutions. Once we begin identifying and paying attention to our talents and gifts and working to claim or improve them, we begin feeling more creative. We enhance our ability to be more inventive through practice.

Make a commitment to explore and develop creativity capacities

We can start by acknowledging that *we are creative* and understand that we *can* enhance and improve our creative abilities. We can be creative! We can replace any negative thoughts with "I am creative" statements. Once we make a commitment to become more creative, we can begin exploring this aspect of our being.

EXERCISE:
Claim Your Creative Nature

Create an "I can" statement that tells you that you CAN be creative, or write yourself a positive note or poem about your creative potential, and place it where you will see it every day:

Exercise creative capacities

We can exercise our minds in a creative manner and get in shape, just like we act to keep the other parts of our body in shape. There are many ways to reenergize, strengthen and support our creativity. Creativity boost the energy we bring to our process of recovery. We can experience the joy of the creative process right away!

Select one or two creative activities that you do now or enjoyed in the past, or that sound interesting or seem to suit you.

What creative activity interests you? How can you get started with it?

Let go of stress

It's hard to be creative if we are really stressed. We need to spend time relaxing and daydreaming to get in touch with our creative potential. Creative ideas flow more freely when we're not trying hard to have them. We need to give ourselves time just to have fun! Having time to reflect gives us the room to organize our thoughts in new ways and allows creative thoughts to flow more freely.

How will you give yourself time for creativity?

Explore the environment; Operate outside habitual ways of seeing and doing

Those of us who feel a lack of creativity are often stuck in set ways of thinking and acting in the world. We may have self-limiting thoughts and very structured ways of going about things. An overly strict routine for performing everyday tasks can restrict creative thinking. We may need to move out of our habitual way of looking at things to gain new perspectives.

Chapter 11

Many of us spend a lot of our time and energy trying to "be normal" or "fit in." This can get us into a rut and stifle the creative juices flowing inside of us. Patch Adams, a doctor who uses humor and creativity for healing, maintains we often live our lives in other people's ruts, rarely venturing out or thinking that we could do things a little differently.

We can let go of the fear that we might do something wrong, make a wrong turn on the recovery path or make a mess, and begin to embrace creative exploration as an opportunity for growth and learning. As we explore new ways of doing things and try things out we open up our world.

The book *Habitual Domains: Freeing Yourself from the Limits of Your Life* (Yu, 1995) describes ways to break out of set ways of looking at the world to make our lives richer and more fulfilling. We can use many methods to free up our thinking such as: identifying with and acting as we believe admired role models would choose to act, by consciously shifting our perspective and dumping our old assumptions, by traveling to different environments or changing the environment we are in, or we can actively brainstorm new solutions.

Embracing our creativity means living with a playful spirit. We can develop, maintain and enhance our creativity by doing things in new ways and exploring new territory. We should stimulate ourselves on a regular basis and expand our horizons. As we embrace new thoughts, and mingle them with old memories, we gain fresh perspectives.

Expand horizons

We can become more creative by treating ourselves to new experiences. Julia Cameron, author of *The Artist's Way* (1982), encourages her readers to take an "artist's date" once a week. This can be anything—a visit to a museum (most have a day without admission charges), a lunch date with ourselves or using our senses in a different way. Whatever it is we decide to do, it should be fun and refreshing!

What will you do to treat yourself to an "artist's date" this week?

"My goal is to say or do at least one outrageous thing every week."
~Maggie Kuhn,
Gray Panthers
Founder

"Adventures don't begin until you get into the forest. That first step is an act of faith."
~Mickey Hart,
Grateful Dead
drummer

We can explore things we feel curious about, reach out to new people and ask questions and explore new aisles at the library. We can participate in adult education classes, workshops, community presentations and attend art shows. As we discover new things, our minds open and we gain a wide set of ideas, images, knowledge and resources to draw upon.

Redesign the environment to support creativity

Our environment can be organized to support creative exploration. We can surround ourselves with things that we think are beautiful and that interest or excite us. We can make a special spot in our home where we can spend time in creative activities and hobbies. This may be a folding card table tucked in our bedroom, a plastic box full of magic markers and a sketch book on our kitchen table or a corner of the basement or garage that we make into a workshop. A bulletin board can hold photos ripped from magazines, a schedule of upcoming community events, a scrap of cloth in a color that energizes us, a postcard collection or our own poems and drawings.

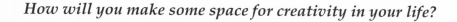

How will you make some space for creativity in your life?

"Creativity is inventing, experimenting, growing, taking risks, breaking rules, making mistakes, and having fun."
~Mary Lou Cook

Associate with creative people

We can learn a lot by studying the lives of highly creative people. When we explore such lives, we find many people who are extraordinarily creative have had mental health challenges.

We can identify a person around us whom we consider to be highly creative and invite the person out to coffee. We can ask them how they define creativity and express themselves and what they have done to enhance their creativity. They may have ideas on how we can explore our own creativity. Many larger towns and cities have working artists who have open studio times, community theater groups, talks by authors or book groups that can expose us to the creative process.

Who do you know that could be a "creativity mentor"?

"The best way to
predict the future
is to create it."
~Peter Drucker

What kinds of things would you like to learn from him or her?

"If you ask me why
I came into this
world, I will tell
you that I came to
LIVE OUT LOUD!"
~Emile Zola

*How will you go about creating your own playful — and creative —
spirit?*

*What is one specific thing that you will do this month to promote your
own creativity?*

CREATIVITY EXERCISE:
Writing and Journaling

Writing is something we do all the time, even if it is making lists and putting them on the refrigerator. Writing can be a positive force for our recovery. Writing down our experiences, our reactions to life events, and our innermost thoughts is often very helpful.

But writing can also make us fearful. Our scariest secrets will be discovered! Our sentence structure or grammar won't be quite right! Writing doesn't have to be in "perfect grammar" nor does it have to be like the letter to our mother that we *had* to do for our therapist. There are lots of writing books (and Internet journaling sites) that we can check out to see what would best fit our style.

Pick an image, symbol or word picture that can characterize your recovery. Write about it or draw a picture of it here:

Write about an experience that stretched you and you called upon inner resources to grow. Use specific details to capture your feelings, the place and the experience you had.

CREATIVITY EXERCISE:
Collage

A collage is a technique of composing a work of art by arranging various materials not normally associated with one another, such as magazine photos, phrases cut from headlines and parts of a greeting card glued onto a surface such as cardboard or paper. Collages are very simple works of art, but they can carry a great deal of meaning.

Begin a collage by gathering pictures, writings or any other objects that catch your eye. You can cut or tear pieces out of old magazines. You may want to think of one or more themes for your collage. Your recovery journey, your strengths, wellness strategies or goals for your life domains could work well if you wanted to focus your collage around recovery. Any theme will work.

Arrange the pieces until they look good to you, then use a glue stick or paste to attach each part onto your background material (later try doing a collage on a more *unusual* surfaces such as an old piece of luggage or a table top). Collage is a great way to bring wonder, creativity and discovery into our lives.

Creativity is one of the greatest resources we have on our road to recovery. We can become more creative today! We can color outside of the lines! We can try a different color! We can become one of the most creative people we know!

Supercharging Strategy # 2:
Walk on the Sunny Side of the Street—
Nurturing an Attitude of Gratitude

Most of us appreciate some aspects of our lives, but we don't consciously examine all that we can be grateful for. We often focus on what we lack and we can feel bitterly wounded by what we have been through. Like the old bluegrass tune, we may see ourselves as a man (or woman) of constant sorrow. We can become so soured about our lot in life that we believe there is nothing happening worthy of thanks giving.

If you have ever participated in a 12-Step type program, you've probably heard about the importance of an "attitude of gratitude." Television personality Oprah Winfrey has popularized the idea of gratitude in her talk show and magazine. An attitude of gratitude can help us heal and speed our recovery.

What is Gratitude?

Gratitude is feeling appreciative or thankful for what we have. All of us have things in our lives that we can be grateful for. We may feel grateful for a supportive family member, a good friend or a safe place to live. We may be thankful for the beauty of last night's sunset.

We often say "thank you" on special occasions by sending a card or calling someone on a special day. We might even remember to tell a friend about that beautiful sunset. Living more fully in a state of gratitude or thankfulness goes much further. When we begin to nurture and experience an "attitude of gratitude," amazing things can happen on our journey of recovery! It turns out we can change the quality of our life by turning the light of our consciousness toward appreciating what we have instead of focusing mostly on what we lack.

What Does an Attitude of Gratitude Give Us?

The greatest benefit of increasing the feeling of gratitude in our lives is that it *makes us feel good*. We may have spent years perfecting negative thinking and then wonder why we are so unhappy! Taking time to be thankful for everything we have helps heal negative thinking. As we shift our attention, we begin to notice the small things that happen every day that increase our enjoyment of life. We worry less and feel better about ourselves. Negative feelings, such as fears and doubts, anger or jealousy, begin to melt away. How can we feel bitter and when we have so much to be thankful for? Gratitude helps unlock the fullness of life.

An attitude of gratitude gives us a greater ability to take on life's challenges. It becomes easier to break down problems into smaller pieces; we feel more patience and persistence in tackling daily concerns. An attitude of gratitude helps eliminate the dreadful feelings of hopelessness because we start to find real things to look forward to — things that show us we are on our way to a more enjoyable future!

Living in a state of gratitude not only has positive psychological effects; it also enhances our physical well-being. When we feel good about ourselves and our situation, it increases our endorphins. This biochemical change boosts our immune system, causing us to feel better and avoid many illnesses. At the same time, feeling good decreases the release of adrenaline. This helps us feel calmer and can reduce our blood pressure.

"Gratitude softens us...If we begin to acknowledge these moments and cherish them...then no matter how fleeting and tiny this good heart may seem, it will gradually, at its own speed, expand."
~Pema Chodron

"You say grace before meals. All right. But I say grace before... I open a book, and grace before sketching, painting, swimming, walking, playing, dancing and grace before I dip the pen in the ink."
~G.K. Chesterton

Chapter 11

347

How Can We Learn to Develop an Attitude of Gratitude?

Tune into even the smallest feelings of gratitude

We can develop our own attitude of gratitude by consciously and actively looking for things for which we are grateful. After a while, it becomes second nature to become more conscious of things to appreciate in our lives. If we tell ourselves that we are grateful for a particular experience, relationship or thing, we soon will be.

Make the decision to be happier

We won't feel happiness unless we make up our minds to do so. If we don't feel joyful, we can look for a role model. We can also try to pattern ourselves after almost any child that we know. Kids don't have to try to be happy...they are in a natural state of awe, delight and wonder at the world.

Think back on a time when you felt gratitude or happiness. Describe how it felt:

Begin to look for the good even in a bad situation

When we have serious challenges in our lives, it is hard to see things positively. Have you met someone who has suffered many major setbacks, but who remains positive, involved and upbeat about life? Chances are, they have developed the art of gratitude. Our lives are full of lessons to be learned. The more we look for the good in situations, the easier it becomes to cope with setbacks.

> "Gratitude is a blessing we give to one another."
> ~Robert Reynolds

> "Sweet are the uses of adversity, which, like the toad, ugly and venomous, wears yet a precious jewel in his head."
> ~William Shakespeare

Can you remember a bad situation in your life in which you were able to find good? What happened? What lessons did you learn?

As I reflect on my life over the past years, I see that I have gone through some major life changes. I'm so grateful for the support and belief in me that has helped transform my life. So many friends, people who care. It's very important for me to keep in mind each day what I have to be thankful for. I've learned that I am important and I do have something to share. I express my gratitude by giving back to my peers through Compassionate Ear, a consumer listening line. I give thanks to my supporters by writing personal cards, notes and postcards. I do this with my family and friends — e-mail has really come in handy. I've now got solid, lasting friendships. At age 61, it can be a challenge to start over, but then again, I'm gutsy. I'm a new person and I love it.

~Pat Schwartz,
Kansas Consumer

Start looking and listening for wonder in your life

Often we're so busy that we don't see — or appreciate — what is around us each and every day. In her book, *Attitudes of Gratitude,* author M.J. Ryan (1999) talks about recapturing our sense of wonderment at any given moment. "All it takes," she says, "is to open our senses and let the world come into us anew...we can touch wonder in every moment as we slow down and perceive the world around us as if for the first time. And when we contact wonder, we know thankfulness for the most ordinary, extraordinary things of life." An attitude of gratitude helps us see the beauty in the small details of our life.

Chapter 11

EXERCISE:
Noticing Your World

The ability to pay attention to details can lead us to a greater appreciation of the world around us. One of the best ways to begin to see "new" things is to take a walk. Spend some time walking around where you live. ***Don't just walk...look***.

Notice what kind of shingles are on your neighbors' roof, the lawn art or graffiti that people have added to the neighborhood, the pattern of cracks in the sidewalk. Check out the clouds; what do they look like today? Try to find your neighbor's cat; do you know her name? Focus on all the small things that you normally take for granted, like the textures of the buildings, the tiny gardens at the base of a tree. If you usually drive a car or ride the bus, you'll notice much more than ever before! What strikes you as beautiful? What raises your interest?

If a walk isn't your idea of a good time, you can try focusing on an ordinary task that you do each day. Maybe it's brushing your teeth or making the bed. Just for today, don't do these things routinely while thinking about other things. Instead, focus intently on this one task. How does it sound? What does it look like? Do you notice anything new or different?

What if we don't feel gratitude?

Some days we find it very hard to feel grateful for anything. When this happens, we don't want to *"should"* all over ourselves...I *should* feel happy today...I *should* feel grateful. The idea isn't to be a sweet smiling phony and lie about what we feel. We can experience what we are feeling (grumpy, closed off, tired, bored, angry, hurt or whatever) and move on. Gratitude is a process that, when allowed, moves gently into our heart and spirit. We don't want to beat ourselves up for not being appreciative! We can be kind to ourselves and know that tomorrow is another day.

Some of us recovering from psychiatric disabilities believe we should follow the old 12-Step adage "Fake it 'til you make it." Other of us totally reject that strategy, because we believe that emotional authenticity, or feeling our own feelings, is too important, and covering up our true feelings gets us in big trouble. **What do you think?**

> "Develop an attitude of gratitude, and give thanks for everything that happens to you, knowing that every step forward is a step toward achieving something bigger and better than your current situation."
> ~Brian Tracy

How Can We Support Our Sense of Gratitude?

Once we begin to live in a state of gratitude, we find ourselves looking for opportunities to appreciate our lives, instead of expecting things to have a negative outcome. There are many things we can do to support and develop an attitude of gratitude. Here are a few ideas:

Create a gratitude inventory

Write a list of all the things in your life that you are grateful for. You can see this list as a beginning and keep the list active by including new things as you we remember them. Begin your gratitude inventory right here.

These are my early life memories for which I am grateful...

These are people in my life to whom I feel gratitude...

These are gifts I have been given for which I am thankful...

"When we live with a grateful heart, we will see endless opportunities to give: a flower from the garden to a coworker, a kind word to your child, a visit to an older person. You will know what to do."
~M.J. Ryan

These are events in my life for which I feel gratitude...

These are times of my life I have loved...

"We are not permitted to choose the frame of our destiny. But what we put into it is ours."
~Dag Hammerskjold

These are places in my life for which I am grateful...

Other things in my life for which I am grateful today...

Create a gratitude journal

Buy a notebook or attractive blank book. You may want to use colored markers or a fancy pen. Each day take the time to record a list of 3-5 things that you appreciated and for which you are grateful.

Try to stay away from things you feel you ought to be grateful for. Stick with what you truly feel thankful for. If you are having a hard time thinking of specific things or experiences from that day, try naming things that you appreciate in general — "I'm thankful for the smell of fresh apples," or "I'm grateful for the sunshine after cloudy days," or "I'm grateful that I knew my grandmother before she died." As you continue this practice, it will become easier to recognize things in your day-to-day experience that brings out feelings of gratitude.

Try to make keeping your gratitude journal into a daily ritual. You'll be surprised how good this makes you feel in a short period of time. Keeping a written journal also gives you something to look back on when you are feeling down.

> *Kansas consumer Barbara Bohm's clergy told her she'd benefit from journaling. She ignored this advice. Sometime later, her sponsor in Over Eater's Anonymous told her keeping a journal would help her. Months later, a counselor told her journaling would allow her to process her thoughts and feelings. A light went on: 'I finally figured out that my higher power was trying to tell me something!' laughs Barbara. She began using a journal as an important wellness and recovery tool.*

Find times to be thankful

Pick a time in your day when you regularly have a few minutes. You might want to consider the time spent standing in line, combing your hair or riding a bus to work. Use these moments to reflect on what you feel grateful for at the time.

A few moments spent being thankful before each meal can be a simple way to express gratitude for all that you have been given. You may want to offer a prayer, have a moment of silence, think about and thank all the people who labored to raise or harvest the food you are eating, or you may want to use a favorite saying to express your gratitude.

"You cannot be grateful & bitter. You cannot be grateful & unhappy. You cannot be grateful & without hope. You cannot be grateful & unloving. So just be grateful."
~Author Unknown

Honor the people in your life, past and present, who have been a positive influence on you

Honoring people who have given something to you can be as simple as offering a mental "thank you," making a phone call or sending a note or card.

Who are the people in your life who you would like to honor? What would you like to do for them?

We can send cards to friends and family. We can thank our veterinarian for taking good care of our pet or a restaurant for serving a great meal. We can thank someone who stood by us when we were going through a lot or our mechanic for keeping our old car on the road.

We can show gratitude to our community by thanking our neighbors, our church members, local businesses or any other group for which we are grateful. We can let them know that we appreciate them. We can offer to volunteer or help with a special project to show our gratitude.

How Can We Maintain an "Attitude Of Gratitude?"

Once we begin to claim a sense of gratitude, there are several things we can do that will help us increase our sense of thankfulness. Some ideas include:

Establish daily rituals of gratitude

- Post notes around the house to help remind you of what you are grateful for.
- Look for role models of gratitude. Talk with them. Find out what they have done to enhance their spirit of thanks giving.
- Change the questions you ask yourself. Instead of saying "Why me,?" ask "Why not me?" or "How can I change this so it's better?"

Gratitude isn't a cure-all for everything that has happened to us. It won't fix everything yet to be. But an "attitude of gratitude" can help move us further in our recovery journey and bring a greater sense of happiness to our life. The challenge is to make gratitude a bigger part of our life; the reward is feeling better about the life we have been given.

Supercharging Strategy # 3: Rest and Deeply Recharge Using Meditation

It used to be thought that meditation could be harmful people with psychiatric disabilities, but recent developments show meditation can actually help heal difficult mental states. For example, forms of mindfulness meditation are very effective in improving the lives of people who have been traumatized (Linehan, 1993; Teasdale, et al., 1995). Holistic health programs often include simple forms of meditation that help the body-mind to heal. In part, meditation helps us through evoking a natural deep relaxation response.

Meditation includes ancient and new ways of directing our minds. There are many forms and ways to meditate. Meditation can be found in all spiritual paths and traditions. We can research different methods until we find one that seems comfortable to us. Information on meditation is available in hundreds of books, videos and instructional tapes. There are also local community centers, schools, recreational programs and yoga centers that offer short courses in meditation.

"Peace can be reached through meditation on the knowledge which dreams give.
Peace can also be reached through concentration upon that which is dearest to the heart."
~Patanjali

MEDITATION EXERCISE:
Deep Breathing

Sit comfortably in a place where you won't be disturbed. If you are sitting in a chair, keep your legs and ankles uncrossed and your feet planted firmly on the floor, or sit cross-legged on the floor with a pillow propping up your bottom and the base of your spine. Place you hands in whatever way you feel comfortable, such as palms cupping each other in your lap or palms open and turned upward on each knee.

Try to breath naturally, breathing in and out of your nose rather than your mouth.

Focus on your breathing. Pay attention to the feeling of your breath as it comes in and out the tip of your nose. With each in-breath, think of a word or short phrase of your choice, such as "Peace," and with each out-breath think of another word or phrase, such as "Love." Or slowly say to yourself, as you breathe in, "I am," and as you breathe out, "Calm." When your mind and body feels calm, you can focus only on your breathing, with no thoughts at all. You can also count your breaths or just pay attention to your breath as it enters and exits your nose.

Continue to focus on your breath for 5-10 minutes and then build up to about 20 minutes once or twice a day. When your mind wanders (which it always will), gently bring it back to watching your breath and repeating the phrase you have chosen. Don't worry if a lot of thoughts come up at first or concentration is difficult to achieve; this happens to nearly everyone at first.

Supercharging Strategy # 4:
See Desired Change Clearly Through Visualization

Many people find it helpful to be able to turn their thoughts from stressful or negative thoughts or situations, and create an image of something more pleasurable in the mind's eye. Visualization works well when we want to see ourselves successfully taking on a new role or building a new habit. Athletes and sports teams often use creative visualization to increase performance and win games. Why shouldn't we use this approach to improve our recovery?

EXERCISES:
Visualization

1. Creating a Place of Peace

Imagine yourself in a place, real or imaginary, that you would like to be.
It should be a place where you can put aside your worries and gain a real sense of peace. Perhaps it is a meadow full of wildflowers or a clearing in the woods with a stream running through it, a beach at the edge of the ocean or the top of a billowing pink cloud floating above the earth.

Gradually begin to imagine the details of this place, including any sights, sounds and smells. Visualize yourself unwinding and reenergizing in the peaceful place.

Gradually return your attention back to where you are.
Bring the good feelings and energy with you and remember them in your current circumstances. Keep going back to your place of peace when you need a break from stress and cares.

2. Succeeding at a goal

Look back over the list of goals you have made and pick one to work on. Now begin to picture a scene in which you have already succeeded at the goal.

Develop a "moving picture" in your head that features you doing the activity really well and feeling good about yourself. If your goal is to make your apartment a better place to live, visualize the changes in detail. If it is to make a friend, visualize yourself doing activities with a trusted companion and really enjoying yourself!

As with other techniques, there are many ways to do visualization and guided imagery. You can learn about them and find the one that feels best for you.

Supercharging Strategy # 5:
Physical Exercise—Walking the Talk

Physical exercise helps us achieve a more relaxed state and increases feelings of well-being. Research shows exercise helps regulate emotions and reduces the impact of stress. Exercise is as effective in many instances as antidepressant medication (Sobel & Ornstein, 1996). A brisk walk can help burn up extra energy. We can use an aerobic exercise in addition to other relaxation techniques. Hatha yoga or tai chi are good forms of non-aerobic activity that promote health, balance and relaxation. Books and videotapes that show how to do these forms of exercise are available from many libraries or from bookstores.

What is your favorite method of exercise? How often do you participate in it? Does exercise help you to feel more relaxed?

> "Exercise is important. You have to stay in shape. My grandmother, she started walking five miles a day when she was 60. She's 97 today & we don't know where the hell she is."
> ~Ellen DeGeneres

Supercharging Strategy # 6:
Using Affirmations to Create a Sense that You Have "Already Arrived"

Affirmations show us the amazing power of our words. What we dwell on in our minds often has an impact on our daily experience. If we say, "I think I'm getting sick," we often do. Using many negative words or phrases reflects how we are thinking—negatively! As long as we continue to think in ways that are self-defeating and pessimistic, we will probably attract more of the same experiences and people that made us feel that way to begin with.

Likewise, if we speak in more positive terms, we are more likely to feel more positive about our lives. An optimistic attitude can lead to more positive, uplifting experiences. It's not always easy to think positively, especially when our recovery journey takes us on bumpy roads.

Affirmations are positive phrases that are repeated in an attempt to change a thought or a whole pattern of thinking that is negative or

> "Nothing in the world has been accomplished without passion."
> ~George Wilhelm Friedrich Hegel

dragging us down. We use these phrases to allow us to think more positively and to shape our beliefs about what is possible in our lives. Affirmations can turn negative thought patterns around and provide us with much needed positive self-reinforcement.

Some people believe our present reality reflects our thinking and if we change our thinking, we can directly change our reality. Research has found that more optimistic ways of thinking do boost our health and increase our chance of success in the world of work and in relationships. Even if affirming thoughts do not directly change the reality "out there" they can make us feel more positive, which changes the quality of our life. Affirmations can lift a sagging mood and connect us with our inner resilient spirit.

How Do We Create Powerful Affirmations?

Writer Jennifer Louden shares many tips on how to write powerful affirmations in her book *Comfort Queen's Guide to Life* (2000). Following these strategies will ensure that we achieve the best results.

- **Affirmations are most effective when stated in the present tense.** We avoid using the future tense or we will always be waiting for things to happen. For example, we say, "I have a beautiful place to live," instead of, "I'm going to have a nice apartment someday."

- **Affirmations should be stated positively.** We affirm what we want, not what we don't want. The more positive things are stated, the more powerful the affirmation. Saying, "I am a healthy person," is better than saying, "I don't want to be so fat."

- **Affirmations should be personalized.** We make our affirmations fit us, not someone else (they can create their own affirmations!). We develop affirmations that reflect exactly what we want, what our dreams and desires are.

- **Affirmations should convey a lot of feeling.** The stronger the feeling we convey in our affirmations, the deeper an impression it will make on us. We should put a lot of action and strong feeling into our affirmations, we should be passionate about them! We think with deep emotion as we say each word; we don't just repeat them without any feeling.

"Renew your energy reclaim your fire and seize the power of your heart's desire. Rebuild your vision, restore your soul, transform the part, and you'll transform the whole."
~from *The Fat Opera* by JoAnn Krestain

"It takes but one positive thought when given a chance to survive and thrive to overpower an entire army of negative thoughts."
~Robert Shuller

- **<u>Affirmations should be short and specific</u>.** Short affirmations are easier to remember.

- **<u>Affirmations should be repeated often</u>. Be persistent.** Repetition imprints the affirmations into our minds. We'll have better results if we use our affirmations regularly instead of using them only once in a while.

- **<u>Believe the affirmations</u>.** This may not happen initially, but the more we use them, the more we believe our affirmations, especially as we begin to see results.

Creating Affirmations for Your Life

You can write affirmations in many areas of life. This section includes sample affirmations in several areas and gives you the chance to start writing your own.

Create affirmations for success
- ❋ I am a success in all that I do.
- ❋ I am productive.
- ❋ Good now flows to me in a steady, unbroken, ever-increasing stream of success, happiness, and abundance.

Write your own affirmations for success...

Create affirmations for daily living
- ❋ I love and accept myself.
- ❋ I am a unique and free being.
- ❋ I am safe and protected.

Write your own affirmations for daily living...

"If you will it, it is no dream."
~Theodore Herzl

"Put love first. Entertain thoughts that give life. And when a thought or resentment or hurt or fear comes your way, have another thought that is more powerful–a thought that is love."
~Mary Morrissey

Create affirmations for health

* ❋ I radiate health!
* ❋ I have abundant energy, vitality and well-being.
* ❋ I am in control of my health and wellness.

Write your own affirmations for health...

Create affirmations for love

* ❋ Love is eternal and everlasting.
* ❋ I am worthy of love.
* ❋ It is safe for me to give and receive love.

Write your own affirmations for love...

Create affirmations for spirituality and peace

* ❋ I am at peace with myself.
* ❋ I am a forgiving and loving person.
* ❋ I am growing as a spiritual being.
* ❋ I am joyful.

Write your own affirmation for spirituality and peace in your life...

"The only person you are destined to become is the person you decide to be."
~Author Unknown

"Shoot for the moon. Even if you miss, you will land among the stars."
~Les Brown

Chapter 11

Create affirmations for problem-solving or overcoming obstacles

✳ I am focused on my goals.
✳ My life is free of tension and worry.
✳ My life is getting easier and happier.
✳ Endless good now comes to me in endless ways.

Write your own affirmation for solving problems or overcoming obstacles in your life...

Caring for Your Affirmations

Now that we have some personalized affirmations, we need to keep them together and use them often. There are many ways to create a useful set of affirmations. We can write our affirmations out and post them all over our home where we will see them regularly. We can stand in front of a mirror and repeat our affirmations aloud to ourselves. We can carry our affirmations with us and repeat them silently to ourselves, anytime, anywhere. We can start watching our thoughts and if we catch ourselves thinking negatively, we can remember our affirmations.

Here are some ideas for building and keeping your personal wealth of affirmations:

Build an affirmation file

Write a single affirmation on a 3 x 5 card. Make one card a day for a month. Continue to write out new affirmations as you need them. Use the affirmation cards year after year, adding new ones as you create them.

Create an affirmation container

Keep your affirmations in a beautiful container. Add positive statements about your strengths—your personal qualities, unique talents and dreams, as well as the affirmations you just created for all parts of your life. Here's how:

Find a nice small container at a yard sale or hobby shop—a potpourri holder, small vase, or music box, or make a special affirmation container. Take a small cardboard gift box and paint a little painting on it or glue a collage of positive phrases or pictures on it that represent your personal hopes and dreams.

Write or type out all your affirmations on little strips of paper, like Chinese fortune cookie fortunes, and fold them or wrap them around a pencil so they become little twists of paper (different colored paper and different typefaces or fancy styles of handwriting make them look especially nice). Pull one affirmation out of the container each day and focus on that one thought. Keep adding new affirmations to your box.

When you have a down day, take all the affirmations out of your container and read through them. It will improve how you are feeling!

We can enjoy using affirmations in our life. They are free, easy and have clear benefits. By using affirmations we find ourselves focusing on what we really want from life, which helps illuminate our pathway to recovery. Here is how one person describes the power of affirmations:

> *The Power of Affirmations*
>
> *Several years ago when I was first hospitalized for my psychiatric disorder, the big thing was to do daily affirmations. All the patients had to sit in a circle and say something positive about themselves — something that they would then repeat inside their head throughout the day to help replace negative feelings/emotions. This practice was supposed to 'boost self-esteem' and help us see our strengths, not our weaknesses. At first saying something like, 'I'm Suzette and I am smart' or 'I'm Suzette and I am a survivor' seemed totally ridiculous. The negative self-talk I did inside my own head negated the effects of the positive words I spoke out loud to the group. There was no way I could see those positive things about myself. But I kept on trying anyway, because I wanted it to work, and was tired of my depression.*
>
> *Continued...*

"Everybody has their ups and downs so I decided to have mine between good and great."
~Daine Hoogterp

"The past is over and done and has no power over me. I can begin to be free in this moment. Today's thoughts create my future. I am in charge. I now take my own power back. I am safe and I am free."
~Louise L. Hay

Over the years I have continued to do affirmations — they take different forms, including finding daily positive statements to feed my soul that particular day, listening to upbeat music and choosing to surround myself with positive, motivating and uplifting people. I also avoid listening to all the 'bad news' in the media or seeing movies that are violent or degrading to humans.

I have found affirmations really work — they are like magical little voices I carry inside that help me fight the daily battles that arise — from depressed thinking, to low self-esteem, conflict resolution, and the struggle to find my gifts in any given situation — they are POWERFUL TOOLS!

The author Louise Hay has created a little box of cards called "Power Thought Cards" that are available in bookstores. I pull one of these cards out each day and lay it on my dresser. I let the card I select set a theme for my day. A few of my favorite Hay Power Cards are:

- *It's only a thought, and a thought can be changed*
- *My work is deeply fulfilling*
- *I am in the process of positive change*
- *My life works beautifully*
- *My healing is already in process*

It wasn't easy at first, but with practice I really began to see how the little seeds of affirmative thinking really started to grow into beautiful, blooming flowers of hope! I've noticed a change in my perception of a lot of things since doing affirmations. I have become much more aware of how much my thinking can dictate my moods, my reactions to people and daily life as well as my memories of past events. My thoughts set the tone for how I live today — as well as how strong my hope is for the future.

Affirmations nicely compliment visualizations and meditation. They are quicker to do, so it's easier to use affirmations at first. As time went by, I began using them with longer visualizations and taking time to meditate. These activities worked wonders and brought inner peace and acceptance — things that added up to true change emotionally, spiritually and even physically. I've discovered a magical stillness inside myself through doing these practices. What was at first extremely uncomfortable silence, has led to incredible discoveries. I'd never have been able to 'hear' some of these lessons if I hadn't taken the time to use these self-healing tools in my recovery.

These 'tools' are like medicine and we are the pharmacist, we can make our own concoctions! We can play with these tools and see what blends work best for us. There are lots of tapes, books and other resources available in the library, at the book store, through church and spiritual centers, etc. that can guide us in learning more about affirmations, visualizations and meditation. If at first we don't believe, try, try that affirmation again!

~Suzette Mack,
Colorado Consumer and Wellness Educator

Supercharging Strategy # 7:
Develop Shock Absorbers by Nurturing a Sense of Humor

It takes a lot to face psychiatric problems and rebound from them. Humor is a great strategy that can give us shock absorbers and springs that bounce us out of some of the roughest territory that we pass through. Humor has been called a rare form of courage. It turns out it is also a very strong force for healing and recovery!

What are the Benefits of Humor?

According to *The Healthy Mind Healthy Body Handbook* (Sobel & Ornstein, 1996) humor and laughter are health-promoting. These authors summarize research that shows humor and laughter relieve anxiety, tension and depression, lowers stress levels and increases our sense of well-being. Humor and laughter have social benefits—they build warm relationships and affirm our shared humanity. Laughter has positive physiological effects: it reduces pain, improves cardiovascular functioning, releases feel-good endorphins and improves immune system functioning!

If we don't have much of a sense of humor we can work to cultivate one. Sobel and Ornstein recommend steps such as exposing ourselves to different forms of humor in movies, books and by listening to comedians, keeping a humor journal, nurturing and telling jokes and learning to laugh at ourselves.

We don't all have the same sense of what is humorous. Humor can be light and fun, but dark or deeply ironic humor can also support us.

> *During my first hospitalization I was very depressed & delusional. When I was admitted I neatly and carefully put my things away — I was very worried about my belongings, and my pride. After spending one night in an observation room, I was transferred to another ward. That night I couldn't find my nightgown, although my husband swore he had packed it.*
>
> *The next evening he & I were able to eat dinner together in the dining room. My roommate from the admission unit swept into the dining room, dressed to the 9's, walking with an air of pride. My husband said, 'Don't you have a dress like that?' I said 'Yes, it looks like my favorite nightgown.'*
>
> *Continued...*

"Laughter is by definition healthy."
~Doris Lessing

"One loses many laughs by not laughing at oneself."
~Sara Jeannette Duncan

"A good time for laughing is when you can."
~Jessamyn West

Chapter 11

Then it dawned on us that it WAS my nightgown, and she was having a ball wearing it! We laughed and laughed, which was a much needed break from the distressing feelings I had been experiencing.

Another time I was admitted to a hospital on Christmas Eve. I was really bummed and embarrassed by the whole situation. There were only about 4 or 5 of us on the unit and we all felt badly about being in the hospital for the holidays.

Late in the day, the music therapist rounded us up — spouses and all. None of us were really in the mood to sing, and I personally hate 'music therapy.' There was nothing else to do though, so we gathered together, and were ready to sing Christmas carols. The music therapist began pounding loudly on the piano, and belted out, 'DO YOU HEAR WHAT I HEAR?' We all looked at each other, stunned, and broke out into a huge gale of laughter. What was so ironic was the music therapist didn't have a clue.

Seeing the humor in difficult situations really helps me heal. It helps me see that I have at least one strength — the ability to see the funny side of what could be seen as the end of the world.

~Amy Steifvater,
Kansas Consumer

I have worked to develop my sense of humor as part of my recovery. Being able to laugh, including laughing at myself, has been a real 'saving grace' for me. Solomon was right when he wrote in Proverbs 'Laughter is good medicine.'

I work three part-time jobs, and they can sometimes be so stressful that I find myself forgetting to lighten up. When I can sit back and realize that I can laugh at situations, it helps my whole body relax.

I love that my newly developed sense of humor becomes contagious to those around me, and that other people appreciate it too.

I visited my brother last year for the first time in 15 years. I was telling him a funny story about what some young children said about my appearance in a bathing suit. He put his arm around me, smiled, and told me how glad he was that I had developed a sense of humor. He said he remembered telling me jokes and I would always say 'That's not funny, John.'

I tell myself now, 'You've come a long way baby. Right on!'

~JoAnn Howley,
Kansas Consumer

Supercharging Strategy # 8:
Keep it in Overdrive: Celebrate Every Accomplishment!

We should celebrate every accomplishment we make on our recovery journey! Celebration pumps us up and gives us the energy we need to replenish our spirit and keep on going. There are many ways that we can celebrate our own positive steps. After all, we've worked hard and we have every right to feel good about it!

What accomplishments in your recovery journey are you most proud of? List several:

How were you recognized for these accomplishments?

How did this recognition, or lack of recognition, make you feel?

"Celebration of passages provides an opportunity for people to remember stories of the experience being observed and to draw new insights from them."
~United Church of Christ *Book of Worship*

"Stop worrying about the potholes in the road and celebrate the journey!"
~Fitzhugh Mullan

If we haven't gotten much recognition for our accomplishments we need to give ourselves some now! If our accomplishments were acknowledged, it never hurts to celebrate successes again! Here are a few ideas for celebration! We deserve this!

Send a congratulations card

We always feel special when we open up our mailbox and see some real mail. In the technological age, there is also the option of an e-mail card. There are lots of free Internet web sites with inspirational cards. We can even send ourself a card!

Create an accomplishment board

We can hang a bulletin board in a special place and begin posting anything that makes us feel good about what we've done. This might include notes from other people, special quotes, an object that reminds us of what we have achieved or other items that inspire us. We can hang it where others will see it when they visit us!

Keep a celebration journal, an accomplishment book or a scrapbook

We can create a celebration journal, write about what we have accomplished, how we did it, who helped in the process, how we felt about our achievements and other tidbits of information. We can then reread the journal regularly for inspiration.

We can also buy a blank journal (the bigger the size, the better) and use this to store thank you notes, certificates of achievement, notes from friends or anything that is special and reminds us of what we have done. If we do something special like finishing a project or conducting an advocacy campaign we can put together a scrapbook documenting what we have done.

We can write down our successes on small pieces of paper, fold them up and put them in our affirmation container. When we're feeling the need for a little pick-me-up, we can reach for some encouragement and savor our accomplishment again and again!

"Success can make you go one of two ways. It can make you a prima donna—or it can smooth the edges, take away the insecurities, let the nice things come out."
~Barbara Walters

"The question isn't who is going to let me; it's who is going to stop me."
~Ayn Rand

Do something special every time we take a positive step or achieve a goal

We want to reward ourselves for progress! This might include making a special meal, buying a book or asking a friend to celebrate our accomplishment. We can plan ahead and create an incentive to boost our pursuit of a goal. This might mean setting a little money aside for a special purchase and then rewarding ourselves with it when we achieve the goal. We can find an object that represents what we have accomplished and keep it in a special place. We can also award ourselves with gold stars and stickers if we like such things.

How will you celebrate your next step on the recovery journey?

"You must embody success for others to generate it."
~Carolyn Warner

Celebrating Others' Success

It's great to celebrate the progress other people have achieved on their recovery journey and honor the all the great and small contributions others have made to our own forward movement. We can use some of the previous tips or do some of the following things to share our good feelings.

Create an achievement award

This may be something like a blue ribbon, certificate of recognition, paperweight in the shape of a star or an uplifting poem that's framed; any kind of thing will do. We can present this item to a friend who has done something outstanding. We can pass our "awards" on to someone else and keep the good feelings circulating.

Write a personal note

A simple handwritten note can have a great impact on someone. While it's nice to hear from others in person or by phone, a heartfelt note can be looked at again and again. Organize a letter writing campaign. Get several people to agree to send a card or letter to a particular person to recognize their hard work. One massive card can be made from a piece of poster board and everyone can sign it.

Give flowers

Giving flowers is a nice way of celebrating someone's successes. Flowers don't have to be expensive arrangements that come from a florist. Consider giving roadside flowers, flowers from your own garden or window box, a small potted plant or even a picture of a floral arrangement.

Hang a banner

Design a banner of celebration and put it up where others can see it and know what the person you are honoring has achieved! (Tip: Some computers can make banners.)

Hold a lunch or party to honor the person

Consider organizing a festive lunch in the person's honor. It takes some organizing and effort to hold an event, but it's an outstanding way to recognize someone who's done something wonderful. An alternative could be arranging a small potluck or baking a cake and having a surprise party.

Create your own award!

We can create our own rituals and award ceremonies. It's a good idea to try and vary the kinds of celebrations. As with anything, if we use something over and over, it can become stale and boring. Above all, we should have fun as we pay attention to the wonderful deeds that occur in our lives!

List one way that you will celebrate the accomplishments of another person.

References & Resources

References

Byrne, C., Woodside, H., Landeen, J., Kirkpatrick, H., Bernardo, A., & Pawlick, J. (1994). The importance of relationships in fostering hope. *Journal of Psychosocial Nursing, 32*(9), 31-34.

Cameron, J. (1992). *The Artist's Way: A Spiritual Path to Higher Creativity*. New York: G.P. Putnam's Sons.

Campbell, J. & Schraiber, R. (1989). *The Well-Being Project: Mental Health Consumers Speak for Themselves*. Sacramento, CA: California Department of Mental Health.

Capacchione, L. (1989). *The Creative Journal: The Art of Finding Yourself*. North Hollywood, CA: Newcastle Publishing Co., Inc.

Csikszenthmihaly, M. (1997). *Finding Flow: The Psychology of Engagement with Everyday Life*. New York, NY: BasicBooks.

Deegan, P. E. (1998). Recovery: The lived experience of rehabilitation. *Psychosocial Rehabilitation Journal, 11*(4), 11-19.

Faust, J.M. *Fight pessimism with gratitude*. Retrieved November 26, 2000 from: http://onhealth.webmd.com/lifestyle/in-depth/item,56932_1_1.asp

Grout, P. (2000). *Art & Soul: 156 Ways to Free Your Creative Spirit*. Kansas City, MO: Andrews McMeel Publishing.

Jackson, M., & Jevne, R. (1993). Enhancing hope in the chronically ill. *Humane Medicine, 9*(2), 121-130.

Kirkpatrick, H., Landeen, J., Byrne, C., Woodside, H., Pawlick, J., & Bernardo, A. (1995). Hope and schizophrenia: Clinicians identify hope-instilling strategies. *Journal of Psychosocial Nursing, 33*(6), 15-19.

Landeen, J., Pawlick, J., Woodside, H, Kirkpatrick, H., & Byrne, C. (2000). Hope, quality of life, and symptom severity in individuals with schizophrenia. *Psychiatric Rehabilitation Journal, 23*(4), 364-369.

Linehan, M. (1993). *Cognitive Behavioral Treatment of Borderline Personality Disorder*. New York, NY: Guilford.

Chapter 11

Littrell, K. H., Herth, K. A., Hinte, L. E. (1996). The experience of hope in adults with schizophrenia. *Psychiatric Rehabilitation Journal, 19*(4), 61-65.

Louden, J. (2000). *The Comfort Queens Guide to Life: Create All That You Need With Just What You've Got.* New York: Random House.

Ryan, M. J. (1999). *Attitudes of Gratitude.* Berkeley, CA: Conari Press.

Sobel, D. S., & Ornstein, R. (1996). *The Healthy Mind Healthy Body Handbook.* New York: Patient Education Media, Inc.

Teasdale, J. D., Segal, Z. V., & Williams, J. H. C. (1995). How does cognitive therapy prevent depressive relapse and why should attentional control (mindfulness) help? *Behaviour Research and Therapy, 33*, 25-39.

Yu, Po-Lung (1995). *Habitual Domains: Freeing Yourself From the Limits of Your Life.* Kansas City, MO: Highwater Editions.

Resources

The Adventures of Harold and the Purple Crayon: Four Magical Stories by Crockett Johnson (HarperCollins Publishers, 1955).

Art & Soul: 156 Ways to Free Your Creative Spirit by Pam Grout (Andrews McMeel Publishing, 2000).

Beyond the Relaxation Response by Herbert Benson & William Proctor (Berkley Publishing Group, 1985).

Claiming Our Creative Self by Eileen M. Clegg (New Harbinger Publications, 1998).

Complete Stretching: A New Exercise Program for Health and Vitality by Maxine Tobias & John P. Sullivan (Alfred A. Knopf, 1992).

An Exploration of Daily Hassles for Persons with Severe Psychiatric Disabilities by S. Miller and R. L. Miller in Psychosocial Rehabilitation Journal 14(4), 1991.

The Roar of Silence: Healing Powers of Breath, Tone, and Music by Don G. Campbell (Theosophical Publishing House, 1989).

Simple Meditation and Relaxation by Joel & Michelle Levey (Conari Press, 1999).

Strong Women Stay Young by Miriam Nelson (Bantam Books, 2000).

www.namh.org
Web site for the National Artists for Mental Health is a non-profit peer organization that advocates participation in the creative, expressive arts as a means to wellness.

Chapter Twelve

Transformations:
Sharing Our Stories of Recovery

This chapter helps you tell your story of recovery and describes the benefits of sharing your recovery story with others.

Introduction

Each of us responds to what life throws at us in different ways. We may go through periods where we feel stuck and terribly alone in our suffering. We may relive the painful parts of our lives over and over in our minds and try to make sense out of what we have experienced. We may try to accept our mental health problems as part of our life. We know other people have gone through difficult and painful life events and rebounded from them, but we can find it hard to deal with our own experiences. Over time, most of us can use our experiences to grow and move toward reclaiming fuller and more satisfying lives.

We have come a long, long way on our journeys of recovery. Now it is time to look back over all the territory we have explored, to assess our progress and tell others what we have experienced and learned. Telling our story of recovery gives us a way to appreciate our progress and support other people on their journey. As we transform and renew ourselves, we naturally come to a place where we want to tell our story and share what we have learned in ways that are helpful and healing.

As the writer Isak Dineson said, "to be a person is to have a story to tell." Every life can be seen as a story and every person's life story is unique. No one else has lived our life. Each of us carries within us a rich collection of stories that are full of our distinctive experiences, special challenges, our sorrows and our joys, our ways of dealing with what we have faced and the lessons we have learned. This chapter helps us create our personal story of recovery and share it with others.

Why is it so Important to Tell Our Stories?

Human beings are storytellers. We learn about the world and ourselves mainly through stories. From the thousand year old pictographs found on canyon and cave walls and hieroglyphics from ancient Egyptian tombs, all the way to the present day, we have always told stories.

Like our ancestors, we share stories over smoky campfires, but we also tell our stories around the kitchen table, in long telephone calls and through the high technology means of Internet and e-mails. Most of us are fascinated by stories of lives. We watch stories on television for hours or crawl under the covers with a novel. We are surrounded by stories each day. But why is telling our story of recovery so very important?

"There is in each of us an ongoing story. It contains our meaning & our destiny. And it goes on inevitably whether we pay attention to it or not...There is an ongoing drama that we do not control and into which we are drawn. And our deepest meaning is to stay with that story. Though we do not know its final outcome, nor even what will come tomorrow, there is nevertheless a great joy and a peace in knowing we are with the story. This is our soul's journey...This is what life is all about."
~Al Kreinheder

Through Telling Our Stories We Re-Make History

Telling our recovery story is a great way to claim our experience. Stories help us take stock and understand what we have lived through. When we tell our stories we bring memories and meaning together and gain a greater sense of coherence and control over our experiences. We put our past into perspective and more fully integrate our life experience.

By telling our recovery story we realize how our life experiences have made us who we are. We see that we wouldn't have learned as much as we have if we had missed out on any of our experiences. We finally see ourselves as people who are imperfect, who have suffered and have had many losses, but also as individuals who have successfully changed the course of our lives, who have strengths, who are survivors!

By telling our stories we are overturning the stories many of us were told that said recovery was not possible. Together we are writing a new story about what it means to live through psychiatric disability and move beyond it. We are telling those who come after us that it is possible to claim our resilience and triumph over psychiatric disability.

We are showing that a psychiatric history is *only one part* of our personal history, that we are *much, much more* than just our psychiatric labels or diagnoses. We see that we don't need to live in a way that justifies other's prejudices — that we are much more than our "disorder" our "mental illness" or our "disability." By telling our story, we reclaim our dignity and our strengths and gain a much stronger and fuller sense of who we are as unique individuals.

As we tell our stories we are building a living history of recovery for others to learn from. Students, providers, family members and other supporters will understand who we are, and what we have been through, much better when they know our stories.

How did another person's story of recovery inspire you on your journey?

"I've come to know that I can be a new person."
~ *Telling Our Story of Recovery* Workshop participant

"I am the only one who can tell the story of my life and say what it means."
~Dorothy Allison

By Telling Our Story and Hearing the Stories of Others, We Gain Perspective and Make Our Lives More Meaningful

Each time we tell our story, or hear another person's recovery story, we deepen our understanding. Each story of recovery reveals important things about a single person's life experiences and the pathways he or she has taken to recovery.

Sharing our stories helps us learn as peers; we find that we share many lessons. When we tell our stories we see that our "brothers and sisters" on the road to recovery have been through many of the situations and emotional spaces that we have passed through. Others have "been there and done that," as the saying goes. We can find a lot of good pointers by sharing stories of our explorations, side trips, detours and successes. We understand our own feelings and actions better when we find that others feel and act in similar ways.

Hearing stories from those who are further along the road to recovery motivates us to keep going. We learn powerful messages from the lives of those who have come before us. The tales we hear of others' recovery journeys renew us and instill or rebuild our hope. We gain and give feedback to one another and share our insights. As we help others, and they help us, we inspire one another. Through our stories we are mapping our collective wisdom.

Our lives gain deeper meaning as we explore and reflect on stories of recovery. We make sense out of things that didn't seem to have any meaning. We come to see that we are really strong and heroic—what we have faced and endured required real courage!

We may even come to find some of our under-appreciated qualities like "stubbornness" were really strengths that allowed us to persist and go on until we could get to a broader understanding and a better place. We may realize what we thought of as "failures" actually led to better things and helped us build even more strengths. Our stumbling blocks become stepping stones on the recovery journey. We see how many of the side roads or detours of the recovery journey seem to join up again and actually add to our progress. There really are no wrong turns that keep us from making progress.

"I haven't a clue as to how my story will end. But that's all right. When you set out on a journey and night covers the road, you don't conclude that the road has vanished. And how else could we discover the stars?"
~Author Unknown

"Don't be satisfied with stories of how things have gone with others. Unfold your own myth."
~Rumi

Chapter 12

What is one story from your life that shaped your recovery journey?

Telling Our Stories Connects Us With Others

By listening to stories of recovery, we discover that we were never really alone. We find we can open up and others will accept us, and we stop feeling so isolated. When we learn what others have suffered and endured, we find we are not the only one with problems. We connect to others who become our role models, kindred spirits, partners and companions in recovery. We realize we all have something to give, and when we open up we are able to make our own special contributions and to receive the wisdom, practical ideas, inspiration, support and gifts that others have to offer. We feel good about expressing our feelings and sharing how others have helped us.

As we share our stories we build healing partnerships. We reach out to people who haven't found their way onto a pathway to recovery and inspire them to make a turnaround. Our story can encourage people who are struggling in ways that seem overwhelming. Through telling our stories we can comfort them, support them and reorient them toward a more positive life path.

By sharing our stories, we achieve solidarity. We come to know that many of our personal problems have their basis in social situations. Some of us join with others to tell our stories to challenge abuse in families and in institutions. We openly tell our stories of hope and recovery to end the terrible stigma and discrimination that exists against people with psychiatric conditions, to build new bridges within the human community.

"Stories...are like the small bag of magic food that is given and when taken by the heart is never used up."
~Gloria Timpanelli

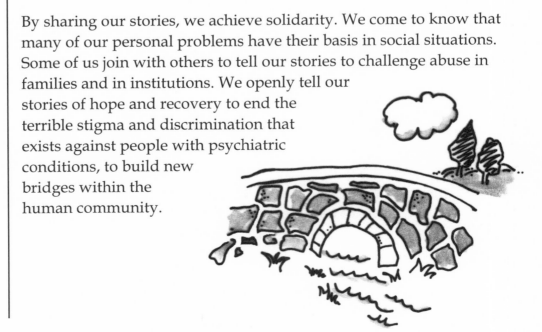

> *Those of us who have been labeled with mental illness are first and foremost human beings. We are more than the sum of the electrochemical activity of our brain. Our hearts are not merely pumps. Our hearts are real and as vulnerable and valuable as yours are. We are people…Those of us who have been diagnosed are not objects to be acted on. We are fully human subjects who can act and in acting, change our situation. We are human beings and we can speak for ourselves. We have a voice and can learn to use it. We have the right to be heard and listened to. We can become self-determining…We can become experts in our own journey of recovery.*
>
> *~Patricia E. Deegan (1996)*
> *From "Recovery as a Journey of the Heart"*

Telling Our Stories Helps Us Heal

Telling our story is very healing. Once we begin to tell our story we are often able to release thoughts of traumatic experiences that previously kept us down. The process of storytelling allows us to explore the feelings that we have about what we have endured. Talking or writing about traumatic past events can be difficult, painful and sad. At the same time it is very healing. Research shows that writing about our worst traumas can improve the functioning of our immune system and these positive effects last several months. Having a well-functioning immune system can improve our health.

Somehow telling our story helps release pain we have stored up within us. We see our challenges and our wounds are not all of who we are, there is a lot more to us! We begin to experience a greater sense of freedom. Our relationships with ourself and others soften and we feel healthier and more hopeful. Telling our story helps us move on.

When we share our story, we get in touch with our emotions, both "positive" and "negative." We identify and understand our reactions and come to accept them. We learn to trust our emotions. We begin to see that strong emotions, such as sadness or anger, are part of being human, they are not psychiatric symptoms. As we trace our history and the road we have traveled, we can see how our feelings have shifted and how we have become more able to contend with, and express, all of our feelings, including strong emotions. We see ways that positive emotions, such as deep self-respect, mutual caring and joy are entering our lives.

"Recovery doesn't end with the telling and hearing of the story...what finally renews people is the belief that their own capacity to love has not been destroyed."
~Author Unknown

Chapter 12

Telling our story helps us discover or rediscover our own strengths, power, and liveliness. We appreciate the inner and outer resources that helped us to take on the challenges we faced. Telling our story stimulates our creativity and gives us a greater feeling of wholeness. Our stories are more than a recitation of difficult experiences. Many of the stories we share are funny or allow us to look at things from a new vantage point or fresh perspective. We may come to appreciate the absurd humor that can be found within the challenges we face.

We can enjoy the stories that others are willing to share and appreciate other people's viewpoints. Sometimes another person's story sparks something in us and gives us the energy, hope or courage we need to go on.

Write about a time in your life that was funny or absurd.

Sharing Our Story Helps Us Learn New Ways to Contend with Our Challenges

Stories provide guidance for us. We have all heard stories from our parents, teachers or friends about their life experiences and how they coped with the challenges they faced. We may have heard parables in our faith communities that contained an important moral to guide our actions. Traditional tribal peoples share many stories to teach their members both the foolish and wise ways to act within the family, clan and community. Similarly, recovery stories also help our "tribe" — those of us recovering from psychiatric disabilities — to learn wise and foolish ways to journey toward recovery.

The process of writing or telling our story helps us to focus on important life experiences and remember how we dealt with them. In the process, we learn about ourselves and what is important in our lives.

What story you have heard that provided a lesson important in your recovery?

We often do not realize how far we have come until we look back over our lives and tell our stories. We are able to see patterns in how we made it through tough times. Storytelling provides an opportunity to discover more about ourselves, how we've survived, how we have coped, how we've endured and how we are growing and improving our lives. As we share our stories, we realize just how well we have handled the difficulties we've encountered and we are better able to accept the challenges we still face. We make further positive life changes by building upon our own strengths and past successes.

Coping strategies are interwoven in stories of recovery and serve as a rich resource for our healing. As we read or listen to other people's stories of recovery, we find new methods of coping and new strategies that help us heal and transform our lives. Sharing our stories opens up choices that are available to us that we had not seen before. The hard-won wisdom others have attained becomes available to us. We try things that work for other people and find some of their wellness strategies work for us as well! We learn new ways to approach our psychiatric disability and identify alternative attitudes, strategies and pathways. By sharing our stories, we increase the storehouse of recovery knowledge and increase our appreciation for our shared humanity.

We find we can speak for ourselves and that we are knowledgeable experts on the processes of resilience and recovery. As we write or speak our truth we feel very proud of ourselves and of our peers. We find developing and sharing our stories is one of the most empowering things that we can do! Telling our stories means that we are speaking for ourselves, that we will not allow others to speak for us and that we will no longer remain silent.

"[There] are the stories that never, never die, that are carried like seed into a new country, are told to you and me and make in us new and lasting strengths."
~Meridel Le Suer

"The universe is made of stories, not of atoms."
~Muriel Rukeyser

Chapter 12

381

I am better than I was before because I have the strengths to deal with life! Strengths that will continue to grow and multiply, building on each other, creating new strengths; strengths that will help me in achieving my goals. There have been some detours, but they have been learning experiences. Like John Lennon said: 'Life is what happens when you are busy making other plans.'

The impact of using the skills I have gained will continue to grow as I continue to learn and adapt them to new situations. How I deal with life's stress is not only important to me…I realize that I am also setting an example for my children, so that they learn healthy coping skills that they can use to meet the challenges of their life. Taking care of my body, mind and spirit will be a life-long effort, allowing me to have a balanced, healthy and fulfilling life.

My journey of recovery isn't over yet! I still have a lot of steps to take. But I am looking forward to what challenges life has in store for me. In the end, I have memories of people who have touched my life. In turn, I am touching their lives. This will continue for the rest of my life and beyond. It has made me stronger.

~Janice Driscoll, RN
Kansas Consumer & Recovery Educator

Write about a time when you were able to cope with a very challenging situation.

Write about a difficult experience that you had in which you were able to gain a sense of healing:

Describe one lesson or wellness strategy that you have learned from hearing someone else's story. How have you applied this strategy or lesson to your own life?

"It isn't easy for any of us to transcend the past, or pain we might have suffered. Yet there are gifts in those pains, and we can choose to let light into the dark places."
~SARK

Telling our recovery stories gives us more confidence and we feel better about ourselves. We no longer see ourselves as victims of circumstance. We find comments from others don't upset us as much as they once did. We feel stronger and become more active. We are more compassionate toward our fellow travelers and ourselves. We begin to see our recovery journey in terms of a deep and abiding capacity for self-healing and transformation.

Describe some positive things that you have learned about yourself on your recovery journey.

By Telling Our Stories, We Become Role Models for Others

"Everybody is talented, original, and has something important to say."
~Brenda Jeland

When we tell our stories, other people begin to view us as a person who has struggled and succeeded against great obstacles. We can become role models for other people who are just beginning their journeys of recovery. Our stories can encourage and support them, just as others' stories helped us and provided us with comfort and support. By teaching with our stories, we can become leaders.

What have you learned that you hope to share with others as a recovery role model?

Chapter 12

383

When I thought about writing about my strengths I did not hesitate. At this point in my life, I know that I am strong in some areas and weak in others. This is an old term, but I am a 'survivor.' I have survived my family, rape, beatings, verbal abuse, shame of my family, numerous jobs, cancer, living with little or no money, being in the state hospital, shock treatments, losing a child, almost losing my husband, my husband's family shunning me, numerous suicide attempts and losing my mind. This was all a lot to live with and to process.

How did I manage? I barely did at times. One of my strengths was my faith that things would eventually get better. My faith has been strong at times and not so strong at other times. I believe in a higher power with all my heart and believe things happen for a reason, however, some things that have happened in my life have spread that notion very thin. Life is an experience and that's how I look at it now. It is the degree in which life bends us that is the test. I do not believe people are basically good. I believe people have dark and light sides and the degree determines what course they will take.

Along with faith, I have a very strong will. It has helped me fight through the dark times. I would will myself to overcome physical illnesses and to go out and find a job. I lost large amounts of weight and this was done strictly with willpower. I willed my life to become better and it did become better but not without a fight. I wanted some things so badly and believed I could have others if I insisted and used willpower.

Another of my strengths is laughter. I love to laugh and have a good time more than anyone I know. I have a sharp wit that can be misunderstood. Sometimes my humor is so good it will pull me out of a dark mood. I love funny movies, comedians and watching my two dogs tease one another. Even at some of my most down times, I could find things to laugh about. One time I went to see my doctor and told him someone had told me to 'pull myself up by my bootstraps.' We both cracked up over that one. Do I ever wish it were that easy! The bootstrap idea is fine is you have wrecked your Volvo and Mercedes on the same day and find out you have no insurance.

Another strength that has come in handy is being able to communicate with different people on almost any level. I can add 'charming' to my list of strengths. I can make all kinds of friends, until they hear I have a mental illness. I have two friends that don't care and like me anyway. In general, dogs give me more pleasure than most people. I have created a world for myself that I love. I have no evil people in my life. I create art. I love music. I have the love of my husband, dogs and a few friends. I love gardening, crafts and traveling. I have been very lucky in some areas of my life. I am calling the score in life even-Steven. I am not lonely, bored or afraid anymore. I have strengths, a very good-hearted doctor and, most of all, my husband.

*~Anonymous,
Kansas Consumer*

How to Begin the Process of Telling Your Story of Recovery

As you progress on your recovery journey, there often comes a time when you may feel the need to tell others about your experience so they can know your story. Sharing your story gives you a chance to honor and celebrate who you are and bear witness to your struggle. There are many ways you can tell your story. Try any or all of the following methods or design one for yourself. Sharing your story is one of the most powerful and important things you can do, both for yourself and for others!

Create a Personal Archive to Draw Upon

Look back over letters, cards, scrapbooks, calendars, newsletters, photo albums, personal journals—even your medical or financial records—to remind you of who you are and what you have done in your life. Collect your ideas or mementos in a special scrapbook or pull them together in a basket or cardboard storage box. You can return to your "personal archives" again and again as you develop your recovery story. Sometimes our personal archives are almost empty because of the disruptions in our lives. Do you have people you could contact to get personal materials?

Create a Memory Box, Shadow Box or Altar

Go over collections that tell about parts of your life story. You can design a memory box to hold some of the items that are special to you by placing them in a nice storage container or displaying them in a deep frame or shadow box. Such materials serve as good reminders of life celebrations. Personal altars are spaces that include items that represent something very meaningful or sacred to you. By grouping items in one place, you create a powerful arrangement of things that focus you and give you extra energy and support.

Cultivate Stories through Arts, Crafts or Using Your Special Talents and Creativity

There are many ways to tell your story using the creative arts. You can act, sing, paint or use other visual arts. Working on a particular art, craft or theater project can help you remember and develop your story. No special artistic talent is needed to create a collage, which is one powerful way to connect to your personal story.

"Each person's life is a story that is telling itself in the living."
~William Bridges

"A person's work is nothing but a long journey to recover, through the detours of art, the two or three simple & great images which first gained access to their hearts."
~Albert Camus

Write Your Story

Begin to tell your recovery story by writing letters to a close friend or write about your recovery in a personal journal or diary just for yourself. New technologies allow us to use innovative formats to document and share recovery stories. The Internet can make it easy to share your story in chat rooms or on recovery web pages.

If you decide to write your story, you can use one of the many books on journaling to help you get started. Most books on journaling are full of great tips. Kathleen Adams wrote *The Way of the Journal* (1993). Adam's ideas include: write in a quiet place, set aside a block of time but give yourself permission to quit whenever you feel like it, write a prayer asking for guidance or center yourself before starting, write quickly without any concern for grammar in early drafts, date what you write, store your writings where they are safe and private and reward yourself for writing with a treat after each writing session.

Select any one of these methods and begin working on your recovery story. What will you need to do in order to begin to create your story?

> "It's very strange, but the mere act of writing anything is a help. It seems to speed one on one's way."
> ~Katherine Mansfield

How will you put aside time to make this project part of your life?

> "Seeing is of course very much a matter of verbalization. Unless I call attention to what passes before my eyes, I simply won't see...It's all a matter of keeping my eyes open."
> ~Annie Dillard

What specific things will you do to empower yourself as you begin the process of discovering your unique story? (Remember, each story is unique. No one else can tell your story for you!)

386

Stages in Creating and Sharing Your Story of Recovery

Developing your story of recovery takes time and effort. Louise DeSalvo's *Writing as a Way of Healing: How Telling Our Stories Transforms Our Lives* (1999), describes stages of storytelling. We've adapted the following DeSalvo stages to the recovery journey.

STAGE 1. Preparation

Begin to pay attention to the things you have experienced and look for ways to express yourself. Your exploration might include reading the recovery stories of others or asking a trusted friend to be your mentor as you begin to explore your story.

STAGE 2. Germination

Begin to gather images and ideas and start to piece your story together. Your ideas will probably feel a little disconnected at first, but you may have a clear picture of where you are heading right from the start. As you begin to explore your recovery story, more thoughts may come and your ideas will become clearer. Certain ideas or images may begin to appear and metaphors, specific objects, symbols or a special quotation may emerge that represent parts of your story. You may experience moments of serendipity or deep intuition in which you make positive discoveries about your story and see connections between experiences that you never understood before.

STAGE 3. Working

Begin to build and develop your recovery story. Add in more details and begin to see where and why things fit together. You may feel deeply emotional as you recall challenges you have faced. Pull your story together in notes or in your mind's eye. You may think you are done at this point, but it is important to continue to refine your story.

You may need to work through layers of feelings; stay with it even if the process is difficult or takes time. In developing your personal account of recovery, it's important to explore old memories or situations that you may have wanted to avoid or ignore because they

> "At bottom every man knows well enough that he is a unique being, only once on this earth; and by no extraordinary chance will such a marvelously picturesque piece of diversity in unity as he is, ever be put together a second time."
> ~Friedrich Nietzsche

might stir up old feelings. We heal as we go through our memories and feel our feelings. It can take a lot of courage to open up about our personal experiences. If you find yourself becoming upset, you may want to work on your story with the support of a safe and trusted friend or advisor.

STAGE 4. Deepening

Continue to revisit and revise your recovery story. Even though you may have spent weeks or months or even years developing your recovery story, during this stage you learn much more deeply what your story is *really* about. Begin to ask questions like "why did all this happen?" or "what lessons have I learned through these experiences?" Your story will take on a deeper and more lasting meaning.

STAGE 5. Shaping

In this stage, begin putting your story into a specific form. This may be a written document, a play, a poem or artwork. Even now your story may not be in its final form. The challenge is to not use this time of shaping to make your story perfect, but to feel a sense of accomplishment or closure about the challenges you have faced.

STAGE 6. Completion

During this time, you will refine your story by adding or deleting elements based on whether you feel they belong. You will probably spend a lot of time working on your story, refining it and gaining even deeper understanding of its meaning. This may be a long, slow process. Don't give up! You will have a story, artwork or image that you are proud of!

STAGE 7. Going public

At this point, you may want to share your story with others. Depending on your own personal style, this may involve sharing your story with a small group of friends or peers, publishing your story or public speaking. This type of sharing allows you to feel that you are part of something greater and expands your story beyond your individual perspective. For more ideas on going public see "Sharing Stories of Recovery" later in this chapter.

Some Things to Consider in Preparing Your Story

There is no set way to create and tell a recovery story. There are probably as many stories of recovery as there are people experiencing recovery! You can be as creative as you want to be and tell your story however you want to tell it. The following list includes some things you may want to think about or include in your story:

- What led to your desire for recovery?
- What got you into recovery?
- What was your turnaround experience like? Was it a gradual awakening or a "Eureka" experience?
- Was there a point where you knew you were on the road to recovery? What happened?
- How did you overcome inertia and get going?
- What or who motivated you?
- What were some of the first steps you made toward recovery?
- What strengths allowed you to move toward recovery and keep going?
- Who helped you along the way? Were there informal supporters who helped, like family members, peers and friends? Did formal helpers boost your recovery? How?
- What did you do for yourself that gave rise to learning, growth and change?
- What detours, barriers or set-backs have you experienced? How did you deal with the set-backs and barriers?
- How did you find hope and meaning?
- How have your personal values and beliefs, including spirituality, supported your recovery?
- What wellness strategies did you use?
- What are the most vivid memories or most profound times of your recovery?
- What has the journey been like for you?
- What are some of your accomplishments so far?
- What lessons have you learned about yourself and about life on your recovery journey so far?
- What gifts did your journey give you that you would like to share with others?
- What is your life like now?
- What are your hopes and dreams for the future?

Sharing Stories of Recovery

Once you have worked on your story of recovery you need to tell or show others what you have learned. Stories are meant to be shared! There are many ways to share recovery stories.

Share Through Peer Support

Peer support can provide us with hope and courage, important relationships, valuable lessons and practical advice. You can show you care by becoming part of a group of mutual self-helpers and role models through peer support. You can tell your story at support group meetings, in peer counseling sessions and at consumer meetings and conferences.

Join a Speakers Bureau

Speakers bureaus help educate the community, school children and civic groups about the experiences real people have with psychiatric disorders. By telling your story you can help break through social stigma. By telling your story before university classes you help future mental health providers develop positive attitudes and become more effective helpers.

Who could benefit from hearing your story?

How will you choose to tell your story of recovery?

"Stories move in circles. They don't move in straight lines. So it helps if you listen in circles. There are stories inside stories and stories between stories, and finding your way through them is as easy and as hard as finding your way home. And part of the finding is the getting lost. And when you're lost, you start to look around and to listen."
~Corey Fischer, Albert Greenberg & Naomi Newman

> *I am a person. A consumer is a person, not some words on paper or a number assigned to them. I have feelings! Don't tell me I do not exist by not giving me options or the ability to express my opinions about my program of recovery. Help me when I need help, but don't take away my right to make my own mistakes…I am who I am & not you!…I can make decisions; I can have triumphs as well as problems. I'm not just one thing. There are many parts to me and I'd like the chance to be those parts & put them together into one person…*
>
> *Times are changing and the future is full of promise. Who would have dreamed 10 years ago that consumers could be providers & that we would be sitting on the Governor's Councils and teaching case management to the 'professional case managers'? After all, we are the experts. It's time we raise our voices. We want to teach you how to treat us. Listen to what we have to say. We are the ones at stake here, so let us say what we want, need and are capable of doing…I live in a real world where there is much diversity, let me live it…Give me a chance for freedom…Freedom to make my choices count for me, whether I fall on my face or walk ten feet tall!*
>
> ~Chris Shore,
> Kansas Consumer

> "Once you have experienced the seriousness of your loss, you will be able to experience the wonder of being alive. It is a fact that once you experience pain, it sensitizes you to joy."
> ~Robert L. Veninga

Put Your Story on an Internet Web Site

There are many Internet sites that provide information on recovery. These sites are helping develop a culture of recovery. Many give us the opportunity to network with others. We can read about other people's journey of recovery & share our own stories on such sites. Some sites have chat rooms where we can meet people online and interact with them, give & receive mutual support & potentially develop friendships. As Sally Clay, a consumer leader from Florida says — this helps those of us in recovery to find a "virtual community" in cyberspace.

Publish Your Story

Many newsletters want short recovery stories. Local newspapers are often looking for inspirational stories about people who are resilient and who have overcome great odds. Several professional mental health journals, such as *Psychiatric Rehabilitation Journal, Psychiatric Services* and *Schizophrenia Bulletin,* publish first person accounts of recovery. Guidelines for authors can usually be found in every copy of the journal. Publishing your story of recovery in a professional journal can have a big impact on the thinking of the field. Some American recovery stories have even been reprinted in Sweden, Israel and Australia.

> "To write about one's life is to live it twice, and the second living is both spiritual and historical, for a memoir reaches deep within the personality as it seeks its narrative form."
> ~Patricia Hampl

Chapter 12

This is about me and the journey that I am on. It is a journey that has no definite beginning. It is a journey that has no definite ending. It is a journey from light to darkness to light. I have a favorite saying "Lux Ex Tenebris;" it is Latin for "light out of darkness." I use this to remind myself of the journey that I have been on and continue to be on. This is the journey of recovery.

Recovery, by definition, is the power to regain something (Webster's dictionary). The power to regain something is a compelling statement. When you receive a diagnosis of any kind you feel like the whole world has been ripped out from under you. You lose your footing and sometimes you lose yourself. Some diagnoses are terminal and some just feel that way. Like a lot of people who receive mental health diagnoses, mine was initially wrong. When everything came to fruition the final truth hit me like a brick wall. I found myself in and out of the hospital, heavily medicated and when I was at home all I did was sleep or sit in a chair and do nothing.

I then began to receive services with the local Community Support Services (CSS) Program. At first I was only partially involved, going once or twice a week for a group or two and isolating a lot at home. I then found myself going to the center every day, riding the vans, and just existing — not doing anything constructive with myself. I felt like I was living in a cloud. I do not remember making a decision to be on a path of recovery, I happened to have found myself there. I did not want to become one of those people who make being a CSS client their profession, identity and ultimately their end. I have found that there are things that I can do to keep myself on the recovery path.

I think learning is a strength that has been useful in my recovery because it keeps me connected to the world. Even in my darkest moments, when all I wanted to do is watch TV, I was still learning even in a small way. Learning keeps me connected to myself, too. I have learned to be introspective and learned about myself as a result. School is an important learning opportunity that I used in the past and am using now.

Using coping skills that I have learned and seeking new skills is another strength I use on a daily basis. I have completed several classes including the Wellness Recovery Action Plan class and have updated my plan a couple of times. I have found that having structure in my daily life, and knowing that I have a plan in place if there were to be a crisis, eases my mind.

My support system is also a strength of mine. This past year my support system underwent several changes due to death and divorce. As a result of these events I was forced to revamp my support system. I have done this by looking to my parents and family. This has helped my recovery by giving me family strength. I also use social supports in the community, such as school and work. The other support that I have found naturally is my beloved pets. Even though they cannot talk back in words that I can understand, I know that they love me and when I am upset and crying they rally around me and let me talk to them. Sometimes all that is needed is the chance to talk without any reply from the other person.

Continued...

The most important strength I have is my own experience and remembering the past. I am careful not to dwell in the past, but when I feel the road ahead is too hard or too bumpy I think about all that I have been through, experienced and all of the ground I have gained. I know that I do not want to go back to the hospital. I know that I do not want to go back to the state of being out of touch with reality and experience constant hallucinations. By remembering these former times and remembering how it felt, I can keep myself on track.

I want to talk about my strength of taking risks. There are, of course, bad risks to take, but I want to focus on the positives. I took a risk applying for the Consumers as Providers training program. I was so scared that I almost did not apply and I am glad that I took this risk. Another risk I took was applying for a peer support job. By taking these risks, and them turning out positively, I have elevated my self-esteem, self-confidence and my sense of purpose in my world. Having a sense of purpose in your world is a corner stone to recovery. Also taking these risks has given me hope, which is the foundation of recovery. I am not a risk taker and to do so takes a lot of effort and faith in myself. The biggest risk I ever took was entering a painting of mine in an art show. I did, and I won one of five awards. This reinforces that good can come from taking a positive risk.

Recovery is a thing that when I started in the mental health system was so very foreign to me. I was given the typical sentence to a life of hospitalizations, unemployment, dependence and misery. My doctor at the time overmedicated me and stuck me in the hospital if I looked at him wrong. I was left to my own devices, my own hopelessness and my own isolation. I have found the path, as have all the others in my class and those who have gone before us, and it gives me hope to see them trailblazing on their own journeys!

~Shelly Scott,
Kansas Consumer Provider

Celebration

Celebrate telling your story! It's great to have come so far and to look back at our real-life adventures. Give yourself credit for making it through so much! Honor your strengths and honor those who have been your travel companions, allies and supporters all along the way. Let's celebrate our best and worst of times, our strengths and our vulnerabilities and find ways to have more pleasure and fun and peace in our lives!

How will you celebrate telling your story?

The Ongoing Journey

The recovery journey doesn't end when we tell our story. Many of us see recovery as a life-long journey of continual self-discovery. We have made a permanent commitment to achieving higher levels of wellness. We know recovery isn't something we accomplish in a single burst of effort. We'll use slow deliberate effort. We'll continue to assess where we are now and where we want to go. We'll continually seek a deeper understanding of ourselves and our purpose, and work to improve our relationships with others and the wider human community. We are eager to continue our explorations, deepen our spiritual connections and join with others to work for social justice. The journey continues…

Head west across the plains,
Journey through a mountain range.
Stop at a river and fill your canteen,
For the land beyond is arid, and water unseen.

Measure your steps – do not hurry.
Focus on your destination –
Do not worry.

And at night when you've eaten,
And made your camp,
With your fire burning bright,
Look up and study the stars.
Find one to guide you,
to guide you with its light.

Your trek ends at ocean's edge.
You cannot go farther.
Yet you build a boat
To carry your dreams,
To carry you across the water.

~Kansan, Michael King Gowdy
November 9, 1990

Our story of recovery isn't finished. As we continue our journey we find new dreams, aspirations and goals to guide us, new paths to follow. As we "keep on trucking," momentum is more and more on our side; things get easier, we learn more and have more stamina. We are encouraged by our own growth, the achievement of our goals and we become freer and stronger. We continue to transform ourselves far into the future.

We continue to take our words and put them into action and walk the talk of recovery, and recovery becomes a powerful force in our lives and the lives we touch. We embrace change and follow our dreams and hearts and continue to explore the territory of recovery even more deeply. We become more fully who we are meant to become.

We develop the knowledge and wisdom we need to continue to transform our lives—physically, emotionally, mentally, socially and spiritually. We use our reclaimed strengths and talents and the lessons that we have learned to make our lives even better. We gain a stronger sense of purpose. Often we want to help others to heal. As we follow our quest, we continue to share our insights, talents and lessons. We connect our life experience to others through our deepening compassion, and head in the direction of having an ever more positive influence on our fellow traveler's, our families, wider groups and our communities. As we live out our life stories we affirm our humanity and accelerate needed change in programs and systems.

The *Pathways to Recovery* workbook ends here, but our journey continues. We may use this workbook for a few months or rely on it for years. We can let go of the workbook and then come back to it. We can revisit the domains and see what sparks new ideas or ambitions. We can continue to use the Personal Recovery Plan format to set new short-term goals. As we achieve our goals, we'll find new areas that take on more importance. We can do some of the exercises again and review our accomplishments, trace our progress and honor the milestones we have passed.

We know that our future will not be a simple straight path; there will be many more twists and turns and uphill treks on our journey. We know there will be challenging times and setbacks. We will need to use all of the tools, positive creative qualities and wisdom we can possibly develop to keep open, gain clarity and keep moving toward freedom.

Our journey continues to unfold, step by step. We find the place inside of us that knows the way and we gain confidence. And most importantly we take the time to celebrate every step we take on our pathways to recovery!

References & Resources

References

Adams, K. (1993). *The Way of the Journal (2nd ed.)*. Lakewood, CO: The Center for Journal Therapy.

Capacchione, L. (1989). *The Creative Journal: The Art of Finding Yourself.* North Hollywood, CA: Newcastle Publishing.

Deegan, P. (1996). Recovery as a journey of the heart. *Psychiatric Rehabilitation Journal, 9*(3), 91-97.

DeSalvo, L. (1999). *Writing as a Way of Healing*. San Francisco: HarperCollins.

Johnson, A. (2001). *Leaving a Trace: The Art of Transforming a Life Into Stories*. New York: Little, Brown and Company.

Keen, S., & Valley-Fox, A. (1989). *Your Mythic Journey: Finding Meaning in Your Life Through Writing and Storytelling* (Rev. ed.). New York: Pedigree Books.

Leete, E. (1989). How I manage and perceive my illness. *Schizophrenia Bulletin, 15*(2), 197-200.

Lovejoy, M. (1982). Expectations and the recovery process. *Schizophrenia Bulletin, 9*(4), 604-609.

Meade, E. H. (1995). *Tell it By Heart: Women and the Healing Power of Story*. Chicago: Open Court Publishing.

Metzger, D. (1992). *Writing for Your Life: A Guide and Companion to the Inner Worlds*. San Francisco: HarperCollins.

Nucho, A. O. (1997). *Listening to Life Stories: A New Approach to Stress Intervention in Health Care*. New York: Springer Publishing.

Pennebaker, J. W. (1997). *Opening Up: The Healing Power of Expressing Emotions (Rev. ed.)*. New York: Guilford Press.

Young-Eisendrath, P. (1996). *The Resilient Spirit: Transforming Suffering Into Meaning and Purpose*. Reading, MA: Perseus Books.

Resources

All About Me by Philipp Keel (Broadway Books, 1998).

At a Journal Workshop: Writing to Access the Power of the Unconscious and Evoke Creative Ability by Ira Progoff (Putnam Publishing Group, 1991).

The Cancer Journals by Audre Lourd (Aunt Lute Books, 1992).

Any of the *Chicken Soup for the Soul* series by Mark Hansen and Jack Canfield (Health Communications, Inc.).

The Beast: The Journey Through Depression by Tracy Thompson (Penguin USA, 1996).

Kitchen Table Wisdom: Stories That Heal by Rachel Naomi Remen (Riverhead Books, 1996).

Leaving a Trace: The Art of Transforming a Life into Stories by Alexandra Johnson (Little, Brown and Company, 2001).

Random Acts of Kindness and *More Random Acts of Kindness* by the Editors of Conari Press.

Recovering: A Journal by May Sarton (W.W. Norton & Company, Inc., 1997).

Stone Soup for the World by Marianne Larned (ed.) (Conari Press, 1998).

Story People by Brian Andreas (available from http://www.storypeople.com).

They Dance in the Sky by Jean Guard Monroe & Ray A. Williamson (Houghton Mifflin Co., 1987).

A Voice of Her Own by Marlene A. Schiwy (Schuster Trade Paperbacks, 1996).

Wouldn't Take Nothing for My Journey Now by Maya Angelou (Bantam Doubleday Dell Publishing Group, 1994).

Writing as a Way of Healing: How Telling Our Stories Transforms Our Lives by Louise DeSalvo (Harper Collins, 1999).

Writing to Heal the Soul: Transforming Grief and Loss Through Writing by Susan Zimmermann (Three Rivers Press, 2002).

Aloha...

We hope *Pathways to Recovery* has helped you to identify and use many of your strengths to move towards recovery. You have used self-assessment, self-discovery and decision-making to know more about where you want to go in life to achieve your dreams and goals! We wish you well in your continuing journey!

There are words like Aloha in the indigenous Hawaiian language or Shalom in the Jewish tradition that mean both hello and good bye. Although we've come to the end of the book, we'd like to open a dialogue with you, the reader.

We'd like to hear what you think about this book!

What suggestions do you want to share with us? What information would you like to see added or expanded upon? If you have ideas for exercises or resources, please let us know. If you want to share you story of recovery or a story of how you have supported others in their recovery, please write us.

We appreciate your time in reading and working through *Pathways to Recovery* and want to hear from you. Your feedback is important as we continue to revise and update this workbook.

Please feel free to contact us:

- For information or technical assistance on the workbook, group facilitator's guide or other activities associated with *Pathways to Recovery*

- For general information about the process used to create *Pathways*

- To share your ideas, thoughts, stories or feedback

- For information on other projects on recovery at The University of Kansas School of Social Welfare

Lori Davidson, Recovery Project Coordinator
The University of Kansas School of Social Welfare
Office of Mental Health Research & Training
1545 Lilac Lane — Lawrence, KS 66044 — U.S.A.
(866) 728-1909 (U.S.A. toll-free)
(785) 864-4270/(785) 864-5277 (fax)
pathways@ku.edu
www.socwel.ku.edu/projects/seg/pathways.html

What we call the beginning
is often the end and to make an end
is to make a beginning.
The end is where we start from...

We shall not cease from exploration
and the end of all our exploring
will be to arrive where we started
and know the place for the first time.

~T.S. Eliot

Meet the Authors and Contributors

Priscilla Ridgway After working over 30 years in the mental health field, I'm suddenly much more optimistic! I've working in direct practice, disability rights, supported housing, policy analysis & best practice research—specifically to understand resilience & advance consumer voice. My own experiences as an accidental mystic, a person with a traumatic brain injury and someone who has struggled with depression & PTSD have given me a greater depth of awareness. I am in love with the power of resilience & creativity that allow us to heal & be transformed. I now work as an assistant professor with the Yale Program for Recovery & Community Health.

Diane McDiarmid At the University of Kansas, I served as Director of the Strengths Recovery, Supported Education & Consumer as Provider projects in the Office of Mental Health Research & Training. I've taught the Strengths Perspective across the U.S. & internationally and served as an adjunct professor, developing course curricula and teaching social work classes in the School of Social Welfare. With many years of experience in direct clinical practice, policy & administration, I've witnessed the positive impact on people's lives from implementing a strengths-based perspective. I am now living in Austin, Texas where you can find me on the water as a competitive rower.

Lori Davidson I've worked in the mental health field for over 20 years, learning from each story that has been shared with me. Over this time, I have come to realize that the line between consumer & provider is very thin, if not non-existant. I consider myself a "provider as consumer," drawing on my own journey with depression as a major factor in supporting individuals to take risks on their own recovery journey. My favorite things are a really good cup of coffee, a fabulous novel &, of course, lilacs. I now work as the Project Coordinator for *Pathways to Recovery* at the University of Kansas.

Julie Bayes During, I served as a consumer provider in the psychosocial program at Bert Nash Community Mental Health Center in Lawrence, Kansas and on the board of directors of Independence, Inc., an independent living resource center. While working as a journalist & television producer, I was diagnosed in 1986 with multiple personality disorder. After struggling with my illness for 10 years, I finally started working on recovery. Through individual therapy & skills work, I learned to relate to the world around me. My motto became "what we think, we become." I live each day by those words & regularly continue my advocacy work.

Sarah Ratzlaff In addition to working on *Pathways to Recovery*, I was the research assistant for the Supported Education Group at the University of Kansas School of Social Welfare, developing research for the Kansas Consumer as Provider program and other supported education initiatives. This was my first job in mental health and I continue to be infinitely inspired by this book, the stories I've read and heard and the people I've met. After receiving my master's degree in sports management, I am now working with Disney Sports Attractions in Lake Buena Vista, Florida.

Cherie Bledsoe "Life is a CELEBRATION of miracles and blessings paved with sparks, bumps & movement." I serve as the Executive Director of S.I.D.E., Inc, a consumer-run organization and am the Consumer Affairs & Development Specialist at the Wyandot Center, both in Kansas City, Kansas. I also work with the Kansas Consumer Advisory Council for Adult Mental Health. My joy is in my relationship with God & my three children–Vernon, Cherie A., & Cicely. I find simple pleasures in doll collecting, warm bubble baths, blowing bubbles & sharing moments with friends & family.

Barbara Bohm I was the "token" mad scientist on the team. I am both bipolar & a nuclear engineer. Keep dreaming—I obtained my Master's against medical advice. Try to allow God a chance to help your life be of service to mankind. Even if it is not the kind of service you had planned on rendering, there is almost always SOME WAY you can help others, if only you look hard enough & are flexible enough to try. For example, due to being a consumer, I am no longer a scientist, a childhood dream of mine. But I continue to serve & am dedicated to working on disability concerns.

Darrin Dressler During my years in the mental health field, I've had the privilege of working with the Consumer as Provider program, helping to educate the community about mental health issues & teaching computer classes. During the writing of *Pathways to Recovery*, I worked as a vocational specialist at Wyandot Center in Kansas City, Kansas, helping people find meaningful work, return to school or volunteer in their community. I'd like to thank everyone I've met along my journey. I hope I've given back all that you have given to me.

Janice F. Driscoll, BSN, RN, CEN I served on the advisory board for *Pathways to Recovery* and collaborated on the early development of the curricula for support groups associated with the workbook. I have been active in peer support initiatives, the Resource Development Advisory Team, the speaker's bureau and the consumer advisory council at my local community support services center in the Kansas City metropolitan area.

Elizabeth A. Gowdy, PhD During the creation of *Pathways to Recovery*, I worked with adult mental health services at Social & Rehabilitation Services' Office of Mental Health Care Policy. My personal & professional journey in mental health has been full of surprises and has renewed my appreciation for the innate power of personal healing in a community of creative, struggling & hope-filled human beings.

Leslie "Les" Higgins I am a consumer, I study cultures, I teach classes on spirituality, I am a reverend and an author. I advocate for people and during the development of *Pathways to Recovery*, I served on the Kansas Consumer Council. I believe in looking, knowing and respecting all of a person. I believe in the balance of life and that healing is possible for everyone.

Tonya Hinman I have worked in the mental health field for the last 15 years. I am honored to learn from consumer mentors who have taught me to truly believe in people. I incorporate creativity to help individuals reach for their potential so they might live their hopes and dreams. I enjoy camping with Wade, Coty & Zac, seeking human connectedness and searching for my heart's desire.

Randy Johnson During the creation of *Pathways*, I worked in the Consumer Affairs & Development office for the Kansas Adult Mental Health Team. I dream of traveling the back roads of the North country in a 1974 Volkswagen "Thing." I currently work as the Senior Director of Advocacy & Support Services for the MHA of the Heartland. I am eternally grateful for my family, my children and for all others who have enriched my world. One of these people might even be you.

Jan Kobe After graduating with a B.F.A. in Illustration, five years of painting for Hallmark Cards and many more years as a freelance artist—I finally perched at Wyandot Center in Kansas City, Kansas, to teach art to those who, like myself, have the experience of mental illness. On one of my many flights, I am proud to have contributed to the art in *Pathways* and I have continued to use its inspiration as the cornerstone of numerous art projects.

Suzette Mack My travels landed me amidst the *Pathways to Recovery* project…called to help, drawing upon my experience in the mental health arena as an occupational therapist, patient/consumer and advocate—but mostly as a human being who works hard to make things better for those whose spirits need some assistance choreographing their own dance of life. When I'm not writing, dancing or doing art, I can be found among Mother Nature, helping paint the colors of her changing seasons.

Shirley Jean Pilger There are a lot of people out there, unhappy, running amok, thinking they are normal. I have a mental health diagnosis—which makes me one of the lucky. I get to use this and similar books to make a better life. I am currently living in California near my family and continuing on my own path of recovery.

Amy Stiefvater I really believe in the *Pathways to Recovery* Workbook. It has helped me grow a lot. I am consumer in Kansas and have worked in and out of the mental health field for about 12 years. I have a MSW from the University of Missouri–Columbia. I live with my husband Jeff and my cats in Overland Park, Kansas.

JoAnn Howley (not pictured)   I am the program director for the Family to Family Program with the National Alliance for the Mentally Ill (NAMI) in Topeka, Kansas. I am the former board president of the Sunshine Connection in Topeka, a consumer-run organization, and I serve on several committees dealing with homelessness, suicide prevention and recovery.

Pathways to Recovery
Group Facilitator's Guide

Since the first printing of the *Pathways to Recovery* workbook, spontaneous groups have sprung up across the globe. Some have been held in formal settings while others were conducted with just two or three people in someone's living room. In most, participants found themselves completing the exercises, discussing the quotations or even arguing about whether certain topics should be included in one chapter or another. With so many different formats emerging, determining how to create a facilitator's guide was quite a challenge.

The *Pathways to Recovery Group Facilitator's Guide* was designed to be easy to navigate and use, even for first-time group facilitators — it's also flexible enough for those who wish to use just parts of the workbook or conduct shorter sessions. Four modules each provide twenty-four, 2-hour sessions and include the following:

- An overview and goals for the topic

- Recommended readings, materials & handouts

- Specific tips for facilitators & notes to guide the session

- Detailed agendas with suggested times & activities

- A coil binding to make it easier for facilitators to use within a group session

The guide gives group leaders all the information needed to facilitate a two-hour *Pathways to Recovery* group, including tips on how to adapt the sessions to meet specific needs. While some groups have taken over a year to cover all the material in the workbook, still others have found it possible to cover one chapter a week. However you decide to conduct your local group, the material you find in this guide will be helpful.

Pathways to Recovery Group Facilitator's Guide
is available for $24/each plus shipping & handling
($6 U.S. — please contact us for international rates)

For ordering information, please contact us at:
pathwaysorders@ku.edu
(877) 458-6804, ext. 108 (USA toll-free)
(785) 856-2884 (fax)

Do you have a <u>Recovery Story</u> to share?

We are interested in collecting written stories, poetry or photographs of artwork from individuals who have used *Pathways to Recovery* &/or participated in a *Pathways* group, possibly for inclusion in a future publication.

Topics for your recovery story could include:

- *How you found hope to begin your recovery journey*
- *How you used courage to take a risk*
- *How a person influenced your recovery path*
- *How you have incorporated spirituality into your life journey*
- *Using "supercharging" techniques to enhance your recovery*
- *Any special experiences that have changed your life goals*

Here's some suggestions & guidelines you may want to consider:

Length Submissions should not exceed 1500 words (3-4 pages, double spaced) although stories or poetry that are shorter or longer will be considered. All edits will be done with the author's permission.

Format If possible, please submit electronically (in Word or PDF format). If submitted by mail, please double space or print submissions.

Release of Information All individuals who have stories selected for publication will be asked to sign a Release of Information form. KU staff will contact you when your story is submitted.

Writing Suggestions There are lots of ideas in Chapter 12 of *Pathways* to get you started but here are some common ideas:

- Read your story out loud. Does it make sense? Will the reader be able to understand it?
- Ask questions to fill in any potential gaps or details that are missing.
- Get a trusted person to provide suggestions & edits.
- Include a title if appropriate. Does it make sense? Will the reader understand why you used this title?

Please submit stories, including detailed contact information (address, phone number, e-mail address), to:

Lori Davidson, Recovery Project Coordinator
The University of Kansas School of Social Welfare
Office of Mental Health Research & Training
1545 Lilac Lane — Lawrence, KS 66044 — U.S.A.
(866) 728-1909 (U.S.A. toll-free)
(785) 856-2884 (fax)
pathways@ku.edu

ORDER FORM
Pathways to Recovery: A Strengths Recovery Self-Help Workbook
Pathways to Recovery Group Facilitator's Guide

Billing Address		Shipping Address (if different from billing address)	
Name		Name	
Agency		Agency	
Address		Address	
City	State/Province	City	State/Province
Postal Code	Country	Postal Code	Country
Phone	Fax	Phone	Fax
E-Mail		E-Mail	

Item	Price	Quantity	Total
Pathways to Recovery Workbook	$24 each		$
Pathways to Recovery Facilitator's Guide	$24 each		$
SUBTOTAL			$
Discount (if applicable)	10% discount on orders of 10-199 books 15% discount on orders over 200 books		$
SUBTOTAL			$
Shipping & Handling (USA Only)	USA shipping rates are $6/book/$17 box of 10 Contact us for ALL international orders		$
TOTAL ORDER	Please allow 10-14 days for processing		$

Payment Information

❑ Enclosed is check # _____ or money order made payable to KUCR (*KU Center for Research*).

❑ Please invoice my organization. Enclosed is purchase order # _____.

❑ Please charge my credit card. **NOTE:** We cannot accept credit card information online.
Credit orders will only be processed via mail, phone or fax only.

❑ Mastercard   ❑ VISA   Name on credit card _____

Credit Card # _____-_____-_____-_____ Exp. Date _____/_____ 3-Digit Card Code _____

Sales & Shipping Information	General Information & Requests
Joanna McCloud 2706 Iowa, Suite C ~ Lawrence, KS 66046 ~ USA (785) 856-2880 or (877) 458-6804, ext. 108 (USA toll-free) (785) 856-2884 (fax) pathwaysorders@ku.edu	**Lori Davidson** 1545 Lilac Lane ~ Lawrence, KS 66044 ~ USA (785) 864-4720 or (866) 728-1909 (USA toll-free) (785) 864-5277 (fax) pathways@ku.edu